RÉGION ET DÉVELOPPEMENT

n° 49-2019

Varia

L'Harmattan

REVUE RÉGION ET DÉVELOPPEMENT

Revue fondée en 1995 par Gilbert Benhayoun et Maurice Catin

Revue semestrielle référencée dans ECONLIT et dans IDEAS (REPEC)

Site web : www.regionetdeveloppement.org

ISSN 2117-0843

5-7, rue de l'Ecole-Polytechnique, 75005 Paris

http://www.editions-harmattan.fr

ISBN : 978-2-343-18622-1

EAN : 9782343186221

Région et Développement

n° 49-2019

Varia

Imène BERGUIGA, Philippe ADAIR 5
The performance of Islamic banks in the MENA region:
Are specific risks a minor attribute?

Ahmed BELLAKHDHAR 25
L'accumulation du capital humain : modèle théorique et
évaluation dans le cas de la Tunisie

Fatima BERAHOU, Saad-Ellah BERHILI, Abdeljebbar ABDOUNI 47
The effects of state dependence on university graduates'
unemployment in Morocco: Analysis using a dynamic model

Ibrahim MOHAMED BELLO 67
Chocs climatiques et migration saisonnière dans la région de Tahoua
au Niger : une approche à partir d'un modèle dichotomique

Michel NAMÉ 81
Transferts de fonds des migrants et sécurité alimentaire dans les pays de
l'Afrique de l'Ouest

Dimitri KARKANIS 109
Un modèle de gravité de la mobilité internationale des demandeurs
d'asile

Bernard MIMBOE NOAH, Samuel FAMBON 127
Interactions fiscales stratégiques entre pays de la CEMAC et flux entrants
d'investissements directs étrangers

Région et Développement

n° 49-2019

www.regionetdeveloppement.org

The performance of Islamic banks in the MENA region: Are specific risks a minor attribute?

Imène BERGUIGA*

Philippe ADAIR**

Abstract- Islamic banks face specific risks related to *Sharia*-compliant contracts. We provide an exhaustive literature review addressing the methodological issues of the measurement of performance and document the main stylised facts regarding the performance of Islamic banks (IBs) in the MENA region. We investigate 53 IBs in 11 MENA countries throughout 2007-2014, first using cross-sectional analysis as of year 2013. A panel data model with instrumental variables estimates the impact of risks upon the returns on assets and equity of Islamic banks. Four salient results emerge: *Sharia* compliance exerts an ambiguous effect upon performance; Islamic specificity is a minor attribute according to the insignificant share of profit and loss sharing (PLS) contracts in total assets; there is no relationship between *Sharia* compliance and specific risk; loan loss provisions do not restrict to specific risks (PLS), hedging all risks.

Classification JEL
C41, G21, N27

Keywords
Islamic banks
Bank performance
Risks
MENA region
Instrumental variables

We acknowledge the useful comments from two anonymous referees. We are grateful to Wafik Grais for assessing a previous version of this paper presented at the ERF 24th Conference on 8-10 July 2018 in Cairo. We are indebted to Nadia Zrelli and Ali Abdallah for drawing our attention to some issues of Islamic banking in a previous version of this paper.

* IHEC, University of Sousse, 3 Route Hzamia Sahloul, 4054 Sousse, Tunisia. imne068@yahoo.fr

** ERUDITE, University Paris Est Créteil, 61 avenue du General de Gaulle, 94000 Créteil, France. adair@u-pec.fr (corresponding author).

INTRODUCTION

Islamic banking is governed by a set of rules prohibiting uncertainty (*maysir*), speculation (*gharar*) and charging an interest rate upon loans (*riba*) that are sources of risk, with the obligation to back up transactions to a tangible asset and share profits as well as losses. Transactions must be assessed by *ex-ante* and *ex-post* auditing from a *Sharia* Board. *Sharia*-compliance prevents IBs from granting subprime loans, leverage, acquiring risky structured products and investing in financial vehicles that lack traceability (Asutay, 2010, pp. 25-29). The remuneration of an Islamic bank is justified by its share, as co-owner, in the profit and loss sharing (PLS) in the case of a venture capital (*Mudarabah*) or a joint venture (*Mucharakah*) and its margin upon the marketing or leasing upon the property of real assets, in the case of a purchase-resale (*Murabahah*) or a lease (*Ijara*). Hence, risk-taking and commercial margin are the only sources of profitability for IBs, whose predominant instrument is *Murabahah*, which substitutes the rate of profit to the interest rate.

Although Islamic Finance assets represent only 1% of the global financial market, Islamic banking (hereafter IB) has been rising, especially since 2009 and Gulf Cooperation Council (GCC) countries detain the lion's share (Ernst & Young, 2015). Several papers have addressed the performance of IBs, especially comparing with that of conventional banking (CBs). However, the risks specific to IBs, such as non-*Sharia* compliance and Islamic contracts, are scarcely considered, whereas panel data analysis is little used to detect stylised facts. Our article fills the gap, using panel data analysis to address the impact of risks specific to IBs upon their performance in the MENA region.

According to (conventional) finance theory, the norm governing financial decisions is the optimisation of the risk (s)/ return ratio. Hence, our research question tackles the following issue: to what extent the risk(s)-return combination proves challenging for IBs?

Section 1 is devoted to the review of empirical literature, addressing the controversial issue of the risks-performance trade-off for IBs. Section 2 displays the data source, sampling and descriptive statistics. Section 3 exhibits the heterogeneous results of a cluster analysis as for key variables. Section 4 presents the estimates of a panel data analysis using instrumental variables. Conclusion highlights four salient findings: the ambiguity of Sharia-compliance and the non-significance of profit and loss sharing contracts, irrespective of the banking system in the MENA region, the absence of relationship between Sharia-compliance and the Islamic contracts, as well as loss provisions hedging all risks that are not restricted to specific risks.

1. LITERATURE REVIEW

1.1. Comparative and intrinsic performance of Islamic banks

Our extensive literature review lists 37 papers on the performance of IBs that can be divided into two strands, whereby the conclusions prove controversial: the first strand is benchmarking the performance of IBs *versus* CBs, whereas the second strand is focusing on the intrinsic performance of IBs.

As for benchmarking, according to a set of nine papers, IBs are more profitable, more liquid and better capitalized; more stable, more competitive and more risk-prone; they were less affected during the 2008 recession. This first set of papers covers (at most) the period 1993-2013 and 70 IBs from 13 MENA countries, using various methods: Data Envelopment Analysis –DEA (Al-Muharrami, 2008); Stochastic Frontier Analysis -SFA (Alam, 2012; Amal and Mohamed, 2015; Regaieg and Abidi, 2015), or Discriminant Function Analysis (Olson and Zoubi, 2011; Ben Khediri et al., 2015); financial ratios analysis - FRA(Parashar and Venkatesh, 2010; Siraj and Pillai, 2012) and panel data econometrics (Rajhi and Hassari, 2013).

In contrast, another set of twelve surveys contend that IBs are less profitable; they bear higher operation risk as well as credit and liquidity risks; they were more affected by the 2008 recession; the influence of age (experience) upon the performance of IBs is controversial. This second set spans throughout 1995-2014 with 40 IBs from 14 MENA countries, using SFA (Abdul-Majid et al, 2010; Srairi, 2010, Ferhi and Chkoundali, 2015), Meta Frontier Analysis (Johnes et al, 2013); financial ratios analysis (Elsiefy, 2013; Fayed, 2013; Miniaoui and Gohou, 2013; Ibrahim, 2015, Rashwan and Ehab, 2016) and panel data econometrics (Beck et al., 2013; Kamarudin et al., 2014; Al-Deehani et al., 2015).

The conclusion from a last set of seven papers is that there was no significant difference in performance between IBs and CBs: the impact of the 2008 recession upon financial markets and the real economy did also affect IBs. Performance is negatively correlated to operation and credit risk, not liquidity risk; Size has a positive influence upon bank performance due to economies of scale. This third set covers the period 1990-2014 and 23 IBs from 12 MENA countries, using DEA (Bader et al., 2008; Hassan et al., 2009; Said, 2013), SFA (Sillah et al, 2015), FRA (Meero, 2015) and panel data econometrics (Hidayat and Abduh, 2012; Zeitun, 2012).

Comparative analysis suggests that the best (worst) performance of IBs *versus* CBs does not depend on the methods that are commonly used in the three aforementioned sets of papers. For instance, parametric methods (SFA) do not prove superior to nonparametric method (DEA) and both often provide the same results (Berger and Humphrey, 1997). It is worth mentioning that performance depends primarily on the size and composition of the sample, as well as on the period of time under review. Most surveys on large samples fail to identify a country effect and do not remove outliers that bias the results, Beck et al. (2013) being excepted. Conversely, surveys on a small size sample, particularly upon the GCC or monographs devoted to a single country, reveal the heterogeneity of banks, although results cannot be extended to the overall MENA region. As for comparative analysis, there is mixed evidence among MENA countries. Some IBs were better-off in 2008-2009 than CBs regarding profitability, with the exception of Bahrain, Qatar and especially the United Arab Emirates that count the largest number of banks in the GCC (Hasan and Dridi, 2010). Boukhris and Nabi (2013) point out there is no significant difference as regards the effect of the financial crisis on the soundness of IBs and CBs. With respect to the size of banks, it is open to question whether large IBs or small ones have resisted better (Said, 2012; Abedifar et al., 2013; Ouerghi, 2014).

The other strand of literature tackles the intrinsic performance of IBs and includes nine surveys upon IBs mostly located in the MENA region. Zarrouk (2012) compares 20 IBs throughout 2005-2009, finding that profitability and liquidity declined after the crisis in Bahrain, Kuwait and UAE. Rosman et al. (2014), applying DEA to 79 IBs from MENA and Asian countries throughout 2007-2010, observe that most IBs proved scale inefficient. Mghaieth and Khanchel (2015), using SFA upon 62 IBs in sixteen countries of the MENA and South-East Asia regions over 2004-2010, conclude that IBs are more efficient for profits than for costs. Unlike Sulfian and Noor (2009), according to Yudistira (2004), Kablan and Yousfi (2013) and Wahidudin et al. (2014) the MENA IBs experience lower performance than their Asian counterparts. IBs operating in high-income countries are more efficient than in other countries (Ahmad et al, 2010).

Among the listed papers, eleven surveys using panel data analysis provide a few stylised facts: IBs are profitable albeit not necessarily more efficient than CBs. IBs are well capitalized, liquid and risk prone, but experience higher transaction costs and do not reach the optimum size to enjoy economies of scale. (Appendix, Table A1). Seven papers compare IBs and CBs with samples mainly covering the MENA countries (except Beck et al., 2013), four of which being exclusively devoted to oil monarchies (Hidayat and Abduh, 2012; Zeitun, 2012; Kamarudin et al., 2014; Al-Deehani et al., 2015). Only three studies focus exclusively on IBs, among which Wahidudin et al. (2014) and Trad et al. (2017) use diverse and large samples.

1.2. Conventional and specific risks

IBs seem to illustrate the positive correlation between risk(s) and return, in line with (conventional) finance theory (Alam, 2012). In as much as IBs face specific risks and well as conventional risks, it remains open to question whether the risk(s)-performance trade-off is comparable for IBs to that of CBs.

Although CBs do not bear the losses and only transfer risks, IBs face the same conventional liquidity risk, credit risk, operational risk and solvency risk. The most important risks for IBs are threefold: credit risk, liquidity risk and operational risk (Hussain and Al-Ajmi, 2012).

Credit risk as well as operational risk are negatively related to performance, while liquidity risk has a non-significant relationship with the efficiency of the MENA IBs (Said, 2013).

Credit risk results from an unforeseen alteration in the credit quality of the issuer or partner and is a source of instability in the banking system (McNeil et al, 2005). Poor cost management goes hand in hand with a higher credit risk (Berger et al, 1997). Ferhi and Chkoundali (2015) suggest that the higher the concentration in IBs, the higher the credit risk. The positive impact of size upon the loan quality is lower for IBs as well as for credit risk.

Liquidity risk is defined as a potential loss and seems to reflect best the genuine characteristics of IBs (Desquilbet and Kalai, 2013). It arises from the inability of IBs to hedge their liabilities or to increase their assets (Idries, 2012), the absence of an Islamic interbank market to refinance and the lack of *Sharia*-compliant financial instruments. Nevertheless, multiple stakeholders imply multiple credit risk, which comes from the issuer of the security, the bank and the entrepreneur when the underlying asset is based on PLS investment, or from the tenant of a lease.

Operation risk creates losses due to inadequate or inconclusive internal practices, personnel and technology, or external events: it influences decision-making (Ray and Cashman, 1999). This risk is significant for IBs and becomes more complicated compared to CBs because of the particular aspects of Islamic contracts and the general legal environment (Marliana et al., 2011). IBs are typically more risk prone than CBs and require more capital to manage their level of risk (Srairi, 2010).

Credit risk as well as operational risk are negatively related to performance, while liquidity risk has a non-significant relationship with the efficiency of MENA IBs (Said, 2013). IBs perform better in credit risk management and solvency maintenance (Muhammad et al., 2012).

In addition to conventional risks, IBs face two main specific risks: risk of non-compliance, risk specific to Islamic contracts. Risk of non-*Sharia* compliance stems from the divergence of interpretation between the members of the *Sharia Board*, which is difficult to circumscribe in the absence of universally recognized religious norms. The specific risk concerns PLS contracts (*Mudharabah* and *Mucharakah*), which require costly monitoring and negotiation of the profit and loss sharing rates (Khan and Ahmed, 2001), and *Ijara* contracts whereupon the bank has to manage and maintain the property leased to avoid value deterioration.

We do not take into account the displaced commercial risk. This business risk is not a risk per se, but a mechanism that links the market risk to a real asset value and the liquidity risk associated with the potential withdrawal of deposits. It is therefore addressed indirectly through the risk specific to Islamic contracts.

The entanglement of risks is due to the simultaneous existence of the various conventional and specific risks encapsulated within each Islamic contract. The regulatory provisions of the Basel III agreements (liquidity standards, leverage ratio and capital adequacy ratio) did not take into account the case of IBs, whose asset transactions must be treated according to different risk weighting. The Islamic Financial Services Council lists all the contracts proposed by IBs, and designed new recommendations to complement the Basel standards with those of the Islamic Finance Regulation (IFSB, 2015). However, there is no credit rating specific to Islamic banking as for the MENA region so far; in addition, no explicit indicator measures the enforcement of *Sharia* regulation (Zins and Weill, 2017).

2. DATA SOURCE, VARIABLES AND METHODOLOGY

In order to design our sample we used the Bankscope database, removing the banks for which only one single observation (year) was available and those with most of the data missing. Our sample over the period 2007-2014 consists in 53 IBs from 11 MENA countries, including five oil producers (Saudi Arabia, UAE, Iran, Kuwait, and Qatar), among which Iran and allegedly Saudi Arabia apply *Sharia* as a source of law as well as Yemen, a non-oil producer. Other non-oil-producing countries not regulated by *Sharia* are Egypt, Jordan, Tunisia, Bahrain and Syria.

Table 1. Variables

Variables	Definition	Formula	Source
Performance	Return on average assets (*ROAA*)	Net operation income before subsidy/ Total average assets	Bankscope
	Return on average equity (*ROAE*)	Net operation income before subsidy/ Total average equity	Bankscope
Specific risk	Loss Loan Provisions (*LLP*)	Loss Loan Provisions upon *Profit and Loss Sharing* (PLS) accounts/Total Assets	Bankscope
	Sharia Board (*Board*)	Number of members on the *Sharia* Board	Annual reports
	Share of specific contracts in total assets (*Specific contracts*)	$\frac{\sum Specific\ contracts(PLS\ and\ Ijara)}{Total\ Assets}$	Annual reports
Credit risk (CR)		Reserve for Non-Performing Loans/ Outstanding gross loans	Bankscope
Liquidity risk	Short-term liquidity ratio (*STLR*)	Liquid Assets/ Client Deposits and short-term financing	Bankscope
	Long-term liquidity ratio (*LTLR*)	Net loans/Total Assets	Bankscope
Solvency risk	*z-score*	$\ln(Zscore) = \ln\frac{E(ROA) + CAR}{\sigma_{ROA}}$ CAR (capital ratio): Equity /Total Assets. ROA standard deviation is calculated for each bank over the period 2007-2014	Bankscope
Bank Charact.	*Age*	Difference between the year of observation and the year of establishment	Bank websites
	Size	Ln(Total Assets)	Bankscope
	Concentration	Bank deposits/Total banks deposits	Bankscope
	Ownership	*Dummy* (Domestic *vs.* Foreign)	
Macroeco. variables	*Inflation*	Inflation rate	WDI
	GDP growth	GDP growth rate	WDI
	Oil-monarchy	*Dummy* (Oil-producer *vs.* non-oil producer)	OPEC

Source: Authors.

Specific risks are addressed with three indicators: (i) Loan Loss Provisions (*LLP*) in the PLS account; (ii) the share of specific contracts (*Specific contracts*) in total assets, including participation schemes upon which the PLS principle applies (*Mudharabah* and *Mucharakah*), as well as *Ijara*; (iii) the number of members on the Sharia Board, assuming that a large number of members should ensure Sharia compliance.

Other risks faced by IBs are related to credit, liquidity and solvency. Credit risk (*CR*) is measured by the provision for Non-Performing Loans. Liquidity risk is addressed with two indicators regarding the long-term (*LTLR*) and the short-term (*STLR*) span of time. *Z-score* is expressed in logarithm (Ln-*zscore*) and gauges the solvency risk.

In addition, bank characteristics (*Age, Size, Concentration* and *Ownership*) and the macroeconomic environment (*Inflation, GDP growth* and *Oil-Monarchy*) are the explanatory variables for bank performance (Table 1).

We assess the impact of specific risks upon the economic (*ROAA*) and financial (*ROEA*) performance of IBs. As a first step, we examine the relationship between performance and specific risks with a cross-sectional analysis. In the second step, we estimate with a panel data model the impact of all the aforementioned risks upon the performance of IBs throughout the overall period.

3. CROSS-SECTIONAL ANALYSIS

We apply a factor analysis including clusters to a sample of 46 IBs in 11 MENA countries as of year 2013 that gathers the largest sub-sample: Bahrain (10), Egypt (2), Jordan (2), Kuwait (7), Qatar (3), Saudi Arabia (2), Tunisia (1), UAE (8), Syria (3) Yemen (3), and Iran (5). The variables used are performance (*ROAE*) and the three specific risk indicators (*LLP, Specific Contracts* and *Sharia Board*).

LLP and *Specific contracts* indicators are broken down into two classes. IBs experience high (*vs.* low) specific risk when the share of provisions and risky assets is below (*vs.* above) median. If the *Sharia* Board is below (*vs.* above) the median of four members, the risk of non-*Sharia* compliance is high (*vs.* low).

The assumption is that a large *Sharia* Board is required to check compliance, which is an opportunity cost affecting profitability. Admittedly, the number of Board members is a loose proxy for *Sharia* compliance, in as much as it does not measure their independence *vis-à-vis* the management of the bank appointing them. In Iran, banks do not have a Board but are all ruled by *Sharia* under the regulation of the Central Bank and are assumed to be compliant. The full sample includes three out of five IBs that comply with *Sharia* (Table 2).

ROEA is used here as the most relevant indicator for IBs, in as much as it encapsulates the shareholders' point of view. It closely correlates with *ROA* (Appendix, Table A2).

Factor analysis is limited here to the most interpretable axes 1-2 that account for 55 per cent of the variance[1] (Appendix: Figure 1). Axis 1 expresses the profitability of banks, displaying a positive relationship between the specific risk and the risk of non-compliance. It contrasts *Board1* and *SP1* with *Board2* and *SP2* oppose IBs whose specific risk and non-compliance are respectively low and high. Axis 2 can be interpreted as the axis of the asset structure; it identifies the relationship between specific risk and profitability, contrasting *ROEA3* and *LLP1* with *ROEA2* and *LLP2*. It thus distinguishes the highly profitable IBs with low loss provisions from those that are less profitable and store high provisions.

Given the absence of CBs in Iran, the banking system is ruled by *Sharia,* without a significant number of Board members, and *Specific contracts* are of minor importance.

[1] Detailed cross-sectional analysis is available upon request.

IBs use conventional products more than participation contracts; hence, they seem to be averse to specific risk.

Table 2. Active variables: specific risks and financial performance (2013)

Code	Variables	IBs	Code	Variables	IBs
Specific risks variables					
Specific contracts / total assets (2 classes): Share of risky assets			*LLP/ Total assets (2 classes): Risky assets hedging*		
SP1	*<median (low specific risk)*	*20*	*LLP1*	< median (deficient risk management)	20
SP2	*≥ median (*high *specific risk)*	*21*	*LLP2*	≥ median (cautious risk management)	21
Sharia Board(2 classes)					
Board1	0-1 members (Iran) and 4-10 members (low *risk of non-compliance*)				25
Board2	1-4 members (high *risk of non-compliance*)				16
Financial performance variable					
ROEA (3 classes)					
ROAE1	<0% (not profitable)				3
ROAE2	≥0% and< median (cost-effective)				17
ROAE3	≥ median (very profitable)				21

Note: The sample is restricted to 41 IBs, due to missing data. Source: Authors.

There are almost as many IBs facing low non-compliance risk and / or specific risks as high non-compliance risk alongside high or low performance. Cluster analysis (Appendix, Figure 1) displays very heterogeneous risk configurations.

Four clusters illustrate a relationship between specific risks and performance that proves either negative (clusters 1 and 3) or positive (clusters 2 and 4).

Cluster 1 gathers six high performing IBs, Saudi Arabia (2), Iran (2) and Egypt (2), whose specific risks (*SP1* and *LLP1*) and non-compliance (*Board1*) are low. These IBs combine high profitability with a small share in specific contracts while complying with *Sharia*.

Cluster 2 includes six less-performing IBs, Iran (2), Bahrain (1), Kuwait (1), Jordan (1) and Syria (1), whose risks are small although they store significant provisions.

Cluster 3 comprises seven low-performing IBs, Bahrain (3), UAE (3) and Syria (1), with a high level of risk (*SP2* and *LLP2)* and non-compliance (*Board2*). IBs combine poor performance with a significant share in specific contracts and significant provisions without complying with *Sharia*.

Cluster 4 includes four performing IBs, Qatar (2), UAE (1) and Jordan (1), with high specific risks and non-compliance. Specific investments are not covered by provisions and profitability is high.

Two other clusters encapsulate an opposite or complementary relationship between specific risk and non-compliance risk. In cluster 5, ten IBs, UAE (4), Kuwait (2), Bahrain (1), Iran (1), Tunisia (1) and Egypt (1), eight of which being highly profitable, combine high specific risk and low non-compliance risk. In cluster 6, five IBs, Yemen (3), Syria (1) and Kuwait (1) combine low specific risk with high non-compliance risk.

4. PANEL DATA ANALYSIS

4.1. Methodology

We designed a panel data model wherein the two performance indicators (*ROAA* and *ROA*E) are the explained variables and all other variables are the explanatory variables. The overall sample consists in 53 banks throughout 2007-2014 (Table 3).

IBs in the sample are distinct from one another according to intrinsic characteristics that may be either fixed (*Within* fixed effects model) or random (*FGLS* random effects model). Both the Fisher test and the Breusch-Pagan test verify the existence of specific effects (probability below 5%), whereas the Hausman specification test points out whether these effects are fixed or random and makes sure *FGLS* is the efficient estimation method (probability over 5%). The random effect estimator takes care of one issue, namely the existence of time-invariant variables (*Sharia Board, Ownership* and *Oil-monarchy*), which a fixed effects model cannot deal with. The other issue is the presence of endogenous variables that we address with the method of instrumental variables (*IV*), using the Hausman-Taylor (*HT*) estimator (Baltagi, 2008). We tested several potential endogenous variables that impact performance and we eventually chose *Size, Age* and *lnZ-score*. *Size* allows for economies of scale; *Age* is related to experience and may capture management practices; *lnZ-score* includes capitalisation and *ROA*.

We follow a step by step approach. The first step includes *Specific contracts* (model 1) and then adds *LLP* (model 2) as specific risks. The second step includes the *Sharia* Board variable (model 3) with respect to non-compliance risk. Eventually, all three indicators of specific risks are simultaneously considered (model 4).The model is first estimated upon the full sample and then upon a sub-sample omitting the Iranian banks, in order to avoid the selection bias previously identified in the cross-sectional analysis and to check the robustness of our results.

4.2. Results and robustness

Estimates of the step-by-step model (Table 3) show a significant and negative effect of the specific risk *(LLP)* and non-compliance (*Board*) upon performance (*ROAA* and *ROEA*).

According to model 1, the *Specific contracts* variable proves non-significant. In model 2, the inclusion of the *LLP* variable that proves significant throughout all models changes the sign of the *Specific contracts* variable that remains non-significant; it suggests that these two indicators are not complementary. According to model 3, the *Sharia* Board is significant and negative: the larger the Board, the lower the risk of non-compliance and the lower the performance of IBs. Model 4 shows an inverse relationship between (high) specific risks on the one hand and (low) risk of non-compliance, as well as (low) performance(*ROEA* and *ROAA*) on the other hand. This corroborates the result from cross-sectional analysis and suggests some complementary relationship between specific risks.

The various models estimated confirm the significant negative impact of specific risks (*LLP* and *Board*), whereas *LTLR* is weakly significant or non-significant in most models, *LnZscore* proves positive and very significant, *STLR* being seldom significant or non-significant in most models. As for the characteristics of IBs, *Age* is non-significant, whereas *Size* proves positive and significant, as well as country effect variables (*Concentration, Inflation* and *GDP growth*), *Oil-monarchy* being non-significant.

We discuss the results of model 4 based on *IV*, with regard first to the determinants of the full sample (Table 3), then to those of the sub-sample without Iran (Table 4).

Table 3. Estimates of performance models: full sample

Dependent variables	ROAA				ROEA			
Models	(1) *FGLS*	(2) *IV*	(3) *IV*	(4) *IV*	(1) *IV*	(2) *FGLS*	(3) *IV*	(4) *IV*
Explanatory variables								
Specific contracts	-0.0002	0.0007		-0.0001	0.0063	-0.0092		0.0158
LLP		-0.8341**		-0.8355**		-5.9438***		-4.9105***
Board			-2.4182**	-2.2206**			-11.4427**	-10.7046**
CR	0.0177	0.0466	0.0400	0.0547	-0.1368	0.0096	-0.0783	0.0189
LTLR	0.0282	-0.0129	-0.0339	-0.0183	-0.0666	0.2141**	-0.1004	-0.0152
STLR	-0.0055	-0.0114*	-0.0111*	-0.0094	-0.0421	-0.0098	-0.0344	-0.0250
lnZscore	0.5333**	3.3443***	3.7102***	3.6099***	14.5435***	2.6640*	16.6384***	16.2788***
Ownership	-0.1045	-0.5552	-3.4678	-3.1809	0.9885	2.6819	-12.7316	-11.3312
Age	0.0014	0.0227	-0.0284	-0.0299	0.4565	0.0501	0.0692	-0.0015
Size	-0.0227	0.8100	1.5176**	1.3402**	4.3447	-0.6633	7.6473**	6.9398**
Concentration	1.3226*	1.4099	1.2294	1.2418	8.5017**	7.5074**	7.3036*	7.0866*
GDP growth	0.1226***	0.1036***	0.1184***	0.1088***	0.4139***	0.3647***	0.4369***	0.3871***
Inflation	0.1304***	0.1213***	0.1158**	0.1231***	0.4995***	0.6715***	0.5075***	0.5454***
Oil-monarchy	0.9745**	2.3817	2.7262	2.7707	6.8155	1.4496	7.6996	7.2413
Observations	220	220	220	220	220	220	220	220
Number of Banks	47	47	47	47	47	47	47	47
R-squared	0.2054	0.252	0.267	0.298	0.3017	0.3656	0.3272	0.2935
Fisher	0.0004	0.0001	0.0002	0.0001	0.0001	0.0000	0.0001	0.0000
Wald	34.10	45.17	49.01	59.96	46.41	68.55	55.15	76.56
Breush Pagan	0.0196	0.0556	0.0977	0.1484	0.0000	0.0000	0.0000	0.0000
Hausman FE vs FGLS	0.0028	0.0000	0.0043	0.0002	0.0014	0.0169	0.0000	0.1409
Sargan	0.2308	0.3001	0.3572	0.4409	0.1265	0.1650	0.3641	0.4418
Hausman HT vs FGLS	0.1068	0.0143	0.0123	0.0026	0.0342	0.5236	0.0319	0.0244

*Note: The sample is restricted to 47 IBs, due to missing data. *** $p< 0.01$, ** $p<0.5$, * $p<0.1$. T-stats are omitted.*
Source: Authors, from Bankscope and bank reports.

Table 4. Estimates of performance models: sub sample (excluding Iran)

Dependent variables	***ROAA***				***ROEA***			
Models	(1) *IV*	(2) *IV*	(3) *IV*	(4) *IV*	(1) *IV*	(2) *IV*	(3) *IV*	(4) *IV*
Explanatory Variables								
Specific contracts	0.0045	0.0064		0.0061	0.0415	0.0556		0.0549
LLP		-0.9711**		-0.9565**		-6.3385***		-6.2931***
Board			-1.2907	-1.1709			-4.0857	-3.2473
CR	0.0568	0.0759	0.0561	0.0769	0.0348	0.1627	0.0116	0.1509
LTLR	0.0568	0.0759	0.0561	0.0769	0.0348	0.1627	0.0116	0.1509
STLR	-0.0311	-0.0167	-0.0332	-0.0197	-0.0938	0.0024	-0.0880	-0.0012
lnZscore	-0.0139**	-0.0125*	-0.0128*	-0.0114	-0.0501*	-0.0409	-0.0464	-0.0377
Ownership	-1.0913	-1.1171	-2.5303	-2.3833	-2.6341	-2.8501	-7.4370	-6.5748
Age	-0.1016	0.6715***	-0.0811	-0.1213	-0.2271	-0.4499	-0.0847	-0.3499
Size	1.9137**	0.3647***	2.1428**	2.1980**	11.3929***	11.4595***	11.2983***	11.5702***
Concentration	1.3226*	1.4099	1.2294	1.2418	8.5017**	7.5074**	7.3036*	7.0866*
GDP growth	0.1582***	0.1443***	0.1572***	0.1464***	0.6790***	0.5890***	0.6563***	0.5928***
Inflation	0.1003*	0.1042*	0.1063**	0.1068*	0.4163*	0.4361**	0.4525**	0.4451**
Oil-monarchy	-1.3145	-1.5126	-0.1716	-0.6337	-13.6698	-15.2365	-8.5188	-11.9243
Observations	193	193	193	193	193	193	193	193
Number of Banks	40	40	40	40	40	40	40	40
R-squared	0.2356	0.2711	0.3080	0.3323	0.3544	0.4140	0.3780	0.4283
Fisher	0.0004	0.0002	0.0002	0.0002	0.0000	0.0000	0.0002	0.0002
Wald	37.30	48.56	70.48	88.57	61.13	88.16	76.34	102.71
Breush Pagan	0.1300	0.2338	0.4581	1.0000	0.1165	0.2138	0.2436	0.3032
Hausman FE vs FGLS	0.1985	0.0000	0.0030	0.0003	0.0001	0.0014	0.0000	0.0003
Sargan	0.3989	0.5309	0.4338	0.6161	0.1960	0.3090	0.2202	0.4014
Hausman HT vs FGLS	0.0493	0.4558	0.0078	0.0259	0.0007	0.0016	0.0001	0.0001

*Note: *** p< 0.01, ** p<0.5, * p<0.1. T-stats are omitted.*
Source: Authors, from Bankscope and bank reports.

As for the full sample, the results show that *LLP* has a negative impact upon performance (both *ROAA* and *ROEA*), in line with conventional finance theory. *LLP* is a risk indicator and not a means of smoothing bank profit as demonstrated by Zoubi and Al-Khazali (2007) and Hassan and Mollah (2014), although IBs may also use loan loss provisions for discretionary managerial actions, when bank capitalization declines. (Soedarmono et al., 2017).

Any increase in the participation contracts portfolio, both on the short-term (*Murabahah*) and the long-term (*Mucharakah*), exerts a positive effect upon profitability in as much as the level of risk remains acceptable (Olson and Zoubi, 2011). We observe that the long-term liquidity ratio (*LTLR*) has little significant impact on *ROAA* and *ROEA*. To mitigate this risk, investment in long-term contracts should decline while maintaining liquidity to cover short-term contracts. However, an excess in liquid assets is detrimental to the profitability and development of IBs (Toumi et al., 2016) due to the opportunity cost of idle money. Hassan and Bashir (2003) conclude that *STLR* has a negative impact upon performance, while we observe a positive impact, although weakly significant.

The risk of bank failure or solvency risk (*LnZscore*) has a positive and significant impact upon performance (*ROAA* and *ROEA*), in line with conventional finance theory. The higher the *LnZscore*, the lower the default risk, the more stable and profitable are IBs. Zehri and Al-Herch (2013) claim that IBs were more stable and profitable during the 2007-2008 crisis, whereas Srairi (2010) asserts there is no difference between IBs and CBs as regards default risk.

Age and *Ownership* prove non-significant, whereas *Size* exerts a positive and significant effect upon performance. *Concentration* is positive and has a significant impact upon *ROEA*. Profitability is the result of significant market power of IBs in the MENA region, which proves oligopolistic and sometimes monopolistic (Kamarudin et al., 2014).

Macroeconomic variables (*GDP growth* and *Inflation*) have a positive and significant effect on performance, whereas *Oil monarchy* is insignificant. Rising demand for deposits and loans positively affects the revenues of IBs, hence their profitability. *Inflation* has a positive impact upon the performance of IBs, if their profits are mainly derived from direct investments, participations and / or other commercial activities (*Murabahah*). This is in line with the conclusion of Olson and Zoubi (2011) and Kamarudin et al. (2014), whereas Wahidudin et al. (2014) find a negative impact on the profitability of the MENA region.

In Table 4, the estimate of the sub-sample of 10 MENA countries, excluding Iran, confirms almost all previous results, with the exception of *Board* becoming non-significant. Provisions for losses in PLS account (*LLP*) and as well as solvency risk (*LnZscore*), *Size* and some macroeconomic variables (*Concentration, GDP growth* and *Inflation*) retain the same signs and remain the determinants of performance. There is no relationship between *Sharia* compliance and the share of specific contracts, which is a minor attribute of IBs. *Age* turns once positive and significant as well as long-term liquidity risk (*LTLR*), while *Size* becomes more significant: large size IBs detain profitable assets and can benefit both from economies of scale and product diversification (Olson and Zoubi, 2011).

There is indeed a selection bias in the overall sample including Iran, which is identified in the sub-sample of 10 MENA countries experiencing a dual Islamic and conventional banking system, which are not affected by the risk of non-*Sharia* compliance. Although being the most mature and following the principles of Islamic finance, Iranian banks are exposed to the risk of non-*Sharia* compliance, which is a hindrance to the development of their products and the diversification of their assets.

CONCLUSION

We explore an aspect of risk that has been little addressed in the literature upon IBs, namely the specific risk relating to provisions for losses in participation contracts, the share of these specific contracts in total assets and non-*Sharia* compliance. We apply first a cross-sectional analysis and then panel data models using instrumental variables upon a sample of 53 IBs in the MENA region throughout 2007-2014.

Loss provisions upon PLS contracts exert a significant negative impact upon performance, whereas the share of these contracts in total assets proves non-significant alongside non *Sharia* compliance. Solvency ratio and, to some extent, liquidity ratios have a positive significant impact, together with some characteristics of IBs and the macroeconomic environment. This pattern corroborates the risk-return combination of conventional finance theory.

Four main outcomes are worth mentioning. First, *Sharia* compliance is ambiguous and is compatible with high or lower performance of IBs operating in a dual Islamic and conventional banking system. Conversely, IBs operating in a fully Islamic banking system (Iran) are risk-averse and nevertheless perform well. Second, whether the banking system is dual or not, the non-significant share of specific contracts in total assets suggests that such contracts are a minor attribute of MENA IBs. Third, there is no relationship between specific risk and the risk of non-compliance, which suggests the absence of specific risk management. Fourth, loss provisions for PLS contracts are used as a means of hedging all risks, not just specific risks. Hence, there is no evidence that the Islamic business model built upon the PLS ~~basic~~ principle, is the core ~~of~~ banking activity for MENA IBs, which are less unconventional than some scholars claim they are.

REFERENCES

Abdul-Majid M., Saal D. S., Battisti G., 2010. Efficiency in Islamic and conventional banking: an international comparison. *Journal of Productivity Analysis* 34(1), 25-43.

Abedifar P., Molyneux P., Tarazi A., 2013. Risk in Islamic Banking. *Review of Finance* 17(6), 2035-2096.

Ahmad N. H. B., Noor M. A. N. M., Sufian F., 2010. Measuring Islamic banks efficiency: the case of world Islamic banking sectors. MPRA Paper 29497. https://mpra.ub.uni-muenchen.de/29497/

Alam N., 2012. Efficiency and Risk-Taking in Dual Banking System: Evidence from Emerging Markets. *International Review of Business Research Papers* 8(4), 94-111.

Al-Deehani, T. M., El-Sadi, H. M., Al-Deehani, M. T., 2015. Performance of Islamic banks and conventional banks before and during economic downturn. *Investment Management and Financial Innovations* 12(2), 238-50.

Al-Muharrami, S., 2008. An examination of technical, pure technical and scale efficiencies in GCC banking. *American Journal of Finance and Accounting* 1(2), 152-66.

Al-Tamimi, H. A. H., Al-Mazrooei, F. M., 2007. Banks' risk management: A comparison study of UAE national and foreign banks. *Journal of Risks Finance* 8(4), 394-409.

Amal, B., Mohamed, I. G., 2015. Competition and Efficiency: Comparative Analysis between Islamic and Conventional Banks of MENA Region. *International Journal of Business and Commerce* 5(3), 20-40.

Ariffin, N., Archer, S., Karim, R., 2009. Risks in Islamic banks: evidence from empirical research. *Journal of Banking Regulation* 10(2), 153-63.

Asutay, M., 2010. *Islamic Microfinance: Fulfilling Social and Developmental Expectations. Islamic Finance: Instruments and Markets*, Bloomsbury Publishing, London.

Bader, M. K. I., Mohamad, S., Ariff, M., Hassan, T., 2008. Cost, revenue, and profit efficiency of Islamic versus conventional banks: international evidence using data envelopment analysis. *Islamic Economic Studies* 15(2), 23-76.

Baltagi, B. H. Ed., 2008. *Econometric analysis of panel data*. John Wiley, Chichester, UK.

Bankscope, World Banking Information, https://bankscope.bvdinfo.com/version-2014103/home.serv?product=scope2006

Beck, T., Demirgüç-Kunt, A., Merrouche, O., 2013. Islamic vs. conventional banking: Business model, efficiency and stability. *Journal of Banking & Finance* 37, 433-47.

Ben Hassine, M., Limani R., 2014. The Impact of Bank Characteristics on the Efficiency: Evidence from MENA Islamic Banks. *Journal of Applied Finance & Banking* 4(3), 237-53.

Ben Khediri, K, Charfeddine, L., Ben Youssef, S., 2015. Islamic versus conventional banks in the GCC countries: A comparative study using classification techniques. *Research in International Business and Finance* 33, 75–98.

Berger, A.N., Humphrey, D.B., 1997. Efficiency of financial institutions: international survey and directions for future research. *European Journal of Operational Research* 89, 175-212.

Berger, P., Ofek E., Yermack, D., 1997. Managerial entrenchment and capital structure decisions. *Journal of Finance* 52(4), 1411-38.

Boukhris, K. and Nabi, S.N., 2013. Islamic and conventional banks' soundness during the 2007–2008 financial crisis. *Review of Financial Economics* 22(2), 68–77.

Desquilbet, J-B., Kalai, F., 2013. Contrat de dépôt et partage du risque de liquidité dans la banque islamique : une approche à la Diamond et Dybvig. *Brussels Economic Review* 56(3-4), 389-412.

Elsiefy, E., 2013. Comparative Analysis of Qatari Islamic Banks Performance vs. Conventional Banks Before, During and After the Financial Crisis. International Journal of Business and Commerce 3 (3), 11-41.

Ernst & Young, 2015, World Islamic Banking Competitiveness Report 2016, ey.com/mena

Fayed, M. E., 2013. Comparative Performance Study of Conventional and Islamic Banking in Egypt. *Journal of Applied Finance and Banking* 3(2), 1-14.

Ferhi, A., Chkoundali, R., 2015. Credit Risk and Efficiency: Comparative Study between Islamic and Conventional Banks during the Current Crises. Journal of Behavioural Economics, Finance, Entrepreneurship, *Accounting and Transport* 3(1), 47-56.

Grais, W., Pellegrini, M., 2006. Corporate governance and Shari'ah compliance in institutions offering Islamic financial services, World Bank Policy Research Working Paper No. 4054, Washington DC.

Hasan, M., Dridi, J., 2010. The Effects of the Global Crisis on Islamic and Conventional Banks: A Comparative Study IMF Working Paper, WP/10/201. International Monetary Fund, Washington DC.

Hassan M. K., Bashir, A.M., 2003. Determinants of Islamic Profitability. Paper Presented at Economic Research Forum 10th annual Conference. www.kantakji.com/media/3016/kabir_bashir.pdf

Hassan, K., Kayed, R. N., 2009. The Global Financial Crisis, Risk Management and Social Justice. *International Journal of Islamic Finance* 1(1), 33-58.

Hassan, T., Mohamad, S., Bader, M. K. I., 2009. Efficiency of conventional versus Islamic banks: evidence from the Middle East. *International Journal of Islamic and Middle Eastern Finance and Management* 2(1), 46-65.

Hassan M. K., Mollah S., 2014. Corporate Governance, Risk Taking and Firm Performance of Islamic Banks during Global Financial Crisis. http://cbagccu.org/files/pdf/3/2.pdf:

Hidayat S. E., Abduh M., 2012. Does Financial Crisis Give Impacts on Bahrain Islamic Banking Performance? A Panel Regression Analysis. *International Journal of Economics and Finance* 4(7), 79-87

Hussain H., Al-Ajmi J., 2012. Risk management practices of conventional and Islamic banks in Bahrain. *Journal of Risks Finance* 13(3), 215-39.

Ibrahim A-J., 2015. Empirical Findings on the Profitability of Banks in Qatar: Islamic vs. Conventional. *International Journal of Business and Commerce* 5(4), 63-78.

Idries M., 2012. Evaluating the riskiness of the banking sector of Jordan. European Journal of Economics, *Finance and Administrative Science* 48, 1-10.

IFSB, 2015. Core principles for Islamic finance regulation (banking segment) (CPIFR).Islamic Financial Services Board. http://www.ifsb.org/standard/IFSB-Core

Johnes J., Izzeldin M., Pappas V., 2014. A comparison of performance of Islamic and conventional banks 2004 to 2009. *Journal of Economic Behavior and Organisation* 103, Supplement, 93-107.

Kablan S., Yousfi O., 2013. What Drives Efficiency of Islamic Banks among Regions? *The Journal of Applied Business Research* 29(5), 1411-20.

Kamarudin F., Nassir A. M., Yahya M. H., Said,R. M., Nordin B. A. A., 2014. Islamic Banking Sectors in the Gulf Cooperation Council Countries: Analysis on Revenue, Cost and Profit Efficiency Concepts. *Journal of Economic Cooperation and Development* 35(2), 1-42.

Khan T., Ahmed H., 2001. Risk Management: An Analysis of Issues in Islamic Financial Industry. *Occasional Paper* 5, Islamic Research and Training Institute.

Mghaieth A., Khanchel I., 2015. The Determinants of Cost/Profit Efficiency of Islamic Banks Before, During and After the Subprime Crisis Using SFA Approach. *International Journal of Accounting and Financial Reporting* 5(2), 74-97.

Marliana, A., Shahida, S., Abdul, I., 2011. Operational risk in Islamic banks: examination of issues. *Qualitative Research in Financial Markets* 3(2), 131-151.

McNeil A. J., Frey R., Embrechts P., 2005. *Quantitative Risk Management: Concepts, Techniques and Tools*. Princeton: Princeton University Press.

Meero A. A., 2015. The Relationship between Capital Structure and Performance in Gulf Countries Banks: A Comparative Study between Islamic Banks and Conventional Banks. *International Journal of Economics and Finance* 7(12), 140-154.

Miniaoui H., Gohou G., 2013. Did Islamic Banking Perform Better During the Financial Crisis? Evidence from the UAE. *Journal of Islamic Economics, Banking and Finance* 9(2), 115-130.

Muhammad H., Mahvish T., Arshiva T., Wajeeh M., 2012. Comparative Performance Study of Conventional and Islamic Banking in Pakistan. *International Research Journal of Finance and Economics* 83, 63-72.

Olson D., Zoubi T. A., 2011. Efficiency and bank profitability in MENA countries. .*Emerging Markets Review* 12, 94-110.

Ouerghi F. F., 2014. Are Islamic Banks More Resilient To Global Financial Crisis Than Conventional Banks? *Asian Economic and Financial Review* 4(7), 941-955

Parashar S.P., Venkatesh J., 2010. How did Islamic banks do during global financial crisis? *Banks and Bank Systems* 5(4), 54-62.

Rajhi W., Hassari S.A., 2013. Islamic banks and financial stability: a comparative empirical analysis between MENA and South-East Asian countries. *Région et Développement* 37, 149-177.

Rashwan, M. H., Ehab, H., 2016. Comparative Efficiency Study between Islamic and Traditional Banks. *Journal of Finance and Economics* 4(3), 74-87.

Ray D., Cashman E., 1999. Operational risks, bidding strategies and information policies in restructured power markets. *Decision Support Systems* 24, 175-82.

Regaieg B., Abidi E., 2015. Les banques islamiques face à la crise des subprimes : étude de *l'x-efficience* par la méthode SFA. *International Journal of Innovation and Applied Studies* 10(1), 45-59.

Rosman R., Wahab N.A., Zainol Z., 2014. Efficiency of Islamic banks during the financial crisis: An analysis of Middle Eastern and Asian countries. *Pacific-Basin Finance Journal* 28, 76-90.

Said A., 2012. Comparing the change in efficiency of the Western and Islamic banking systems. *Journal of Money, Investment and Banking* 23, 149-180.

Said A., 2013. Risks and efficiency in the Islamic banking systems: the case of selected Islamic banks in MENA region. *International Journal of Economics and Financial Issues* 3(1), 66-73.

Sillah B. M. S., Khokhar I., Khan M. N., 2015. Technical Efficiency of Banks and the Effects of Risk Factors on the Bank Efficiency in Gulf Cooperation Council Countries. *Journal of Applied Finance & Banking* 5(2), 109-122.

Siraj, K. K., Pillai, P. S., 2012. Comparative study on performance of Islamic banks and conventional banks in GCC region. *Journal of Applied Finance & Banking* 2(3), 123-161.

Soedarmono W., Eko Pramono S., TaraziA., 2017. The procyclicality of loan loss provisions in Islamic banks. *Research in International Business and Finance* 39, 911-919.

Srairi S. A., 2010. Cost and profit efficiency of conventional and Islamic banks in GCC countries. *Journal of Productivity Analysis* 34(1), 45-62.

Sufian F., Noor M.A.N.M., 2009. The determinants of Islamic bank's efficiency changes: Empirical evidence from the MENA and Asian Countries Islamic banking sectors. *International Journal of Islamic and Middle Eastern Finance and Management* 2(2), 120-138.

Toumi K., Viviani J-L., Belkacem L., 2016. A Comparison of Leverage and Profitability of Islamic and Conventional Banks. 6th International Finance Conference on Financial Crisis and Governance. Cambridge Scholars Publishing (Ed.). April.

Trad N., Trabelsi M. A., Goux, J. F., 2017. Risk and profitability of Islamic banks: A religious deception or an alternative solution? *European Research on Management and Business Economics* 23(1), 40-45.

Wahidudin A. N., Subramanian U., Kamaluddin A. M., Bahari M. Z., 2014. Factors of Profitability in Islamic Banking - Difference between MENA and ASEAN countries, *Social Science Research Network*, March 21, papers.ssrn.com/sol3

Yudistira, D., 2004. Efficiency in Islamic banking: An empirical analysis of eighteen banks. *Islamic Economic Studies* 12(1), 1-19.

Zarrouk H., 2012. Does Financial Crisis Reduce Islamic Banks' Performance? Evidence from GCC Countries. *Journal of Islamic Finance and Business Research* 1(1), 1-16.

Zehri F., Al-Herch N., 2013. The impact of the global financial crisis on the financial institutions: A comparison between Islamic banks and conventional banks. *Journal of Islamic Economics Banking and Finance* 9, 69-88

Zeitun R., 2012. Determinants of Islamic and Conventional Banks Performance in GCC Countries Using Panel Data Analysis. *Global Economy and Finance Journal* 5(1), 53-72.

Zoubi T.A., Al-Khazali O., 2007. Empirical testing of the loss provisions of banks in the GCC region. *Managerial Finance* 33(7), 500-511.

Zins A., Weill L., 2017. Islamic banking and risk: The impact of Basel II. *Economic Modelling* 64, 626-637.

APPENDIX

Table A1. A review of panel data surveys upon IBs in the MENA region

Authors	Sample and coverage	Period	Method	Outcomes
Performance of Islamic banks (IBs) compared to conventional banks (CBs)				
Olson and Zoubi (2011)	80 banks; 10 MENA countries: 14 IBs; 66 CBs	2000-2008	DFA, panel data	IBs are less efficient (cost), more risk-prone and profitable than BC.
Zeitun(2012)	51 banks; GCC: 13 IBs; 38 CBs	2002-2009	Panel data	Property and the age of banks do not influence performance: IBs do not differ from CBs. Profitability correlates positively with GDP and negatively with inflation.
Hidayat and Abduh (2012)	37 banks; Bahrain: 23 IBs ; 14 CBs	2005-2010	Panel data	Lag in the impact of recession.
Abedifar et al. (2013)	553 banks; 118 IBs (86 MENA); 354CBs	1999-2009	Panel data (random effects)	Small leveraged IBs have lower credit risk and are more stable than CBs. During the crisis, large IBs are less stable than large CBs.
Beck et al. (2013)	500 banks; one third in the MENA region: 88 IBs ; 422 CBs	1995-2009	Panel data	IBs are better capitalized, more liquid and profitable than CBs, but size effect reduces the advantage.
Rajhi and Hassari (2013)	557 banks; 16 countries (10 MENA): 90 IBs; 467 CBs	2000-2008	Panel data (GMM)	Positive link between stability (*z-score*) and size.
Al-Deehani et al. (2015)	25 banks; GCC: 13 IBs; 12 CBs	2001-2012	GLM (General Linear Model - Multivariate)	IBs are more risk prone and less profitable during the recession.
Kamarudin et al. (2014)	74 banks; GCC: 27 IBs; 47 CBs	2007-2011	DEA, GLS (Generalized Least Squares)	IBs are less efficient (cost, profit and income) than CBs.
Ouerghi (2014)	94 banks;5 Oil monarchies + Malaysia30 IBs; 60 CBs	2007-2010	GLS (Generalized Least Squares)	IBs are less efficient and profitable, more prone to credit risk than CBs. Large IBs perform better than large CBs.
Performance of Islamic banks (IBs) without comparison with conventional banks (CBs)				
Wahidudin et al. (2014)	91 banks; 19 countries (14 MENA): 69 IBs; 21 IBs (including Southeast Asia)	2004-2009	Panel data	Higher operation costs for MENA IBs.
Ben Hassine and Limani (2014)	22 IBs; MENA countries	2005-2009	Panel data	Inefficiency is rather technical or organisational than regulatory or allocative.
Trad et al. (2016)	78 banks; 13 countries: 12 MENA (74 IBs) + Pakistan (4 IBs)	2004-2013	Panel data (GMM)	Profitability (ROA, ROE) and liquidity risk negatively correlated. IBs well capitalized. Ambiguous impact of macro- economic variables.

Source: Authors.

Table A2. Correlation matrix

	ROAA	ROAE	LLP	Sharia Board	Specific contracts	CR	LTLR	STLR	Lnzscore	Size	Concen-tration	Age	Owner-ship	Oil-Monar.	Infla-tion	GDP growth
ROAA	1.00															
ROAE	0.76*	1.00														
LLP	-0.28*	-0.22*	1.00													
Sharia Board	-0.13*	-0.29*	-0.08	1.00												
Specific contracts	0.02	-0.001	0.13*	0.11*	1.00											
CR	-0.17*	-0.17*	0.05	0.07	0.18*	1.00										
LTLR	0.22*	0.30*	-0.07*	-0.17*	0.32*	-0.54*	1.00									
STLR	-0.15*	-0.17*	0.008	0.07	-0.16*	0.02	-0.49*	1.00								
Lnzscore	0.13*	0.16*	-0.1	-0.10*	0.15*	-0.13*	0.16*	-0.01	1.00							
Size	0.02	-0.11*	-0.14*	0.62*	0.26*	-0.16*	0.05	0.003	-0.05	1.00						
Concentration	0.16*	0.19*	-0.11*	0.10*	-0.03	-0.15*	-0.04	-0.05	0.03	0.34*	1.00					
Age	0.01	0.12*	-0.06	-0.24*	0.14*	-0.03	0.10*	-0.25	0.009	-0.23*	-0.06	1.00				
Ownership	0.09	0.09	0.04	-0.20*	0.08	0.02	0.35*	-0.42*	0.06	-0.05	-0.13*	0.07	1.00			
Oil-monarchy	0.02	-0.04	0.006	0.03	0.19*	-0.08	0.33*	-0.1	-0.13*	0.10*	-0.33*	0.07	0.29*	1.00		
Inflation	0.09	0.21*	0.14*	-0.18*	-0.16*	0.23*	-0.20*	0.02	-0.11*	-0.26*	0.09	0.06	-0.23*	-0.39*	1.00	
GDP growth	0.12*	0.06	-0.13*	0.19*	0.07	-0.15*	-0.02	0.11*	-0.002	0.21*	0.12*	-0.12	-0.07	0.06	-0.36*	1.00

** $p<0.1$. Source: Authors.*

Figure 1. Clusters according to axes 1-2

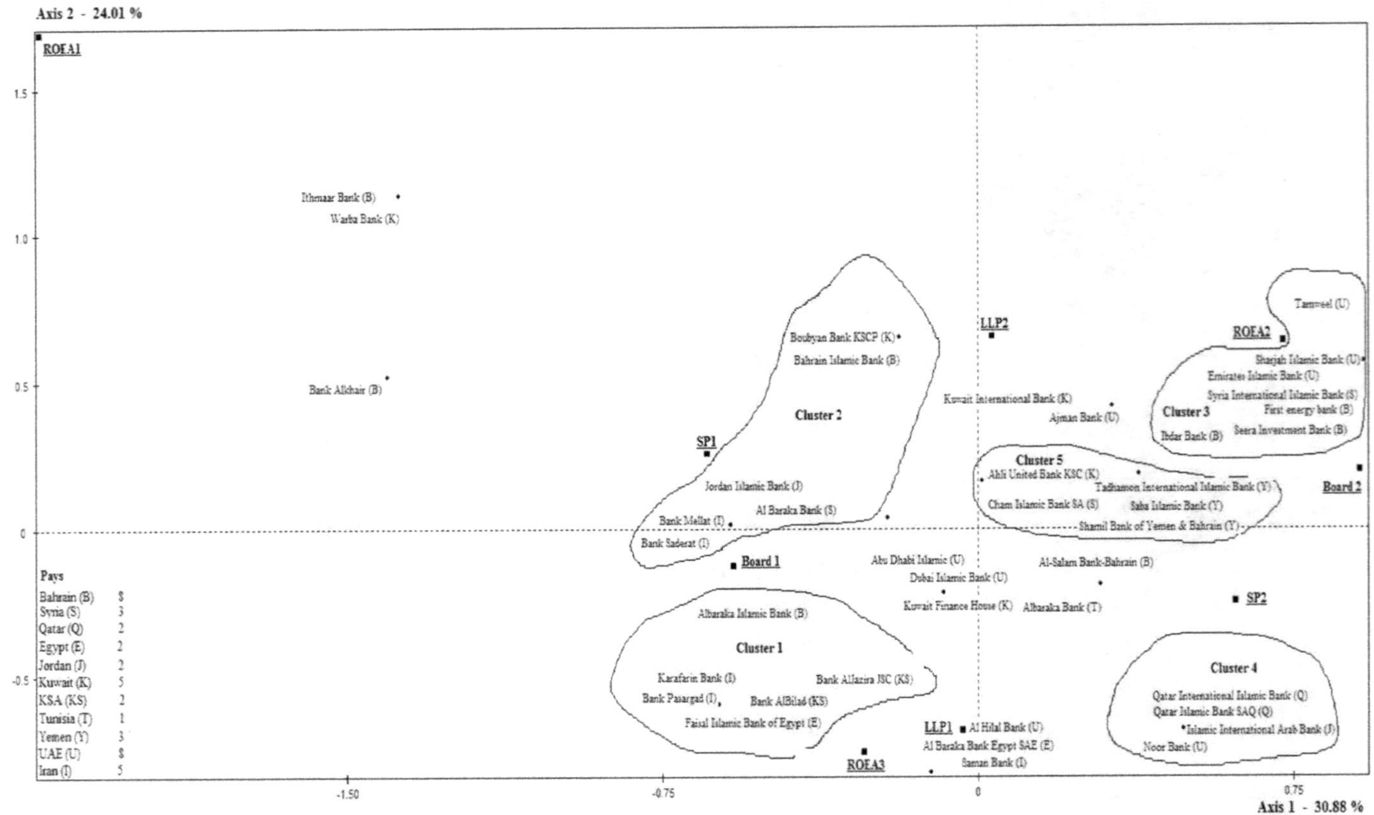

La performance des banques islamiques en région MENA : les risques spécifiques sont-ils un attribut mineur ?

Résumé - Les banques islamiques (BI) font face à des risques spécifiques liés à la conformité des contrats au regard de la *Chariaa*. Nous étudions 53 BI dans 11 pays de la région MENA entre 2007 et 2014, en utilisant d'abord une analyse transversale appliquée à 2013. Un modèle de données de panel avec variables instrumentales estime l'impact des risques sur les rendements des actifs et des capitaux propres. Quatre résultats saillants émergent : la conformité à la *Chariaa* exerce un effet ambigu sur la performance; la spécificité islamique est un attribut mineur au regard de la part insignifiante des contrats de partage des profits et des pertes (PLS) dans l'actif total; il n'y a pas de relation entre la conformité à la *Chariaa* et le risque spécifique; les provisions pour pertes couvrent l'ensemble des risques et non les seuls risques spécifiques (PLS).

Mots-clés

Banques islamiques
Performance des banques
Risques
Région MENA
Variables instrumentales

Région et Développement

n° 49-2019

www.regionetdeveloppement.org

L'accumulation du capital humain : modèle théorique et évaluation dans le cas de la Tunisie

Ahmed BELLAKHDHAR*

Résumé - Les études empiriques utilisant le capital humain sont sensibles à la manière dont il est mesuré et amènent parfois des résultats divergents. Comme causes invoquées, l'utilisation du nombre moyen d'années d'étude comme proxy du capital humain ou encore l'ignorance de la qualité de l'éducation. En ce sens, nous proposons un modèle théorique d'accumulation de compétences qui intègre simultanément les aspects quantitatifs et qualitatifs de l'éducation et qui tienne compte d'un rendement scolaire décroissant. Ce modèle est utilisé pour estimer un modèle structuré de type Macro-Mincer intégrant aussi l'expérience professionnelle. Comme application, nous avons pris le cas de l'économie tunisienne sur la période 1976-2010. Les résultats empiriques obtenus montrent que la négligence de la dimension qualité mène à un effet positif non statistiquement significatif du nombre moyen d'années d'étude et que le taux de rendement social associé est surestimé. Par contre, l'estimation d'un modèle qui intègre sous une certaine forme les deux aspects de l'éducation, qualité et quantité, montre que leurs effets sont statistiquement significatifs.

Classification JEL

C51, H52, J21

Mots-clés

Accumulation de capital humain
Qualité de l'éducation
Taux de rendement scolaire
Modèle Macro-Mincer
Tunisie

* Institut Supérieur de Gestion de Tunis ; bellakhadar@yahoo.fr

1. INTRODUCTION

Le capital humain peut être défini comme « l'ensemble des compétences, qualifications et autres capacités possédées par un individu à des fins productives. Il peut être inné ou s'acquérir durant le cursus scolaire, universitaire ou au cours d'expériences professionnelles, par la transmission de savoirs et qualifications » (Simonnet, 2003). Dans cette logique, les investissements éducatifs peuvent être évalués, comme tout autre investissement, en termes de taux de rendement. Pour les individus, l'éducation peut permettre d'améliorer leur productivité, d'augmenter leurs revenus et leurs chances d'employabilité.

Malgré les efforts de formulation théorique d'un modèle d'accumulation de capital humain, le manque de précision dans les indicateurs mesurant le capital humain a été souligné et pose de sérieuses difficultés méthodologiques. L'utilisation du nombre moyen d'années d'étude comme proxy du capital humain et l'ignorance des aspects qualitatifs de l'éducation constituent les principales critiques qui ont été évoquées. Pour mieux comprendre les mécanismes régissant le lien entre l'éducation, l'accumulation de savoir et la croissance économique en général, il est donc requis de donner une définition adéquate du capital humain. Quelle est la spécification théorique la plus cohérente qui retrace le processus d'accumulation des compétences ? Est-ce que les moyens plus ou moins accordés à la formation du capital humain par les politiques publiques jouent un rôle particulier ?

Dans cet article, notre démarche consiste à formuler dans un premier temps un modèle théorique sur la relation éducation/croissance qui intègre à la fois la dimension qualité et la dimension quantité du capital humain. Cette formulation théorique est par la suite utilisée pour élaborer un modèle empirique de type « Macro-Mincer » intégrant de plus l'expérience professionnelle. Une application est donnée dans le cas de l'économie tunisienne sur la période allant de 1976 à 2010. Le paramètre fondamental à estimer est le taux de rendement scolaire. Il constitue l'élément principal dans l'évaluation empirique de capital humain. Pour tester à quel niveau la variable qualité d'éducation considérée est déterminante dans l'évaluation du rendement scolaire, deux modèles alternatifs seront estimés : le premier est formulé sans tenir compte de la dimension qualité et le deuxième intègre les deux aspects quantitatifs et qualitatifs de l'éducation. Le but est d'évaluer les impacts directs de la quantité (nombre moyen d'années d'éducation) et de la qualité (à travers les ressources financières engagées par les pouvoirs publics) de l'éducation, ainsi que leur effet global sur le rendement de l'investissement en capital humain.

Le présent article est structuré comme suit. La section 2 présente le modèle théorique d'accumulation de capital humain. Dans une section 3, le modèle empirique est estimé. La section 4 analyse l'évolution du rendement scolaire au cours du temps et ses déterminants. La dernière section conclut.

2. MODÈLE D'ACCUMULATION DE CAPITAL HUMAIN

Les études empiriques montrent qu'un rapport positif entre le capital humain et la croissance économique n'est pas toujours validé. Le manque de consensus empirique est lié principalement à l'absence d'une définition adéquate et à une évaluation imprécise du capital humain. Pour surmonter ces insuffisances, on essaye de développer un modèle théorique d'accumulation de compétences qui intègre les aspects quantitatifs et qualitatifs de l'éducation et qui tienne compte du rendement scolaire décroissant. La spécification retenue propose une mesure agrégée du capital humain à travers l'estimation d'un modèle empirique structuré de type Macro-Mincer comme chez Soto (2006) et Krueger et Lindahl (2000).

2.1. Spécification du modèle théorique

On considère le cas d'un individu (ménage) représentatif à durée de vie infinie, dont les préférences sont représentées par une fonction d'utilité qui dépend de sa consommation c. Cette fonction d'utilité est de type Ramsey à élasticité de substitution intertemporelle constante (σ^{-1}), avec $\sigma \neq 1$. Le taux de préférence pour le présent est paramétré par ρ.

$$\int_0^\infty \frac{c_t^{1-\sigma} - 1}{1-\sigma} e^{-\rho t} dt, \quad \rho > 0 \tag{1}$$

Ce ménage détient des actifs indiqués par la variable a. Il choisit son niveau d'épargne, sa consommation c, la part du temps consacrée à l'éducation u_h et ses dépenses scolaires privées $\overline{D}$ afin de maximiser sa fonction d'utilité, sous la contrainte d'accumulation de son capital humain et de son budget. Le capital humain est accumulé suivant la fonction suivante :

$$\dot{h} = B(u_h h)^{\vartheta} \overline{D}^{1-\vartheta} \tag{2}$$

où h est le niveau du capital humain par travailleur et $\dot{h}$ sa variation. B est le paramètre reflétant l'efficacité de la « reproduction des savoirs ». Le paramètre ϑ est supposé positif et inférieur à l'unité. On remarque que ce modèle d'accumulation prend la forme mathématique d'une équation différentielle de Bernoulli. Par hypothèse, le temps disponible est normalisé à l'unité. Une fraction u_h du temps est consacrée à la formation, $0 < u_h < 1$, et le complément $(1 - u_h)$ à d'autres activités. Dans la pratique, la valeur empirique de la fraction u_h est non observée directement. Elle est souvent modélisée par le nombre moyen d'années d'étude atteint dans une économie S divisé par l'espérance de vie à la naissance L_e soit $u_h \approx (S/L_e)$.

À chaque période, on suppose que l'actif total du ménage est la somme du salaire réel après impôt, $(1-\tau_w)w(1-u_h)h$, et des encaisses financières nettes d'impôt obtenues à la fin de période, $[(1-\tau_k)r]a$. Le ménage répartit ses ressources entre consommation privée, dépenses scolaires et épargne. Sa contrainte budgétaire est donnée par l'équation suivante :

$$\dot{a} = (1-\tau_k)ra + (1-\tau_w)w(1-u_h)h - c - (1-s_d)\overline{D} \tag{3}$$

où $\dot{a}$ est l'épargne restante, r est le taux d'intérêt réel et w le salaire réel par unité de capital humain. Dans ce modèle, on suppose que l'Etat peut intervenir pour subventionner les dépenses scolaires privées à un taux s_d et financer ses dépenses publiques en éducation. Ses ressources principales proviennent de la taxation des salaires des ménages à un taux τ_w et de la taxation des revenus du capital à un taux τ_k. Les données empiriques sur la Tunisie montrent que les deux types de dépenses scolaires (privées et publiques) sont en moyenne proportionnelles. On suppose alors une relation linéaire entre les deux variables définie comme suit : $D_{priv} \approx \ell D_{pub}$, où ℓ est une constante positive.

Soit g_x le taux de croissance d'une variable x, $g_x = \dot{x}/x$ et x_0 sa valeur initiale. La résolution de l'équation différentielle (2) et du programme de maximisation d'utilité dans la logique d'optimisation aboutit aux solutions suivantes :

$$\begin{cases} logh = logh_0 + B\left(\ell \times \frac{u_y}{u_h}\right)^{1-\vartheta} \left(\frac{y_0}{h_0}\right)^{1-\vartheta} \left(\frac{D_{pub}}{Y}\right)^{1-\vartheta} u_h & (5) \\ g_h = \vartheta B(1-\alpha)^{1-\vartheta} \left(\frac{1-\vartheta}{\vartheta}\right)^{1-\vartheta} \left(\frac{1-\tau_w}{1-s_d}\right)^{1-\vartheta} \left(\frac{y_0}{h_0}\right)^{1-\vartheta} u_h & (6) \end{cases}$$

La subvention de l'éducation s_d favorise l'accumulation des compétences, par contre le taux d'impôt τ_w exerce un impact négatif. Ces résultats sont confirmés par différentes études empiriques (Hanushek et Kimko, 2000 ; Pritchett, 2001 ; Soto, 2006 ; Chenu, 2016).

Dans l'évaluation du capital humain, le taux de rendement scolaire reste l'ingrédient principal. Il mesure l'impact marginal d'une année d'étude sur le revenu moyen (*généralement approximé par le PIB par travailleur*). Les travaux empiriques réalisés à ce niveau montrent que cet effet marginal est décroissant. Dans notre cas, on note le taux de rendement scolaire par $\hat{\rho}(S)$. Il est exprimé par :

$$\hat{\rho}(S) = \frac{dlog(y)}{dS} \approx \frac{dlog(h)}{dS} = \vartheta B(\ell \times L_e \times u_y)^{1-\vartheta} \left(\frac{y_0}{h_0}\right)^{1-\vartheta} \left(\frac{D_{pub}}{Y}\right)^{1-\vartheta} S^{\vartheta-1} \quad (7)$$

Étant donné que le paramètre ϑ est positif et inférieur à l'unité, on déduit alors que le taux de rendement marginal est décroissant en fonction du nombre moyen d'années d'étude (*Indicateur de la quantité d'éducation*) et croissant en fonction de la part des dépenses scolaires publiques dans le PIB (*indicateur macroéconomique de l'effort quantitatif fourni par un pays afin d'améliorer la qualité de son enseignement)* (Dessus, 2000). L'effet global est la résultante des deux effets quantité et qualité d'éducation.

En se basant sur les résultats précédents, il est possible de réexprimer le taux de croissance du capital humain comme suit :

$$g_h = \frac{dlog(h)}{dt} \approx \frac{log(h_t) - log(h_0)}{\Delta t} = \underbrace{\vartheta B\left(\ell \times \frac{u_y}{u_h}\right)^{1-\vartheta} \left(\frac{y_0}{h_0}\right)^{1-\vartheta}}_{\alpha_h} \left(\frac{D_{pub}}{Y}\right)^{1-\vartheta} u_h \quad (8)$$

Ceci implique que

$$\alpha_h \left(\frac{D_{pub}}{Y}\right)^{1-\vartheta} = \vartheta B(1-\alpha)^{1-\vartheta} \left(\frac{1-\vartheta}{\vartheta}\right)^{1-\vartheta} \left(\frac{1-\tau_w}{1-s_d}\right)^{1-\vartheta} \left(\frac{y_0}{h_0}\right)^{1-\vartheta} \approx Constante \quad (9)$$

Ce résultat nous permet de définir le niveau du capital humain éducatif dans une économie en fonction de variables agrégées comme suit :

$$H = H_0 \times e^{\alpha_h \left(\frac{D_{pub}}{Y}\right)^{1-\vartheta} S} \quad (10)$$

où H est le niveau agrégé de capital humain éducatif, S est le nombre moyen d'années d'étude et $\left(\frac{D_{pub}}{Y}\right)$ est la part des dépenses scolaires publiques dans le PIB. α_h est le taux de rendement d'une année d'étude corrigée par l'indice qualité. C'est le paramètre principal à estimer. Cette spécification théorique sert de base à la construction d'un modèle empirique structuré qui permet d'évaluer le capital humain à partir des données disponibles. L'estimation de ce modèle macroéconomique d'accumulation des compétences permet de saisir les externalités associées au capital humain.

2.2. Construction du modèle économétrique et méthode d'estimation

La construction du modèle empirique s'appuie sur les méthodes adoptées notamment par Mincer (1974), Klenow & Rodriguez Clare (1997), Hall & Jones (1999), Bils & Klenow (2000), Pritchett (2001) et Aiyar & Feyrer (2002). Une des hypothèses de base du modèle standard de capital humain est que les salariés sont rémunérés à leur productivité marginale et que celle-ci augmente avec le stock de connaissances accumulées. Le bénéfice net marginal d'une année de scolarisation peut alors être estimé à partir du revenu des individus selon leur niveau d'éducation. Il est supposé constant, indépendamment du moment et du système éducatif existants.

Mais certaines critiques sont à adresser à cette hypothèse. Le taux de rendement d'une année d'étude n'est pas constant mais peut être variable avec le niveau scolaire selon le niveau de développement (Barro et Lee, 2010). Les résultats de Pritchett (2003) et Soto (2006) montrent également que lorsque les pays sont pris comme homogènes en termes de qualité d'éducation, le taux de rendement moyen de Mincer est dans la plupart des cas surestimé. Le coefficient associé au nombre d'années d'étude dans les équations de régression traditionnelles de Mincer peut ainsi inclure les deux effets de la quantité et de la qualité d'éducation.

Tableau 1. Processus d'évaluation par étape du capital humain

1	• *Collecte des données disponibles sur les principales variables de modèle* $\left[y, S, \left(\frac{D_{pub}}{Y}\right), L_e \text{ et } Exp\right]$
2	• *Évaluation empirique du paramètre ϑ par l'estimation du modèle* $S\left(\frac{D_{pub}}{Y}, L_e;\ \boldsymbol{\vartheta}\right) = \mu_0 - \boldsymbol{\vartheta} L_e log\left(\frac{D_{pub}}{Y}\right) + \varepsilon \quad \Rightarrow \quad (\widehat{\boldsymbol{\vartheta}} = ?)$
3	• *Construction de la variable DYVS sachant $(\boldsymbol{S},\ \boldsymbol{D_{pub}/Y}\ \&\ \widehat{\boldsymbol{\vartheta}})$* $\boldsymbol{DYVS}\left(S, \frac{D_{pub}}{Y}, \hat{\vartheta}\right) = \left(\frac{D_{pub}}{Y}\right)^{1-\hat{\vartheta}} S$
4	• *Introduction de DYVS dans le modèle principal et estimation de $(\boldsymbol{\alpha_h}, \boldsymbol{\alpha_2}, \boldsymbol{\alpha_3})$* $log\left(\frac{y}{y_0}\right) = \boldsymbol{\alpha_h} DYVS + \boldsymbol{\alpha_2} Exp + \boldsymbol{\alpha_3} Exp2 + \varepsilon \ \Rightarrow\ (\widehat{\boldsymbol{\alpha}}_h = ?\ \widehat{\boldsymbol{\alpha}}_2 = ?\ \widehat{\boldsymbol{\alpha}}_3 = ?)$
5	• *Construction du stock de capital humain par travailleur* $\boldsymbol{h}$ $log\boldsymbol{h} = log h_0 + \widehat{\boldsymbol{\alpha}}_h \left(\frac{D_{pub}}{Y}\right)^{1-\hat{\vartheta}} S + \widehat{\boldsymbol{\alpha}}_2 Experience + \widehat{\boldsymbol{\alpha}}_3 (Experience)^2$

Par comparaison à la spécification standard de Mincer, limitée aux données microéconomiques, l'estimation d'un modèle macroéconomique permet de comprendre comment l'éducation agit globalement sur l'économie et avec quelle ampleur. Elle peut aider à la formulation de politiques éducatives globales en allant au-delà des évaluations de rentabilité microéconomique. Pour mieux comprendre les mécanismes régissant le lien entre l'éducation, l'accumulation de savoir et la croissance économique en général, il est donc fondamental de savoir à quel niveau la correction par l'indice de qualité d'éducation peut améliorer la significativité du coefficient associé au nombre moyen d'années d'étude. Est-ce que l'impact de la qualité d'éducation sur le rendement scolaire est positif ? Quelle est l'importance de l'apprentissage postsecondaire dans l'accumulation des connaissances, dans notre cas d'étude en Tunisie ?

Nous retenons comme modèle empirique à estimer un modèle macroéconomique structuré de type Macro-Mincer qui modélise la relation entre le taux de croissance du PIB par travailleur et le nombre d'années d'étude corrigé par la qualité d'éducation. Ce modèle intègre en plus l'expérience professionnelle et son carré pour tenir compte de l'importance de l'apprentissage dans l'accumulation des connaissances. La forme quadratique permet une représentation de la concavité du profil des gains dus à l'investissement postscolaire en capital humain, c'est-à-dire des taux de rendement décroissants.

$$log\left(\frac{y}{y_0}\right) = \boldsymbol{\alpha_h}\left(\frac{D_{pub}}{Y}\right)^{1-\vartheta} S + \boldsymbol{\alpha_2}Experience + \boldsymbol{\alpha_3}(Experience)^2 + \varepsilon \qquad (11)$$

où y est le niveau de PIB par travailleur au coût des facteurs à prix constant, y_0 est le niveau de production par travailleur d'un actif ayant un capital humain éducatif nul et sans expérience professionnelle, ε est le terme d'erreur. Ainsi, la division par rapport à y_0 permet de détecter l'impact spécifiquement lié à la compétence (éducation et formation professionnelle). Les variables $y, S, \left(\frac{D_{pub}}{Y}\right)$ et $(Experience)$ sont établies à partir des bases de données disponibles. Les différents paramètres $(\alpha_h, \alpha_2, \alpha_3)$ vont être estimés à partir du modèle empirique qui prend la forme économétrique générale suivante :

$$log\left(\frac{y}{y_0}\right) = \boldsymbol{\alpha_h}DYVS + \boldsymbol{\alpha_2}Exp + \boldsymbol{\alpha_3}Exp2 + \varepsilon \qquad (12)$$

Dans cette équation, les variables explicatives sont (i) le niveau de scolarité corrigé par la qualité d'éducation (analytiquement exprimé par $\left(\frac{D_{pub}}{Y}\right)^{1-\vartheta} S$) et indiqué par *DYVS*, (ii) l'expérience professionnelle et son carré indiqués respectivement par les variables *Exp* et *Exp*2. Pour obtenir la valeur de la variable *DYVS*, on a besoin d'établir dans un premier temps une évaluation du poids ϑ suivant les données disponibles. Pour cela, on a adopté une méthode économétrique similaire à celle utilisée par Bils et Knelow (2000) et Schoellman (2011). Le modèle empirique obtenu prend la forme générale suivante (voir Annexe) :

$$S = \boldsymbol{\mu_0} + \boldsymbol{\mu_1}L_e log\left(\frac{D_{pub}}{Y}\right) + \boldsymbol{\varepsilon} \qquad (13)$$

Il s'agit d'une équation de régression qui relie le niveau scolaire optimal à la qualité d'éducation. ε désigne le terme d'erreur, μ_0 est un terme constant et μ_1 est l'estimateur de $(-\vartheta)$ tel que $(\hat{\vartheta} = -\hat{\mu}_1)$. Une fois les différents éléments du modèle obtenus, il devient possible de construire le stock de capital humain par travailleur défini par la relation suivante :

$$logh = \underbrace{logh_0}_{Capital\ Initial} + \underbrace{\alpha_h\left(\frac{D_{pub}}{Y}\right)^{1-\vartheta} S}_{Capital\ Educatif} + \underbrace{\alpha_2 Experience + \alpha_3(Experience)^2}_{Capital\ par\ Expériences\ Professionnelle} \qquad (14)$$

Cette spécification montre que le capital humain total est la somme d'un capital initial, d'un capital éducatif et d'un capital-compétence généré par l'expérience professionnelle sur le marché du travail. Le premier type de capital revêt des formes diverses. Le capital éducatif représente l'ensemble des compétences acquises par l'investissement en éducation et nécessite une attention particulière. Le tableau 1 résume le processus d'évaluation du capital humain étape par étape.

Dans ce qui suit, on va présenter les variables du modèle, les estimations empiriques nécessaires et interpréter les résultats obtenus.

3. ÉVALUATION DU CAPITAL HUMAIN

3.1. Évaluation du poids de la qualité d'éducation

Dans notre analyse, la valeur du paramètre ϑ est déterminante. En effet, pour une valeur égale à l'unité la dimension qualité d'éducation est ignorée, le taux de rendement scolaire est constant comme chez Lucas (1988). Dans ce cas, la plupart des résultats empiriques trouvés sont non convaincants et parfois contradictoires.

Van Leeuwen (2007), Földvári et van Leeuwen (2005), Krueger et Lindah (2001), Schoellman (2011) et Paltrinieri (2013) ont montré que le taux de rendement scolaire est variable au cours du temps. Il peut connaître des phases de croissance, de décroissance ou de stabilité.

Le paramètre ϑ est supposé positif et inférieur à l'unité. Nos résultats théoriques obtenus dans le cadre de ce modèle montrent l'existence d'un effet quantité microéconomique (où le taux de rendement privé est décroissant avec le nombre moyen d'années d'étude) accompagné d'un effet macroéconomique positif exercé par la qualité d'éducation sur le taux de rendement scolaire. L'importance de l'effet global dépend du poids relatif de chacun de ces deux effets. De manière précise, l'importance de l'effet global dépend étroitement de la valeur de ϑ. Pour estimer ce paramètre, le modèle empirique utilisé prend la forme générale suivante :

$$S = \boldsymbol{\mu}_0 - \boldsymbol{\vartheta} L_e logDY + \boldsymbol{\varepsilon} \tag{15}$$

Dans cette équation de régression, la variable expliquée est le nombre moyen d'années d'étude de la population âgée de 15 ans et plus. Elle est extraite de la base de données réalisée par Barro et Lee (2010). Les données que nous avons utilisées concernent uniquement le cas de la Tunisie. La variable explicative est le produit de l'espérance de vie à la naissance par le *log* de la qualité d'éducation. Elle est indiquée par $L_e LogDY$.

3.1.1. Présentation des données

Notre étude est appliquée au cas de la Tunisie sur la période 1976-2010, soit 35 observations pour chaque variable du modèle. Dans l'équation (15), la variable à expliquer S mesure le nombre moyen d'années de scolarisation de la population âgée de 15 ans et plus. Elle est obtenue à partir de la base de données réalisée par Barro et Lee (2010). Les données montrent l'existence d'une croissance régulière de la variable S sur toute la période d'étude. Elle est passée de 2.5 années scolaires en 1976 à plus de 7 en 2010. Cette augmentation est largement due au retrait de la population active âgée de 60 ans et plus dont le niveau d'éducation est relativement faible (environ une année d'étude) et à l'entrée progressive de la population active de 15-24 ans, dont le niveau de scolarité est voisin de 6 ans sur la période considérée.

Les données sur l'espérance de vie à la naissance indiquée par L_e sont obtenues à partir de Penn World Table (PWT version 6.3). S'agissant de la part des dépenses publiques d'éducation dans le PIB, notée par DY, on a utilisé la base tunisienne constituée par l'Institut d'Études Quantitatives (IEQ). Actuellement, 25% du budget de l'Etat est consacré à l'éducation. Les dépenses publiques totales de fonctionnement et d'investissement en éducation ont nettement progressé durant les trois dernières décennies. Elles sont passées de 5,2% du PIB en 1980 à 6,5% en 2000 pour dépasser 7% du PIB en 2010. Les ressources publiques affectées par la Tunisie à l'éducation sont parmi les plus élevées des pays à revenu moyen et des pays de même niveau de développement. La dépense totale de l'Etat en éducation s'élevait à 6,7 % du PIB en 2002, par rapport à une moyenne de 5,1 % pour les pays à revenu moyen et de 4,9 % pour les pays de l'OCDE.

3.1.2. Estimation et interprétation

Les résultats des estimations données dans le tableau 2 montrent que la valeur estimée du paramètre ϑ est de 0,2. Elle est positive et statistiquement significative à un risque d'erreur de 5%. La valeur estimée $\hat{\vartheta}$ est inférieure à l'unité ce qui confirme les hypothèses théoriques de notre modèle intégré d'accumulation de capital humain. La valeur du R^2 corrigé excède 87% et la p-value du modèle, indiquée par la statistique ($Prob > F$), est inférieure à la valeur critique 0.05. La relation positive entre la qualité d'éducation et le niveau de scolarité apparaît donc statistiquement significative.

Tableau 2. Estimation de l'effet de la qualité d'éducation

Variable dépendante : Nombre moyen d'années d'étude S	
L_eLogDY	-0.20**
	(-6.576)
cons	-34.2**
	(-5.7)
Fisher	43.25
Prob > F	0.001
AdjR-squared	0.875

( ) indique la statistique de Student. (**) implique que le coefficient est significatif à un risque d'erreur de 5%. Source : Calcul de l'auteur.

Une fois le paramètre ϑ estimé, il est possible de construire la variable principale de l'équation de régression (12) qui est le niveau de scolarité corrigé par la qualité d'éducation.

3.2. Estimation du taux de rendement scolaire

Comme tout investissement, celui en capital humain peut faire l'objet d'un calcul du taux de rendement marginal, associé à une dépense ou une année d'étude supplémentaire. Ce rendement peut être évalué comme le rapport entre, d'un côté, le surcroît des revenus du travail que cet investissement permettra d'obtenir sur le restant de la vie active et, de l'autre côté, l'ensemble des coûts occasionnés par cet investissement ou la durée du temps consacrée à l'éducation.

Dans notre étude, le paramètre fondamental à estimer et à traiter de manière détaillée est le taux de rendement scolaire. Pour tester à quel niveau la qualité d'éducation est déterminante dans l'évaluation du rendement scolaire, deux régressions alternatives seront estimées. La première est formulée sans tenir compte de la dimension qualité et la deuxième régression va intégrer simultanément les deux aspects quantitatifs et qualitatifs de l'éducation, tout en tenant compte des rendements scolaires décroissants.

3.2.1. Estimation du taux de rendement sans l'effet qualité de l'éducation

Si on ignore l'effet de la qualité d'éducation ($\vartheta = 1$), le taux de rendement obtenu est similaire à celui déterminé par Lucas (1988). Il est supposé constant et exprimé par $\hat{\rho}(S) = B$.

Ce résultat amène un modèle d'accumulation de capital humain estimé par l'équation de régression suivante :

$$log\left(\frac{y}{y_0}\right) = BS + \boldsymbol{\alpha}_2 Exp + \boldsymbol{\alpha}_3 Exp2 + \varepsilon \qquad (16)$$

Dans ce modèle log-linéaire, on suppose que chaque année d'éducation additionnelle accroît le salaire annuel moyen de B %. Il est donc possible de construire une proxy du capital humain, similaire à la spécification de Mincer. Les variables explicatives sont le nombre moyen d'années d'étude, défini comme précédemment, la variable expérience et son carré. L'expérience professionnelle est calculée suivant la formule $Exp = \hat{a}ge - 6 - S$. La variable $\hat{a}ge$ représente l'âge moyen de la population active pendant une période de temps particulière. La valeur est obtenue à partir des données disponibles produites par l'Institut National de la Statistique (INS). La variable dépendante est le log de PIB réel par travailleur y rapporté à son niveau initial y_0 calculé au début de chaque période. Il est mesuré au coût des facteurs à prix constant de 1990. Les données sont extraites de la base de données de l'IEQ.

Tableau 3. Estimation du rendement scolaire sans l'effet de la qualité d'éducation

	Variable dépendante : $Log\left(\frac{y}{y_0}\right)$
S	0.118 (1.654)
Exp	0.0001 (0.029)
Exp2	-0.0013 (-1.856)
Fisher	15.932
Prob > F	0.0109
AdjR-squared	0.5649

( ) indique la statistique de Student. Source : Calcul de l'auteur.

Sur la période d'étude 1976-2010, les données montrent que la valeur moyenne (en log) du PIB par travailleur est de 1,68. C'est équivalent à un taux de croissance annuel moyen de 3,5%. Une analyse détaillée montre l'existence de certaines phases distinctes dans l'évolution du PIB par travailleur. Au cours de la période allant de 1976 à 1981, le PIB par travailleur (en dinar constant) a connu une croissance annuelle moyenne importante de près de 8%. Entre 1982 et 1991, la variable est passée de la valeur 1,28 à 1,53, soit un taux de croissance annuel moyen qui ne dépasse pas 2%. Sur la période 1991-1994, le niveau moyen du PIB par travailleur s'est stabilisé à une valeur moyenne de 1,65. A partir de 1995, le PIB par travailleur a augmenté à un rythme régulier passant de 1,7 en 1996 à 2,3 en 2010, soit un taux de croissance annuel moyen de près de 2,5%.

Le tableau 3 donne les résultats de l'estimation du paramètre B par la méthode des moindres carrés ordinaires. Sa valeur estimée représente une estimation ponctuelle du taux de rendement scolaire. Elle est positive (11,8%) mais statistiquement non significative pour un intervalle de confiance de 95%.

La littérature empirique montre que la plupart des auteurs qui ont adopté ce modèle standard de Mincer (sans tenir compte de l'effet de la qualité d'éducation) ont trouvé des résultats non satisfaisants en termes de signe et de significativité. Plusieurs explications ont été proposées à ce problème. Une des principales explications met l'accent sur la nécessité de distinguer entre la quantité et la qualité de l'éducation (Pritchett, 2001). Pour surmonter ces insuffisances, on a essayé de construire un modèle qui intègre simultanément les aspects quantitatifs et qualitatifs de l'éducation et qui tienne compte des rendements scolaires décroissants.

3.2.2. Estimation du taux de rendement avec l'effet qualité de l'éducation

On doit à Psacharopoulos (1985 ; avec Woodhall, 1985 ; 1994 ; avec Patrinos, 2002) les études sur la rentabilité de l'investissement éducatif. Les résultats empiriques montrent que les taux de rendement scolaire diminuent avec l'acquisition d'une année d'étude additionnelle. Les travaux de O'neill (1995) indiquent qu'en moyenne la contribution de l'éducation dans l'explication du PIB par travailleur est voisine de 58% dans les pays développés et de 64% dans les pays moins développés durant la période 1967-1985. Par ailleurs, les études macroéconomiques réalisées par Hanushek et Kimko (2000), Pritchett (2001) et Soto (2006) montrent que les pays ayant un taux de rendement scolaire privé réduit ont un taux de rendement social supérieur. Par contre, pour les pays ayant un taux privé élevé, le taux social est faible et non significatif. Dans le même cadre d'analyse, les estimations de Soto (2006) montrent que le taux de rendement mincérien corrigé par l'indice de qualité atteint sa valeur maximale pour un niveau élevé de qualité d'éducation et perd sa significativité statistique pour les niveaux faibles. Ainsi, l'ignorance de la dimension qualité peut donner des résultats biaisés.

Tableau 4. Estimation du rendement scolaire avec l'effet de la qualité d'éducation

	Variable dépendante: $Log\left(\frac{y}{y_0}\right)$
DYVS	0.878** (3.070)
Exp	0.0069** (3.163)
Exp2	-0.00157** (-3.239)
Fisher	31.921
Prob > F	0.0030
AdjR-squared	0.8998

( ) indique la statistique de Student. (**) implique que le coefficient est significatif à un risque d'erreur de 5%. Source : Calcul de l'auteur.

Notre modèle empirique de base qui intègre l'indice de qualité prend la forme économétrique générale donnée par l'équation 12. Les résultats de l'estimation sont présentés dans le Tableau 4. Dans cette régression où $\hat{\vartheta} = 0{,}2$, la valeur estimée du coefficient associé à la variable composée *DYVS* est de 0,878. Elle devient significativement positive par comparaison au modèle sans indice de qualité. La probabilité p-value ($Prob > F$) qui était de 0.010 dans le tableau 3 est améliorée, passant à 0.003 dans le tableau 4 lorsque la qualité de l'éducation est incorporée dans le modèle.

Ces résultats d'une certaine manière permettent de comprendre le signe négatif et l'absence de la significativité statistique des estimations obtenues par la plupart des études empiriques qui supposent une homogénéité en termes de qualité d'éducation.

3.2.3. Taux de rendement privé et social

L'éducation est porteuse à la fois d'une rentabilité privée et d'une rentabilité sociale. La rentabilité privée est inhérente à chaque individu où on peut considérer que chaque année de scolarisation supplémentaire est synonyme d'une augmentation de ses revenus futurs. Le rendement social établit un rapport entre l'ensemble des ressources investies dans l'éducation et l'ensemble des bénéfices de l'éducation.

En se basant sur la définition théorique du Taux de Rendement Scolaire Privé (TRSP), on peut dériver son expression analytique dans le cas de notre modèle intégré comme suit :

$$Taux\ de\ Rendement\ Scolaire\ Privé = \left(\frac{dlog\left({}^{y}/{}_{y_0}\right)}{dS}\right) \approx \hat{\alpha}_h \overline{\left(\frac{D_{pub}}{Y}\right)}^{1-\vartheta} \qquad (17)$$

où $\overline{\left(\frac{D_{pub}}{Y}\right)}$ est la valeur annuelle moyenne de la part des dépenses publiques en éducation dans le PIB, calculée sur toute la période d'étude. Elle est égale à 0,114. $\hat{\alpha}_h$ est un estimateur de α_h. Dans le cas où la dimension qualité est intégrée dans le modèle, $(0 < \vartheta < 1)$, le coefficient α_h associé au nombre moyen d'années d'étude corrigé par l'indice de qualité est estimé à 0,878. Il est positif et statistiquement significatif à un risque d'erreur de 5%. Pour $(\vartheta = 1)$, la valeur estimée du coefficient B représente une estimation ponctuelle du taux de rendement scolaire privé. La valeur estimée $\hat{B}$ (11,8%) est statistiquement non significative pour un intervalle de confiance de 95%. Nos résultats montrent que la valeur estimée du rendement scolaire privé est égale à 10%.

Selon Soto (2006), le Taux de Rendement Social Mincérien (TRSM) est défini analytiquement par l'expression suivante :

$$Taux\ de\ Rendement\ Social\ Mincérien \approx (1-\alpha)B \tag{18}$$

Il désigne l'impact moyen d'une année d'étude supplémentaire dans la production agrégée sans tenir compte de la dimension qualité. Dans cette expression, le paramètre $(1-\alpha)$ désigne l'élasticité associée au capital humain dans la fonction de production finale. Le Taux de Rendement Social Mincérien est estimé, dans le cas du modèle standard de Mincer $(\vartheta = 1)$, à 8,3% pour une valeur $\alpha \approx 0,3$.

S'agissant du Taux de Rendement Mincérien Moyen (TRMM), il est défini comme étant le Taux de Rendement Social Mincérien corrigé par l'indice de la qualité d'éducation. Analytiquement, le TRMM est exprimé comme suit :

$$Taux\ de\ Rendement\ Mincérien\ Moyen = (1-\alpha) \times \hat{\alpha}_h \overline{\left(\frac{D_{pub}}{Y}\right)}^{1-\vartheta} \tag{19}$$

Nos estimations empiriques donnent un Taux de Rendement Mincérien Moyen de 7%. Pour $\vartheta = 1$, les deux taux de rendement coïncident à une valeur de 8,3%. Il apparaît donc que négliger la dimension qualité aboutit à un taux de rendement social biaisé à la hausse de 1,3 point.

En conclusion, on peut noter que nos résultats confirment l'hypothèse selon laquelle la qualité d'éducation exerce un effet positif sur le taux de rendement scolaire et que son ignorance aboutit à une surévaluation de celui-ci – ce qui a été justifié par plusieurs auteurs (Hanushek et Kimko, 2000 ; Pritchett, 2001 ; Soto, 2006 et Schoellman, 2011).

3.3. Construction de la série de capital humain total

3.3.1. Capital humain éducatif

Il est communément admis que l'éducation formelle est le facteur le plus important pour l'acquisition des compétences individuelles et la formation du capital humain. On note h^{edu} le capital humain éducatif. Il représente le capital dont dispose un individu ayant passé S années scolaires à l'école, dans un pays qui consacre une part de son PIB au financement des dépenses publiques en éducation $\left(\frac{D_{pub}}{Y}\right)$. Analytiquement, il est exprimé par la relation suivante :

$$log h^{edu} = \alpha_h \left(\frac{D_{pub}}{Y}\right)^{1-\vartheta} S \tag{20}$$

Sachant que les données de tous les éléments de ce modèle sont disponibles pour la Tunisie, il est possible de constituer une série de capital humain éducatif par travailleur. Sa représentation graphique (en Log) au cours du temps est donnée dans la figure 1. Ce graphique montre que le capital humain passe de la valeur de 1.25 en 1976 à plus de 2,1 en 2010, correspondant à un taux de croissance annuel moyen de 2%.

Figure 1. Stock de capital humain éducatif par travailleur sur la période 1976-2010 en Tunisie

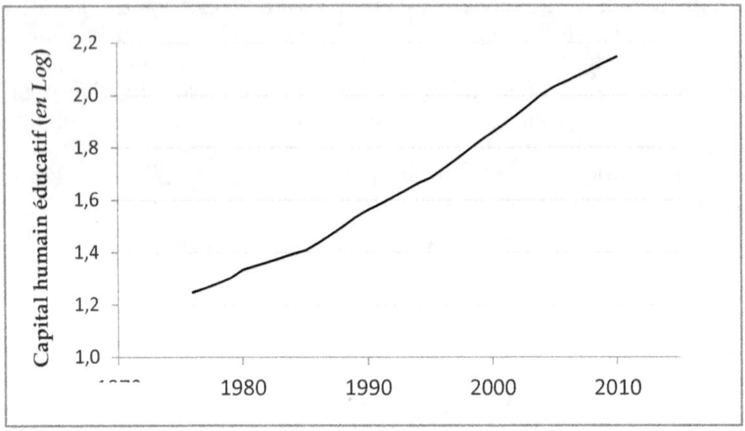

3.3.2. Capital humain total

La valeur annuelle moyenne du capital éducatif par travailleur sur la période 1976-2010 est de 1,58. S'agissant du capital-compétence généré par l'expérience professionnelle, les valeurs estimées des paramètres α_2 et α_3 sont très proches de zéro. Ceci implique une valeur très faible pour $\alpha_2 Experience + \alpha_3 (Experience)^2$.

Pour construire le capital humain total, on a besoin de déterminer également la valeur du stock de capital humain initial. Ce dernier sera déterminé à partir de la relation d'équilibre $\left(h_0 = (1-\alpha)\frac{y}{w \times h^{edu}}\right)$ où w est le taux de salaire réel par unité de capital humain et α est supposé égal à 0,3. Nos estimations montrent qu'en Tunisie le capital humain par travailleur h s'est accru à un taux annuel moyen de 2 % sur la période 1976-2010. Il est net que l'augmentation du stock de capital humain par travailleur peut être attribuée en grande partie à la hausse du nombre moyen d'années d'étude et à l'amélioration de la qualité d'éducation.

La figure 2 montre l'existence de trois grandes phases dans l'évolution du capital humain. Une première période allant de 1976 à 1987 est marquée par une croissance régulière à un taux annuel moyen de 4,9 %. En 1988, on peut constater une réduction importante de 0.3 points du niveau de capital humain par travailleur. Au cours d'une deuxième période allant de 1989 à1995, le taux de croissance annuel moyen du capital humain s'est limité à 0,6%. Durant cette période, la valeur annuelle moyenne (en log) du capital est de 0.44.

Après 1995, le stock du capital humain a connu une augmentation importante. Le capital humain par travailleur atteint sa valeur maximale de 2,4 en 2009 contre 1,7 en 1996, soit un rythme de croissance annuel moyen de 3%. Sur la période 1996-2010, les données montrent que le nombre moyen d'années d'étude et la part des dépenses publiques en éducation dans le PIB ont augmenté à des taux annuels moyen de 2,4% et 0,5% respectivement. La hausse du niveau de scolarité de la population active et l'augmentation de l'investissement en éducation apparaissent comme les deux principaux facteurs de l'élévation du capital humain par travailleur.

Figure 2. Évolution du stock de capital humain par travailleur sur la période 1975-2010 en Tunisie

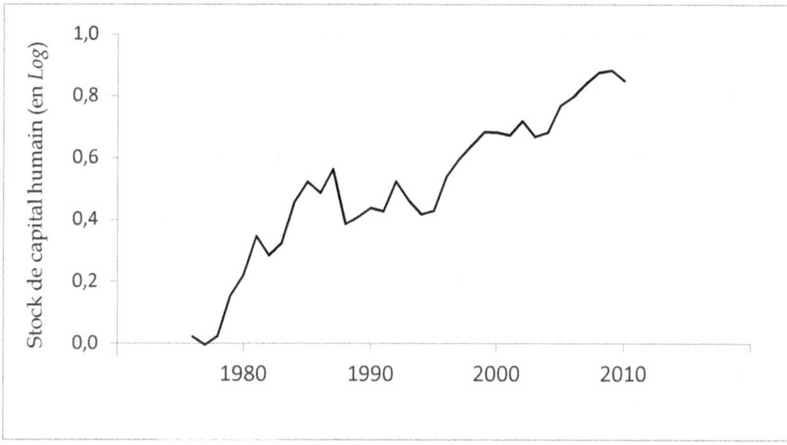

L'évolution du taux de croissance du capital humain sur la période d'étude est illustrée par la figure 3. Le taux de croissance du capital humain en Tunisie est caractérisé par une évolution en dents de scie. Sous les soubresauts conjoncturels, le taux de croissance moyen de capital humain est de 2,4%.

Figure 3. Taux de croissance du capital humain total durant la période 1975-2010 en Tunisie

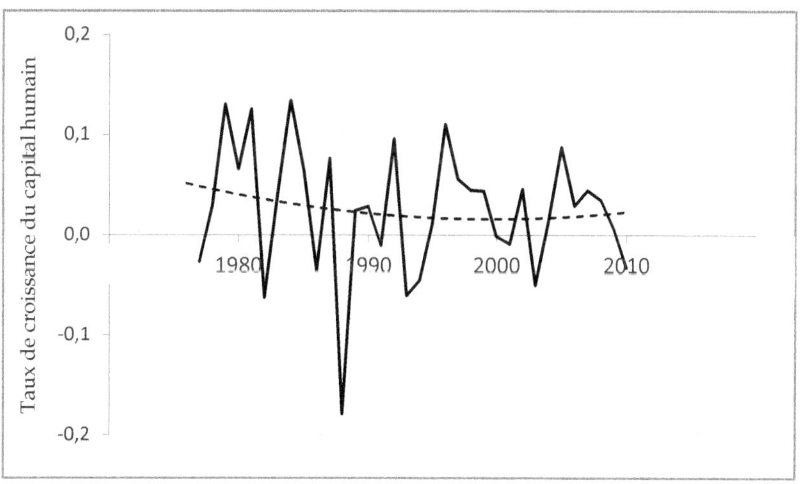

La période de 1976 à 1987 connaît un taux de croissance annuel moyen important du capital humain qui dépasse 4,5%. Au cours de la deuxième période 1988-1995, le taux de croissance annuel moyen du capital humain est voisin de -1,7%. Les taux de croissance faibles réalisés durant cette période marquent la limite des efforts qui ont été déployés pour l'éducation. Entre 1996 et 2010 et à la différence de la période précédente, le taux de croissance du capital humain s'élève à 2,8%, activé par la croissance du nombre moyen d'années d'étude et de la part des dépenses d'éducation dans le PIB.

4. LES DÉTERMINANTS DE LA VARIATION DU RENDEMENT SCOLAIRE

Dans les sections précédentes, le taux de rendement scolaire a été défini par la relation analytique suivante :

$$log\hat{\rho}(S) = log\left(\underbrace{\vartheta\ B\left(L_e \times \ell u_y\right)^{1-\vartheta}\left(\frac{y_0}{h_0}\right)^{1-\vartheta}}_{\kappa}\right) + (1-\vartheta)log\left(\frac{D_{pub}}{Y}\right) - (1-\vartheta)log(S)$$

avec ϑ un paramètre positif et inférieur à l'unité et κ un terme constant à l'équilibre et indépendant de $\left(\frac{D_{pub}}{Y}\right)$ et de S. Ceci implique que toutes les variations de $log\hat{\rho}(S)$ sont liées principalement à celles des variables scolaires. Conformément aux résultats des études macroéconomiques empiriques, cette formule montre l'existence simultanée d'un effet microéconomique négatif exercé par l'augmentation du nombre moyen d'années d'étude sur le taux de rendement accompagné d'un effet macroéconomique positif lié à la qualité scolaire. L'importance de l'effet final dépend du poids relatif de chacun de ces deux effets. Pour montrer si les données sur la Tunisie confirment ce résultat théorique, on peut présenter graphiquement le taux de rendement scolaire par rapport à chacune de ces variables.

4.1. Variation du taux de rendement en fonction du niveau de scolarité

À l'échelle microéconomique, les études empiriques montrent que le rendement marginal privé d'une année d'étude dans l'accumulation de capital humain est décroissant. Sur le plan théorique, les analyses développées dans le cadre de notre modèle montrent que la dérivée première du taux de rendement scolaire par rapport au nombre moyen d'années d'étude est négative et la dérivée seconde est positive. Ceci implique que la fonction $\hat{\rho}(S)$ est convexe et décroissante en fonction de la variable S. En utilisant nos données, la figure 4 retrace les valeurs de [$\vartheta B\left(\frac{\ell u_y}{u_h}\right)^{1-\vartheta}\left(\frac{y_0}{h_0}\right)^{1-\vartheta}\left(\frac{D_{pub}}{Y}\right)^{1-\vartheta}$] en fonction de S.

Figure 4. Variation du taux de rendement scolaire en fonction du niveau de scolarité

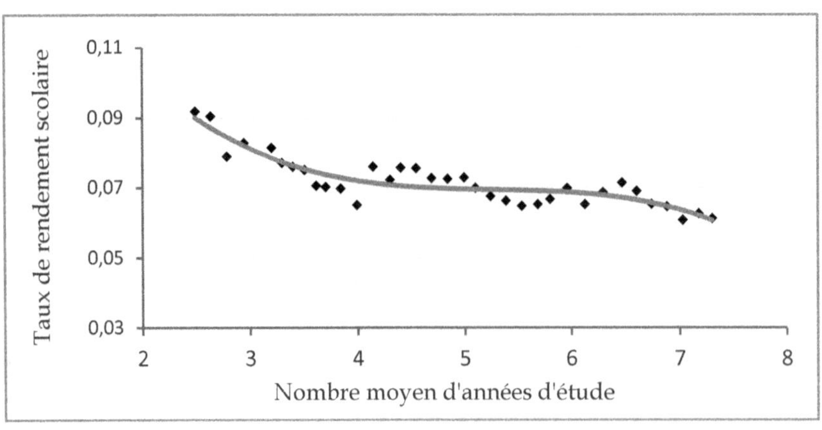

Le graphique montre que le taux de rendement scolaire est décroissant en fonction du nombre moyen d'années d'étude. Ceci confirme les résultats trouvés par

Psacharoupolos sur des données microéconomiques. Il apparaît que pour un niveau de scolarité inférieur à 2,8 années d'étude, le taux de rendement est à son niveau le plus élevé. Au-delà de cette valeur, le rendement scolaire commence à décroitre jusqu'à atteindre 7,2% pour un niveau de scolarité de 4,3 années. Pour un nombre moyen d'années d'étude supérieur à 5, le taux de rendement se situe à une valeur relativement stable en moyenne autour de 7%. Pour des niveaux scolaires supérieurs à 5,5 années d'étude, le taux de rendement continue à diminuer mais à un taux moyen faible de 0,2%.

Les études macroéconomiques réalisées par Soto (2006), Hanushek et Kimko (2000) et Pritchett (2001), parmi d'autres, montrent que la variable qualité d'éducation exerce un impact significatif sur le taux de rendement scolaire. Le taux de rendement atteint en effet sa valeur maximale pour un niveau élevé de qualité d'éducation et perd sa significativité pour des niveaux plus réduits. Étant donné qu'un nombre d'années d'étude élevé est associé à une bonne qualité scolaire, alors le taux de rendement sera biaisé à la hausse si on ignore la dimension qualité (Soto, 2006 et Schoellman, 2011).

4.2. Variation du taux de rendement en fonction de la qualité d'éducation

Le taux de rendement marginal d'une année scolaire est exprimé par la formule :

$$\hat{\rho}(S) = \underbrace{\vartheta B \left(\ell \times \frac{u_y}{u_h}\right)^{1-\vartheta} \left(\frac{y_0}{h_0}\right)^{1-\vartheta}}_{\alpha_h} \left(\frac{D_{pub}}{Y}\right)^{1-\vartheta}$$

où $0 < \vartheta < 1$ et le paramètre α_h est positif (0,878). On peut démontrer analytiquement que la dérivée première du taux de rendement scolaire par rapport à la qualité d'éducation est positive et la dérivée seconde est négative. Ceci implique que la fonction $\hat{\rho}(S)$ est concave et croissante en fonction de la variable $\left(\frac{D_{pub}}{Y}\right)$.

Figure 5. Variation du taux de rendement scolaire en fonction de la qualité d'éducation

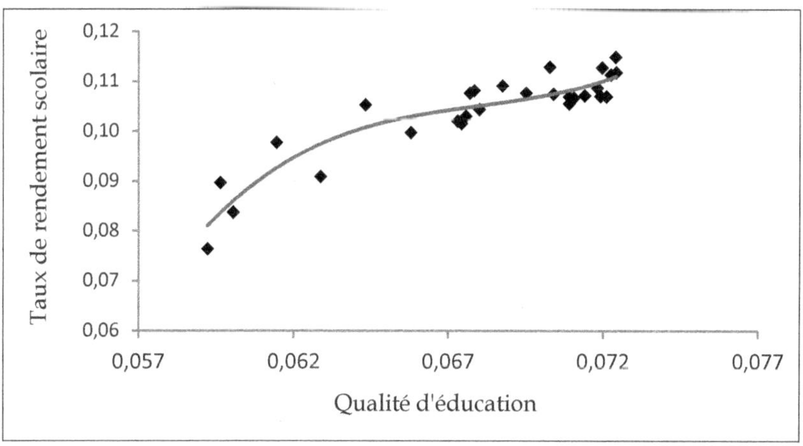

La figure 5 illustre la variation du taux de rendement scolaire pour les différentes valeurs de la qualité d'éducation en Tunisie. La courbe confirme la relation positive qui existe entre le taux de rendement scolaire et la variable qualité. Une lecture détaillée montre que le taux de rendement scolaire est à son niveau le plus bas (7,3%) pour un niveau faible de la qualité d'éducation (5,9%). Suite à une augmentation de la part des dépenses publiques en éducation dans le PIB de 5,9% à 6,4%, le taux de rendement scolaire enregistre une croissance sensible, de l'ordre de 3,3% en moyenne. Au-delà du seuil de 6,5% de la part des dépenses publiques dans le PIB, le taux de rendement progresse à un rythme décroissant. Ces résultats confirment la forme concave et la relation qui existe entre la qualité d'éducation, mesurée par la part des dépenses d'éducation dans le PIB, et le taux de rendement scolaire.

En résumé, nos résultats montrent l'existence d'un effet microéconomique exercé par l'augmentation du nombre moyen d'années d'étude sur le taux de rendement privé accompagné d'un effet macroéconomique positif exercé par la qualité d'éducation. L'importance de l'effet final dépend du poids relatif de chacun de ces deux effets.

4.3. Tendance du taux de rendement scolaire au cours de temps

La figure 6 retrace l'évolution du taux de rendement scolaire. En 1983, le taux de rendement est supérieur à 10%. Durant la période 1983-1987, le taux a connu une certaine baisse, passant de 10,3% en 1983 à 8,7% en 1987. Une explication possible de cette décroissance est que l'impact positif de la qualité d'éducation soit resté insuffisant par rapport à celui du niveau d'étude. C'est l'effet négatif du niveau de scolarité qui domine. Cette décroissance au niveau de taux de rendement scolaire confirme les résultats microéconomiques de Psacharoupolos (1994).

Figure 6. Variation du taux de rendement au cours de temps

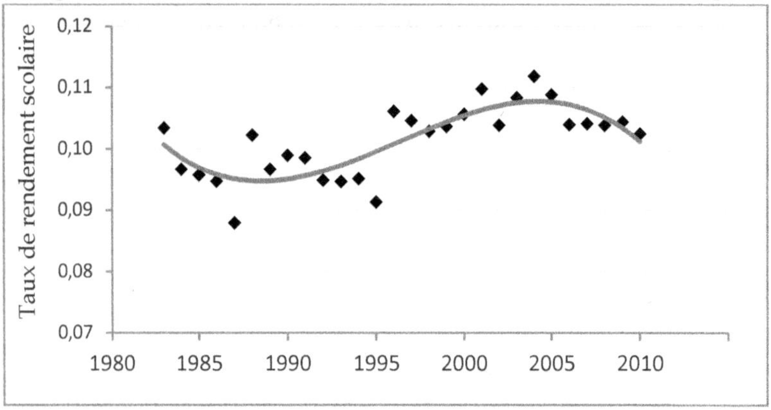

Entre 1987 et 1992, la figure montre une stabilité du taux de rendement scolaire autour de 9,4%. De 1992 à 2004, le taux de rendement scolaire connaît une tendance à la hausse. En se basant sur les résultats graphiques précédents, on remarque que la période 1987-2004 est caractérisée par un impact réduit de la quantité d'éducation sur le taux de rendement, et à l'inverse par un effet positif important des dépenses publiques d'éducation. Il apparaît donc que c'est l'effet qualité qui prédomine sur cette période. Entre 2004 et 2006, le taux de rendement se stabilise de nouveau à une valeur moyenne de 10,8%. Par la suite, une certaine décroissance est enregistrée.

En résumé, il paraît important de souligner que les résultats empiriques obtenus confirment nos hypothèses théoriques selon lesquelles le taux de rendement marginal d'une année d'étude est décroissant, la qualité d'éducation exerce un impact positif et que la variation globale du taux de rendement scolaire est la résultante des effets de la qualité et de la quantité d'éducation.

5. CONCLUSION

Dans cet article, nous avons essayé de spécifier dans un premier temps un modèle théorique non linéaire d'accumulation de capital humain qui incorpore simultanément les aspects quantitatifs et qualitatifs de l'éducation et qui tienne compte d'un rendement scolaire décroissant. La spécification obtenue a été utilisée dans un second temps pour la construction d'un modèle empirique structuré de type Macro-Mincer. L'application a porté sur l'économie tunisienne au cours de la période 1976-2010. Le paramètre fondamental à estimer est le taux de rendement scolaire. Les estimations obtenues montrent que négliger la dimension qualité donne une valeur positive mais statistiquement non significative du coefficient associé au nombre moyen d'années d'étude. Par contre l'estimation d'un modèle intégré montre que l'impact exercé par la qualité d'éducation sur le taux de rendement scolaire est positif et statistiquement significatif. Ceci peut expliquer le signe négatif et l'absence de la significativité statistique des estimations obtenues dans plusieurs études empiriques qui supposent une homogénéité en termes de qualité d'éducation.

Concernant la variation du taux de rendement scolaire, nos résultats théoriques et empiriques montrent l'existence d'un effet microéconomique décroissant exercé par l'augmentation du nombre moyen d'années d'étude, accompagné d'un effet macroéconomique croissant exercé par la qualité scolaire mesurée par la part des dépenses publiques dans le PIB. L'importance de l'effet final dépend du poids relatif de chacun de ces deux effets. Ce résultat peut présenter un certain apport à la littérature sur le capital humain.

Dans notre analyse appliquée, le taux de rendement atteint une valeur maximale de 11% pour un niveau élevé de qualité d'éducation et perd sa significativité pour des niveaux plus réduits. Étant donné qu'un nombre d'années d'étude élevé est associé à une meilleure qualité d'éducation, alors le taux de rendement est en quelque sorte surestimé de 1.3 points dans un modèle qui ignore la dimension qualité. Ces résultats infirment l'hypothèse de linéarité de Mincer qui considère que le taux de rendement de l'éducation est constant et que les années d'étude ont le même poids dans la fonction d'accumulation des compétences indépendamment du moment et du système éducatif dans lequel elles se sont situées. Le caractère de non linéarité pourrait aussi résoudre le problème de la non significativité du coefficient associé au nombre moyen d'années d'étude.

Il est important toutefois de souligner que malgré la pertinence des résultats obtenus, notre application empirique ne concerne qu'un seul pays et non un panel. De plus, avec uniquement 35 observations et un poids-qualité fixe dans la fonction d'accumulation du capital humain, il est difficile en l'état de considérer nos conclusions comme pouvant être générales.

REFERENCES

Aiyar S. and Feyrer J., 2002. A Contribution to the Empirics of Total Factor Productivity, mimeo, Darmouth College (http://www.darmouth.edu)

Banque mondiale, 2000. Rapport sur le développement dans le monde 1999-2000.

Banque mondiale, 2007. World Development Indicators, CD-ROM.

Barro R.J. and Lee J., 2010. A New Data Set of Education Attainment in the World, 1950-2010, National Bureau of Economic Reseach, document de travail n° 15902.

Bils M. and Knelow P.J., 2000. Does Schooling Cause Growth?, *American Economic Review*, 90, 5, 1160-1183.

Chenu F., 2016. Éclairer les performances par une analyse après coup pour évaluer des compétences professionnelles, *Mesure et évaluation en éducation*, 39, 1, 23-44.

Dessus S., 2000. Capital Humain et Croissance : Le rôle retrouvé du système éducatif, *Économie publique*, 2, 6, 95-115.

Földvári P. and Van Leeuwen B., 2005. An Estimation of the Human Capital Stock in Eastern and Central Europe. *Eastern European Economics*, 43, 6, 53-65.

Hall R. and Jones C., 1999. Why Do Some Countries Produce So Much More Output Per Worker Than Others, *Quarterly Journal of Economics*, 114, 1, 83-116.

Hanushek A. and Kimko D., 2000. Schooling, Labor-Force Quality, and the Growth of Nations, *The American Economic Review*, 90, 5, 1184-1208.

Heston A. and Summers R., 2009. The Penn World Tables (Mark 6.3), Center for International Comparisons of Production, Income and Prices, CIC.

Klenow J. and Rodriguez-Clare A., 1997. The Neoclassical Revival in Growth Economics: Has It Gone Too Far? In NBER Macroeconomics Annual, Edited by B. S. Bernanke and J. J. Rotemberg, MIT Press.

Krueger A. and Lindhal M., 2001. Education for Growth: Why and for Whom, *Journal of Economics Literature*, 39, 1101-1136.

Lucas R., 1988. On The Mechanics of Economic Development, *Journal of Monetary Economics*, 22, 1, 3-42.

Mincer J., 1974. Schooling, Experience and Earnings, National Bureau of Economic Research, Columbia University Press, New-York.

O'Neill D., 1995. Education and Income Growth: Implications for Cross-Country Inequality, *Journal of Political Economy*, 103, 6, 1289-1301.

Paltrinieri L., 2013. Quantifier la qualité. Le « capital humain » entre économie, démographie et éducation, *Raisons politiques*, 4, 52, 89-107.

Pritchett L., 2001. Where Has All the Education Gone? *World Bank Economic Review*, 15, 3, 367-391.

Psacharopoulos G., 1984. The contribution of education to economic growth: international comparisons. World Bank reprint series; n° 320. Washington, D.C. Revised in Kendrick J. (Ed), *International productivity comparisons and the causes of the slowdown*, Cambridge, Mass, Ballinger, 15, 3, 367-413.

Psacharopoulos G., 1985. Returns to Education: A Further International Update and Implications, *Journal of Human Resources*, 20, 583-604.

Psacharopoulos G., 1994. Returns to Investment in Education. A Global Update, *World Development*, 22, 1325-1345.

Psacharopoulos G. and Patrinos A., 2002. Returns to Investment in Education: A Further Update, *Policy Research Working Paper Series*, 2881, The World Bank.

Psacharopoulos G. and Woodhall M., 1985. *Education for Development: An Analysis of Investment Choice*, Oxford University Press.

Schoellman T., 2011. Education Quality and Development Accounting, Working paper, Arizona State University.

Simonnet V., 2003. Le capital humain, dans Allouche J., *Encyclopédie des Ressources Humaines*, Vuibert.

Soto M., 2006. The Causal Effect of Education on Aggregate Income, Working Paper, Instituto de Análisis Económico, Barcelona.

Van Leeuwen B., 2007. *Human capital and economic growth in India, Indonesia, and Japan. A quantitave analysis, 1890-2000*, Utrecht University, Netherlands.

ANNEXE

Spécification du modèle estimant le paramètre ϑ

Soit la fonction de production par travailleur définie par : $y = k^{\alpha}(Au_y h)^{1-\alpha}$, où k est le capital physique, h est le capital humain par travailleur et A le niveau technologique. On note par $\dot{A}$ le flux de nouvelles connaissances, qui est déterminé en suivant le modèle :

$$\dot{A} = \delta(u_R h)^{\theta} \left(\frac{M}{Y}\right)^{\epsilon} \left(\frac{IDE}{Y}\right)^{\tau} \left(\frac{A_{sup} - A}{A_{sup}}\right)^{\gamma} A^{\emptyset}, \quad \delta > 0, \qquad 0 < \theta < 1, \qquad 0 < \emptyset < 1$$

où δ indique la productivité de la R&D et $(u_R h)$ représente la part de capital humain consacré à l'innovation. La fraction u_R peut être modélisée par $\left(\frac{L_R}{L}\right)$, où L est l'effectif total de la population active dans l'économie et L_R désigne le nombre d'emplois dans le secteur de R&D. IDE et M sont les volumes respectifs des investissements directs étrangers entrants et des importations de produits manufacturiers intensifs en technologie. A_{sup} est le niveau technologique à la frontière ("leading-edge technology"). Le terme $\left(\frac{A_{sup}-A}{A_{sup}}\right)$ est la difference relative dans la productivité totale des facteurs de l'économie par rapport au niveau supérieur des pays partenaires. Le paramètre θ décrit le phénomène de duplication. Il est supposé $0 \leq \theta < 1$. $\emptyset$ est un paramètre indiquant l'effet inter-temporel de la technologie existante sur la productivité future de création des connaissances. Les paramètres ϵ et τ sont les élasticités du flux de nouvelles connaissances par rapport à (M) et (IDE) respectivement. À l'équilibre de marché, on a les relations suivantes : $r = \alpha^2 \frac{Y}{K}$ et $w = (1-\alpha)\frac{y}{h}$ où r est le taux de profit réel et w est le salaire réel par unité de capital humain. On note par $\mho$ le terme $\left(\frac{1-\emptyset}{\theta}\right)$.

Dans cette économie, le modèle de décision d'un ménage représentatif sur l'investissement optimal en capital humain est fondé sur une comparaison entre les coûts des études et le supplément de revenus anticipés. On note par W_0 la valeur actuelle escomptée des revenus futurs nets des frais de scolarité qu'un ménage représentatif peut générer par son capital humain. Elle est exprimée par :

$$W_0 = \int_S^{\infty} (1 - u_h) w_t h(S)\, e^{-(1-\tau_k)rt} dt - \int_0^S (1 - s_d)\overline{D}_t e^{-(1-\tau_k)rt}\, dt$$

où w_t est le taux de salaire par unité de capital humain, $(1 - u_h)$ est la fraction du temps consacrée au travail, $\overline{D}_t$ est la dépense scolaire privée supportée par un étudiant représentatif, s_d est le taux de la subvention accordée par l'Etat sur les dépenses d'éducation, h_t est le stock du capital humain d'un ménage représentatif ayant atteint S années d'étude à la période t. La dépense individuelle $\overline{D}_t$ est exprimée par $\overline{D}_t = \ell u_y \frac{D_{pub}}{Y} y_t$.

À l'équilibre, on peut exprimer l'équation en dynamique du PIB par travailleur y_t par $y_t = y_0 e^{g_y^* t}$, où g_y^* est le taux de croissance à l'état stationnaire. De même pour le taux de salaire par unité de capital humain w_t, il est exprimé par $w_t = w_0 e^{g_A^* t}$, où g_A^* décrit le progrès technique à l'équilibre. Cette équation reflète l'hypothèse selon laquelle le progrès technique lié au capital humain est un facteur de plus en plus productif. Ceci implique que la dépense privée est exprimée par l'équation suivante :

$$\overline{D}_t = \left(\frac{\ell u_y}{1-\alpha}\right)\left(\frac{D_{pub}}{Y}\right) y_0 e^{g_y^* t}$$

On déduit que la valeur actuelle escomptée W_0 est exprimée comme suit :

$$W_0 = w_0(1 - u_h)h(S) \int_S^{\infty} e^{(g_A^* - (1-\tau_k)r)t}\, dt - (1 - s_d) w_0 h_0 \left(\frac{\ell u_y}{1-\alpha}\right)\frac{D_{pub}}{Y} \int_0^S e^{(g_y^* - (1-\tau_k)r)t} dt$$

La résolution de la fonction intégrale aboutit à l'équation suivante :

$$W_0 = w_0(1 - u_h)h(S)\left[\frac{e^{(g_A^* - (1-\tau_k)r)t}}{g_A^* - (1-\tau_k)r}\right]_S^\infty - (1-s_d)w_0 h_0\left(\frac{\ell u_y}{1-\alpha}\right)\frac{D_{pub}}{Y}\left[\frac{e^{(g_y^* - (1-\tau_k)r)t}}{g_y^* - (1-\tau_k)r}\right]_0^S$$

Pour que la richesse escomptée soit bornée, il faut vérifier si $g_A^* - (1-\tau_k)r < 0$. Les résultats à l'équilibre montrent que le quotient $g_A^* - (1-\tau_k)r = -\vartheta\left(\frac{g_h}{u_h}\right) < 0$. Ceci implique que notre condition est vérifiée. Le développement de l'expression de W_0 donne l'équation suivante :

$$W(S) = \left(\frac{(1-s_d)\ell u_y y_0 \frac{D_{pub}}{Y}}{g_y^* - (1-\tau_k)r}\right) + \frac{w_0 h_0 (1-u_h)}{(1-\tau_k)r - g_A^*} e^{(g_y^* - (1-\tau_k)r)S}$$

$$- \left[\frac{\frac{w_0 h_0 (1-s_d)\ell u_y}{(1-\alpha)}\left(\frac{D_{pub}}{Y}\right)^\vartheta}{\frac{\vartheta\alpha_h \mho}{\sigma(\mho+1)-1}\left(1 - \frac{\rho}{\vartheta^2 B(1-\alpha)^{1-\vartheta}\left(\frac{1-\vartheta}{\vartheta}\right)^{1-\vartheta}\left(\frac{1-\tau_w}{1-s_d}\right)^{1-\vartheta}\left(\frac{y_0}{h_0}\right)^{1-\vartheta}}\right) - \vartheta\alpha_h}\right] e^{(g_y^* - (1-\tau_k)r)S}$$

La condition de premier ordre du problème $Max_S W(S)$ est définie par l'équation suivante :

$$W_S' = 0$$

$$= w_0 h_0 \left[\frac{(1-\tau_k)r(1-\sigma) - \rho}{\sigma}\right]\left[\frac{(1-u_h)}{(1-\tau_k)r - g_A^*}\right.$$

$$\left. - \frac{\frac{(1-s_d)\ell u_y}{(1-\alpha)}\left(\frac{D_{pub}}{Y}\right)^\vartheta}{\frac{\vartheta\alpha_h \mho}{\sigma(\mho+1)-1}\left[1 - \frac{\rho}{\vartheta^2 B(1-\alpha)^{1-\vartheta}\left(\frac{1-\vartheta}{\vartheta}\right)^{1-\vartheta}\left(\frac{1-\tau_w}{1-s_d}\right)^{1-\vartheta}\left(\frac{y_0}{h_0}\right)^{1-\vartheta}}\right] - \vartheta\alpha_h}\right] e^{(g_y^* - (1-\tau_k)r)S}$$

Ce résultat implique que la relation suivante doit être vérifiée.

$$(1-u_h) = \left((1-\tau_k)r - g_A^*\right)\left(\frac{\ell u_y\left(\frac{1-s_d}{1-\alpha}\right)\left(\frac{D_{pub}}{Y}\right)^{\vartheta}}{\frac{\vartheta\alpha_h\mho}{\sigma(\mho+1)-1}\left[1-\frac{\rho}{\vartheta^2B(1-\alpha)^{1-\vartheta}\left(\frac{1-\vartheta}{\vartheta}\right)^{1-\vartheta}\left(\frac{1-\tau_w}{1-s_d}\right)^{1-\vartheta}\left(\frac{y_0}{h_0}\right)^{1-\vartheta}}\right]-\vartheta\alpha_h}\right)$$

À l'équilibre, la quantité $\left((1-\tau_k)r-g_A^*\right)$ peut être exprimée comme suit : $(1-\tau_k)r-g_A^* = (1-\tau_k)r-\left(\frac{\theta}{1-\emptyset+\theta}\right)\left(\frac{(1-\tau_k)r-\rho}{\sigma}\right) > 0$, où $\mho = \frac{\theta}{1-\emptyset}$. Si on remplace $((1-\tau_k)r-g_A^*)$ par son expression, on obtient

$$(1-u_h) = \left[\frac{\left[(1-\tau_k)r-\left(\frac{1}{\mho+1}\right)\left(\frac{(1-\tau_k)r-\rho}{\sigma}\right)\right]\ell u_y\left(\frac{1-s_d}{1-\alpha}\right)\left(\frac{D_{pub}}{Y}\right)^{\vartheta}}{\frac{\vartheta\alpha_h\mho}{\sigma(\mho+1)-1}\left(1-\frac{\rho}{\vartheta^2B(1-\alpha)^{1-\vartheta}\left(\frac{1-\vartheta}{\vartheta}\right)^{1-\vartheta}\left(\frac{1-\tau_w}{1-s_d}\right)^{1-\vartheta}\left(\frac{y_0}{h_0}\right)^{1-\vartheta}}\right)-\vartheta\alpha_h}\right] \times \left(\frac{D_{pub}}{Y}\right)^{\vartheta}$$

Et en appliquant la fonction logarithmique :

$$Log(1-u_h) = Log\left[\frac{\left[(1-\tau_k)r-\left(\frac{\theta}{1-\emptyset+\theta}\right)\left(\frac{(1-\tau_k)r-\rho}{\sigma}\right)\right]\ell u_y\left(\frac{1-s_d}{1-\alpha}\right)\left(\frac{D_{pub}}{Y}\right)^{\vartheta}}{\frac{\vartheta\mho\alpha_h}{\sigma(\mho+1)-1}\left(1-\frac{\rho}{\vartheta^2B(1-\alpha)^{1-\vartheta}\left(\frac{1-\vartheta}{\vartheta}\right)^{1-\vartheta}\left(\frac{1-\tau_w}{1-s_d}\right)^{1-\vartheta}\left(\frac{y_0}{h_0}\right)^{1-\vartheta}}\right)-\vartheta\alpha_h}\right] + \vartheta Log\left(\frac{D_{pub}}{Y}\right)$$

Étant donné que la fraction u_h est inférieure à l'unité, il est alors possible d'utiliser l'approximation logarithmique suivant laquelle $Log(1-u_h) \approx -u_h$.

Ce résultat implique l'égalité suivante :

$$S^* \approx -L_e Log \left[\frac{\left[(1-\tau_k)r - \left(\frac{\theta}{1-\emptyset+\theta}\right)\left(\frac{(1-\tau_k)r-\rho}{\sigma}\right)\right] \ell u_y \left(\frac{1-s_d}{1-\alpha}\right)\left(\frac{D_{pub}}{Y}\right)^{\vartheta}}{\frac{\vartheta\alpha_h \mho}{\sigma(\mho+1)-1}\left(1-\frac{\rho}{\vartheta^2 B(1-\alpha)^{1-\vartheta}\left(\frac{1-\vartheta}{\vartheta}\right)^{1-\vartheta}\left(\frac{1-\tau_w}{1-s_d}\right)^{1-\vartheta}\left(\frac{y_0}{h_0}\right)^{1-\vartheta}}\right)-\vartheta\alpha_h} \right] - \vartheta L_e Log\left(\frac{D_{pub}}{Y}\right)$$

À partir de cette équation, on déduit le modèle empirique qui permet d'estimer le poids de la qualité d'éducation dans le taux de rendement scolaire ϑ, conformément aux données disponibles. L'équation de régression à estimer peut prendre la forme générale suivante :

$$S = \mu_0 + \mu_1 L_e log\left(\frac{D_{pub}}{Y}\right) + \varepsilon$$

D'où le résultat.

The accumulation of human capital: Theoretical model and evaluation for the case of Tunisia

Abstract - Empirical studies using human capital are sensitive to the measures associated to this capital and sometimes lead to diverging results. The uses of the average number of years of schooling as a proxy for human capital or the ignorance of the quality of education are the major causes. In this sense, we propose a theoretical model of skill accumulation that simultaneously integrates the quantitative and qualitative aspects of education and takes into account decreasing return to schooling. This model is used to estimate a Macro-Mincer structured model that also integrates the professional experience. As an application, we took the case of the Tunisian economy over the period 1976-2010. The empirical results obtained show that the neglect of the quality dimension leads to a non-statistically significant positive effect of the average number of years of schooling and that the associated social rate of return is overestimated. On the other hand, estimating a model that integrates the two aspects of education, quality and quantity, shows that their effects are statistically significant.

Key-words

Human capital accumulation
Quality of education
Return to schooling
Macro-Mincer model
Tunisia

Région et Développement
n° 49-2019
www.regionetdeveloppement.org

The effects of state dependence on university graduates' unemployment in Morocco: Analysis using a dynamic model

Fatima BERAHOU*, Saad-Ellah BERHILI**
Abdeljebbar ABDOUNI***

Abstract - This paper examines the causal relationship that exists between an individual's unemployment experience and his or her future employment prospects. In literature, such relationship is termed "state dependence". The data of the present study comes from a survey addressed to a representative sample of Moroccan graduates from three universities covering all their faculties and schools. A dynamic random-effects probit model is applied to the data to test for state dependence effects for Active Moroccan University Graduates. In this model, an individual's unemployment probability at a given point in time, during a period of three years after graduation, is primarily dependent on his or her professional status in the previous time point and personal characteristics. After controlling both for observed and unobserved population heterogeneity, results strongly suggest that past unemployment increases individuals' chances of current unemployment, validating the "scar theory" of unemployment, which stipulates that a previous unemployment spell precludes the accumulation of work experience and may bring the deterioration of human capital.

Classification JEL
C23, C25, J22

Mots-clés
Human capital
Labor Market
Dynamic random-effects probit model
Panel data
Stigmatization effects

* National Authority of Evaluation, Higher Council of Education, Training and Scientific Research in Rabat-Morocco ; LARETA, Faculty of Legal, Economic and Social Sciences, Hassan 1st University in Settat-Morocco; fatima.berahou@gmail.com.
** National Authority of Evaluation, Higher Council of Education, Training and Scientific Research in Rabat-Morocco ; saadellah@gmail.com.
*** LARETA, Faculty of Legal, Economic and Social Sciences, Hassan 1st University in Settat-Morocco; a.abdouni27@gmail.com.

INTRODUCTION

The idea that, there is a causal relationship between an individual's past employment or unemployment and his future labor force status, is of considerable interest in the theory of unemployment. Furthermore, the 'scar theory' of unemployment holds "that unemployment experience alters one's future probability of being unemployed because individuals lose valuable work experience while they are unemployed, or because they are marked as 'losers' by potential employers" (Heckman and Borjas, 1980, p. 250). This means that unemployment, especially a long-term one, may lead to a depreciation of human capital or gives a negative signal for companies, and then affects an individual's future employment prospects.

Becker (1975) predicted this scarring theory. Following him, although general skills increase an individual's marginal productivity in different sectors, these skills are non-transferable and specific to the company providing the investment. A consequence of unemployment is the depreciation of general skills and the loss of company specific skills.

Pissarides (1994) thinks that low quality companies recruit unemployed individuals but lose them to high quality companies that pay well, and this loss of a good job may decrease the probability of having a better-paid job later.

Several previous empirical studies have tried to investigate the extent of state dependence in employment or unemployment. Heckman (1981a) shows that there is significant state dependence in the employment probabilities of US married women. Furthermore, Hyslop (1999) also finds strong state dependence in employment for US married women in the 1980s.

Omori (1997) finds that if the duration of previous non-employment increases, the duration of current non-employment increases as well. However, Corcoran and Hill (1985) find that past unemployment does not raise the probability of current unemployment for men at prime age. For Britain, Narendranathan and Elias (1993) and Arulampalam et al. (2000) find strong state dependence in unemployment. Frijters, Lindeboom, and Van den Berg (2009) for Holland, Haan (2006) for Germany and Islam (2006) for Sweden, also found this result. Le Maire and Scheuer (2006) have also found a positive and significant state dependence for groups with weak labor market participation in the Danish case. Furthermore, Lynch (1985) shows that the length of previous unemployment spells does not have a significant effect on the current duration of unemployment for British youths. In the same way, Gregg (2001) finds that early-cumulated duration of unemployment significantly affects the unemployment experience in the future. A study of Denise and Doiron (2008) analyses the level of state dependence in labor force outcomes for young low-skilled Australians. They found that having experienced an employment spell in the past increases the probability of future employment and also, unemployment spells raise the probability of future unemployment, but the duration of past spells does not matter. Moreover, using data from the German Socioeconomic Panel (GSOEP) to estimate the probability of being unemployed conditional on the employment state of the previous period, Biewen and Steffes (2008) found that the disadvantage from being in unemployment in the previous period is smaller for individuals in times of relatively high aggregate unemployment and larger when aggregate unemployment is low.

In addition to that, some studies show that unemployment may be examined in conjunction with the type of job taken after exiting unemployment. State dependence in unemployment is also viewed as a result of non-accumulation of new human capital during an unemployment spell or during a low-paid employment period. Therefore, low-wage jobs have similar adverse effects to unemployment.

Layard et al. (1990) argue that being in a low-quality job may be a bad sign as well as being in unemployment. McCormick (1990) argues that employers use the type of job held as well as the unemployment duration (Blanchard and Diamond, 1994) as indicators of future productivity. Stewart and Swaffield (1999), Weber (2002) and Stewart (2007) have considered an example of persistence in low pay, among others.

To explain Moroccan graduates' labor force behavior during a period of three years after graduation, we estimate a dynamic random-effects probit model and test for state dependence effects with respect to both observed and unobserved population heterogeneity.

The initial conditions' problem arises in a dynamic context. It is caused by the presence of the past value of the dependent variable, an unobserved heterogeneity term in the dynamic equation and the correlation between them. Heckman (1981a, 1981b) was the first to address this problem and proposed an approximation to "the initial conditions" by a reduced-form equation for the initial observation (at the beginning of the observation period). The maximum likelihood is estimated here using the full set of sample observations. However, the Heckman estimator remains a very time-consuming one. This has led to the suggestion of other alternative estimators that have the advantage of using standard software such as the estimators suggested by Orme (1997, 2001) and Wooldridge (2005).

This paper therefore provides an examination of the relationship that exists between an individual's unemployment experience and his or her current labor force status. Special attention is paid to account for the unobserved heterogeneity and initial conditions' problem using the Heckman, Orme and Wooldridge estimators, and comparing the results of each one.

The remainder of the paper proceeds as follows. The data used are presented in section 1 and the econometric model is set out in section 2. The main results of the paper are contained in section 3.

1. DATA DESCRIPTION

The data of the present study come from a survey carried out in 2012 by the National Authority of Evaluation in Morocco affiliated to the Higher Council of Education, Training and Scientific Research. The survey was addressed to a representative sample of graduates from three universities covering all their faculties and schools: Hassan 1st University-Settat, Hassan II University-Casablanca and Mohammed V University-Rabat. It is based on a three-year monthly retrospective calendar, aiming to collect monthly data about occupational status of young graduates. The longitudinal sample consists *of young students who graduated in 2009* from the three universities.

The graduates' sample was stratified based on school and diploma of the graduate, then a systematic sampling was used within each stratum to obtain a representative sample of the population. The starting sample contains 45,500 observations for 1625 individuals (active and inactive). The data contains information on: the curriculum studied up to graduation in 2009, the monthly occupational status between 2009 and 2012, the first and the last unemployment spell details, the first and the last employment details, the student's family background and personal characteristics.

For the present analysis, the sample was reduced to 22,518 observations for 834 graduates by focusing on active graduates only. Individuals who were inactive, state employees and those who were pursuing their studies along the period of observation were withdrawn. We focused on unemployment experienced by active population during the 36 months after graduation

The dependent variable used is the professional status of the individual i at time t, disaggregated into the categories 'unemployed' and 'employed'. The unemployment indicator used is constructed following the ILO/OECD's definition of unemployment. Thus, a person is unemployed if he or she does not have a job during a specified period and is available for work. The sample included self-employed persons, full time and part time employees, graduates with fixed term, temporary and casual contract, paid trainees whether in formal or informal sector. State employees are excluded from the sample because they definitely come back working in their home institution. Table 1 summarizes the definitions of the main explanatory variables used in the analysis and presents summary statistics (means and standard deviations) for these variables.

Table 1: Definitions of variables and summary statistics

Variable	Description	Mean (SD)
chom	Current Labor force status (at time t) (0 = employed, 1 = unemployed)	0.218 (0.413)
chomlag	Labor force status in the previous month (t-1)	0.226 (0.419)
Gender	(0 = Female, 1 = Male)	0.533 (0.499)
Age	Age completed at the time of graduation	26.053 (4.928)
French	Level of fluency in the French language	0.796 (0.403)
Residence	Living with parents	0.632 (0.482)
Nb_empl_broth	The number of employed brothers and sisters	1.928 (1.782)
Mobility	The mobility between the region origin and the region of university where the laureate graduated (0= Non mobile, 1 = Mobile)	0.256 (0.437)
High_parents_Educ	The highest education level of one of the parents *No schooling* *Primary school level* *Secondary school level* *Tertiary school level*	 0.184 (0.388) 0.183 (0.387) 0.331 (0.471) 0.302 (0.459)
Qualif_degree	Qualification degree *Bachelor and less* *Master* *Engineering qualification* *Doctoral qualification*	 0.484 (0.499) 0.313 (0.464) 0.134 (0.341) 0.068 (0.252)

Source: Author's calculation (for the sample of active graduates).

In our dataset, females represent 47% of the sample and individuals are aged between 19 and 56 years at the time of gradation.

We have distinguished between three age groups[1]. The first group includes individuals who are under 25 years of age, the second concerns graduates aged between 25 and 34 years and the third category is associated with individuals being over 34 years of age. Most of our graduates are young individuals. Thus, 10% of the university graduates are aged under 25 years at the time of the interview, while 81% of them are aged between 25 and 34 years.

Moreover, 84% of graduates in our reduced sample declared that, while they were studying, their fathers were employed, 14% said that their fathers were inactive and only the fathers of 2% of the graduates were unemployed. In addition to that, mothers of about 83% of graduates did not have a job (80% were inactive and 3% were unemployed).

1 This categorization is considered by the High Commissioner for Planning in Morocco.

In addition, 20% of our graduates have parents without schooling level while 29% of them have at least one of their parents with tertiary school level.

Most of the graduates were living with their parents while studying (62%). Some 14% of our university graduates were heading up a household in which they lived alone or with one or more friends, 5% were living with a spouse in their own household and 20% lived in university campus.

Most of the students (71%) graduated from open access institutes (Faculty of Science, Faculty of Legal, Economic and Social Sciences and Faculty of Letters and Human Sciences). Concerning the qualification degree, 49% of our graduates have Bachelor degree and less while 31% have Master degree. Surprisingly, 76% of the graduates declared that they have excellent or high level of French language.

Unemployment rates between the time of graduation and 36 months later

The feature implemented to measure the unemployment rates consists of the administration of a retrospective monthly calendar tracking the situation of the individuals during a period of 36 months after the graduation.

Using different professional situations declared by the individuals in this monthly calendar (employment, unemployment, inactivity), we calculated the unemployment rate for each month and we derived the unemployment rate for specific times: one month, six months, twelve months, eighteen months and two years after graduation. Inactive graduates (students and other inactive graduates) are not taken into account in the calculation of these rates.

Figure 1 shows that unemployment rate one month after leaving the university is 46%. This rate gradually decreases to 16% after 36 months from the time of graduation. Women have higher unemployment rates than men, with a gap of 12 points at the time of the interview (22% for women and 10% for men).

Figure 1: Unemployment rates between the time of graduation and the time of the interview

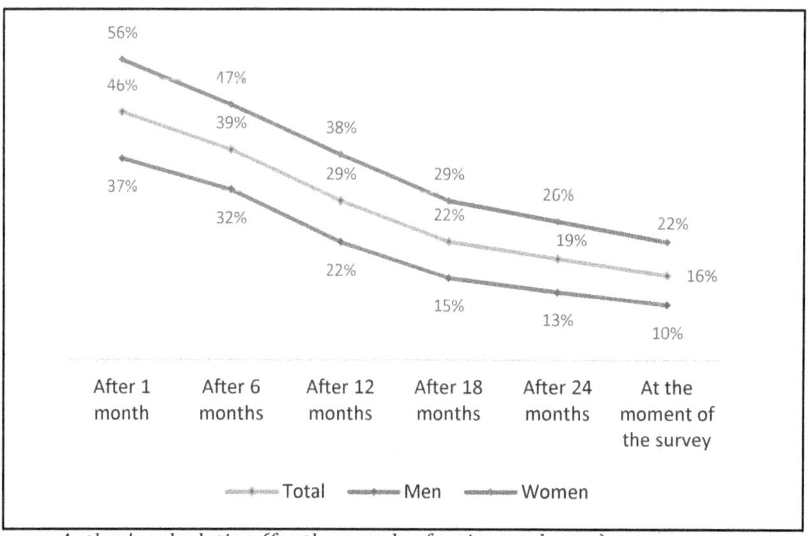

Source: Author's calculation (for the sample of active graduates).

Table 1 presents the distribution of active university graduates according to the duration of unemployment between the time of graduation and the time of the interview. Results show that 42.46% of our graduates have never had an unemployment spell during the studied period, 18.19% have been unemployed for one to six months, and 16.41% have had a long unemployment duration exceeding two years in the observed period. Differences in length of unemployment duration between men and women are important. Thus, more men (51.17%) than women (32.70%) have never had an unemployment spell after leaving the university. However, a visible gender gap is observed regarding the long unemployment duration exceeding two years: 10.94% of men and 22.53% of women.

Table 1: Length of graduates' unemployment according to gender

	Total	Women	Men
0 months	42,46%	32,70%	51,17%
From 1 to 6 months	18,19%	18,61%	17,82%
From 7 to 12 months	10,26%	9,88%	10,60%
From 13 to 18 months	7,39%	9,93%	5,12%
From 19 to 24 months	5,29%	6,35%	4,34%
Over 24 months	16,41%	22,53%	10,94%

Source: Author's calculation (for the sample of active graduates).

Unemployment rates at the time of the interview

At the time of the interview (36 months after the completion of the university studies), 16% of the active graduates were unemployed and 84% were employed. The unemployment rate for men peaked at 10%, while the one for women peaked at 22%.

In our dataset, the most people affected by unemployment are individuals aged between 25 and 34 years with a rate of 18% at the time of the interview. Nonetheless, individuals aged under 25 years are associated with an unemployment rate of 5%. The lowest unemployment rate is around 3% for graduates aged over 34 years.

Figure 2: Distribution of the unemployment durations observed 12 months after graduation

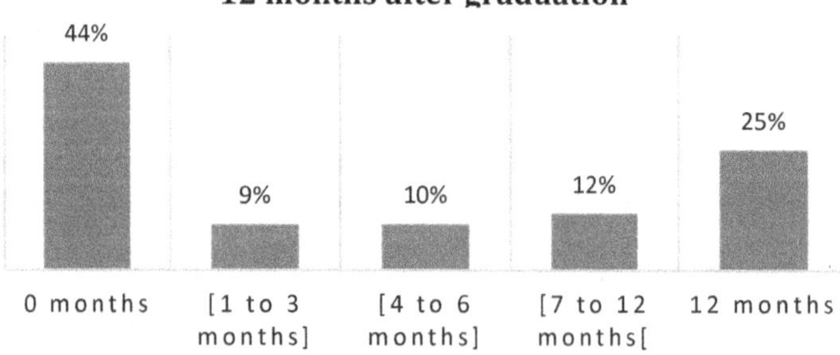

Source: Author's calculation (for the sample of active graduates).

Study results show also that unemployment rate is high among university graduates who hold a bachelor's degree or less, standing at 26%. However, the percentage of unemployed graduates who hold a Master's degree stands at 8% while a percentage of 3% only was recorded for individuals who hold doctoral degree.

Graduates that can speak and write French fluently are less likely to be unemployed. Thus, the unemployment rate for individuals with excellent or high level of French language amounts to 11%, 36 months after graduation.

Moreover, the unemployment rate stands at around 14% for university graduates whose fathers were employed and at only 6% for those whose mothers were employed. However, 40% of individuals who have unemployed fathers and 47% of graduates who have unemployed mothers were unemployed at the time of the interview.

In addition, graduates who have at least one of their parents with tertiary school level of education are less likely to be unemployed. Only 6% of them were unemployed 36 months after graduation.

Figure 2 shows the distribution of the unemployment durations observed twelve months after graduation. 44% of graduates have never been in unemployment between graduation and twelve months later. However, 37% of graduates have not found an employment six months after leaving the university. This percentage stands at 25% within the period between the graduation and 12 months after. The unemployment history has a significant effect on the probability of unemployment.

Interregional mobility

Figure 3 shows that 71% of our graduates studied in the region of origin while 29% of them moved to study from their region of origin to another region. 56% of the graduates who already moved to study don't stay where they studied after graduation. This percentage is largely lower among those who studied in the region of origin (10%). This shows the impact of the graduate's mobility for studies on the post-graduation decision. Therefore, a graduate is more likely to move after graduation if he or she previously moved to study (Davanzo, 1983). One reason of the mobility to study is to look for a better performing university, and after graduation, this university from where the student graduated will be a signal to employers (Spence, 1973) and may affect his employability.

In addition, 63% of the graduates who move to study and move again after graduation go back to their region of origin, and among them, 15% are moving to a city different to the city of origin.

Figure 3: Interregional mobility for the graduates of the three Moroccan universities

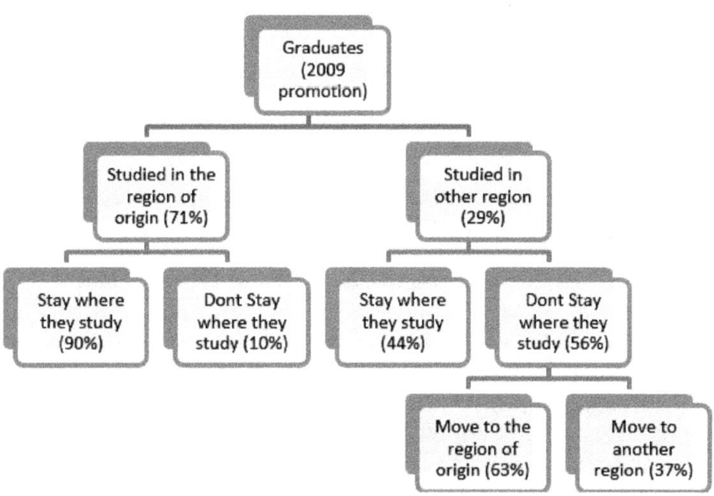

Source: Author's calculation (for the sample of active graduates).

Intercity mobility and unemployment

Almost 27% of the students who graduated from Hassan 1st University located in the city of Settat stayed in Settat three years after graduation and 22% of them migrated to Casablanca (economic capital of Morocco). Among them, only 4% of active graduates are unemployed 3 years after graduation.

Figure 4: Mobility between the city of the university and the city of residence 3 years after graduation

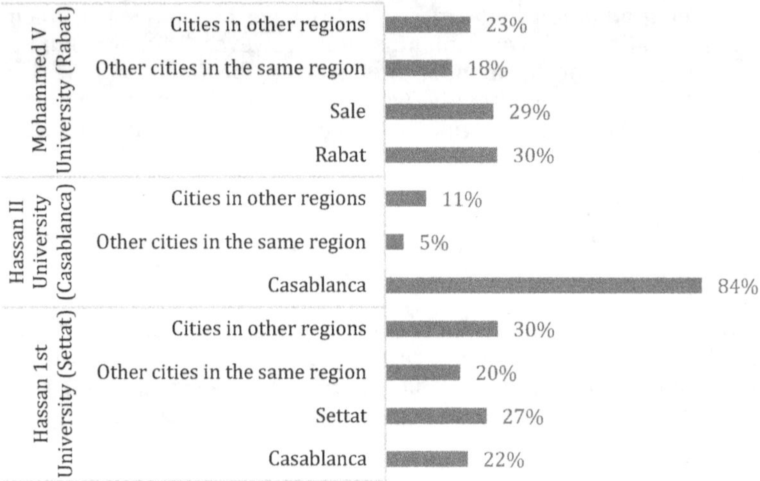

Source: Author's calculation (for the sample of active graduates).

In the same way, the percentage of the graduates of Mohammed V University, located in Rabat, who stayed in Rabat stands at 30% and 29% migrated to Sale (city on the outskirts of Rabat) having the lowest unemployment rate (14%).

Casablanca is the city characterized by the lowest percentage of post-graduation migration (16%). Thus, only 5% of the graduates of Hassan II University located in this town migrated to another city in the same region and 11% of them migrated to a city in another region.

Table 2: Unemployment rates according to the intercity mobility

University	City of residence after graduation	Unemployment
Hassan 1st (Settat)	Casablanca	4%
	Settat	28%
Hassan II (Casablanca)	Casablanca	20%
Mohamed V (Rabat)	Sale	14%
	Rabat	20%

The low unemployment rates for the graduates who migrate may be explained in part by the fact that they are moving to areas where unemployment is low and the employment perspectives are larger. However, the graduates' mobility does not always increase employability opportunities. It depends strongly on the type of mobility and the regions concerned.

Unconditional and conditional probabilities of unemployment

Table 3 presents unconditional and conditional probabilities of unemployment on the previous status at t-1. The unconditional probability of being unemployed at a point in time is 21.8%. The probability of being unemployed at t is over 94.8% for those who were unemployed at t-1, so someone unemployed at t-1 is more likely to be unemployed at t than someone employed at t-1. This result shows that there is strong state dependence in unemployment. However, part of this dependence could be due to heterogeneity. The probability of unemployment is higher for those with medium or low level of French language, for those who live with their parents, for those who have less than 3 brothers and sisters at work, for those whose parents have never reached school, for the graduates who studied in their region of origin and for those with bachelor degree and less, among others.

Table 3 presents also unconditional and conditional unemployment probabilities for various subgroups of graduates differentiated by gender, age, language, number of employed brothers and sisters, parents' education, experience, residence, mobility and educational level. These factors are likely to influence the probability of unemployment. We first estimated a general specification of the random-effects probit model by including these variables as explanatory variables.

Table 3: Conditional and unconditional probabilities of unemployment

	Unconditional	**Employed at t-1**	**Unemployed at t-1**
All	0.218	0.004	0.948
Gender			
Male	0.159	0.003	0.937
Female	0.286	0.005	0.955
Level of fluency in the French language			
Excellent or high level	0.174	0.004	0.938
Medium or low level	0.389	0.007	0.965
Residence			
With parents	0.275	0.005	0.954
Alone or with others	0.119	0.003	0.925
Number of employed brothers and sisters			
One or two	0.227	0.004	0.949
Three and more	0.166	0.003	0.934
Mobility between region of origin and region of university			
Mobile	0.159	0.002	0.917
Non mobile	0.306	0.005	0.949
Parents' highest education level			
No schooling	0.278	0.006	0.966
Primary school level	0.254	0.006	0.958
Secondary school level	0.244	0.004	0.944
Tertiary school level	0.129	0.002	0.918
Qualification degree			
Bachelor and less	0.313	0.007	0.960
Master	0.178	0.003	0.933
Engineering qualification	0.020	0.001	0.721
Doctoral qualification	0.119	0.002	0.896

Source: Author's calculation (for the sample of active graduates).

2. ECONOMETRIC SPECIFICATION

In this section, we present the dynamic probit model used to analyze the effects of employment or unemployment experience of Moroccan University Graduates on the probability of being unemployed later. The model includes the previous state among the explanatory variables to allow for state dependence. An important focus has been made to the treatment of unobserved heterogeneity and initial conditions.

2.1. A dynamic random-effects probit model

In our model, the dependent variable y^*_{it} depends on a vector x_{it} of measured exogenous variables, on the unemployment status in the previous period y_{it-1} and on the error term ε_{it}.

The latent equation for the random-effects dynamic probit model to be considered is specified as:

$$y^*_{it} = \gamma y_{it-1} + \beta' x_{it} + \alpha_i + \varepsilon_{it} \tag{1}$$

where the subscript i indexes individuals (i = 1,..., N) and t time periods (t = 2,..., T). y^*_{it} is the latent dependent variable for individual i in period t describing an individual's unemployment propensity, x_{it} is a vector of exogenous explanatory variables, α_i are (unobserved) individual-specific random effects, and the ε_{it} are assumed to be distributed $N(0, \sigma^2)$.

The observed binary outcome variable y_{it} is defined as:

$$y_{it} = \begin{cases} 1 \; si \;\; y^*_{it} = \gamma y_{it-1} + \beta' x_{it} + \alpha_i + \varepsilon_{it} > 0 \\ 0 \; si \;\; y^*_{it} \leq 0 \end{cases} \tag{2}$$

The presence of the lagged outcome variable y_{it-1}allows us to test the hypothesis of true state dependence. However, the error term may be serially correlated, for a given individual, which would lead to spurious state dependence[2]. Therefore, in order to test for true state dependence, we have to control for unobserved individual effect. The Heckman's estimator allows us to resolve this problem.

2.2. Heckman's estimator and initial conditions problem

The following dynamic reduced form model is specified:

$$Prob[y_{it} = 1 | y_{it-1}, x_{it}, \alpha_i] = \Phi[\gamma y_{it-1} + x'_{it}\beta + \alpha_i] \quad i=1,\ldots, N \tag{3}$$

Heckman (1981b) proposed the approach to the initial conditions' problem that involves specifying a linearized reduced form equation for the initial period:

$$\mathrm{Prob}[y_{i1} = 1 | \alpha_i] = \Phi[z'_{i1}\lambda + \theta\alpha_i] \quad i=1,\ldots, N \tag{4}$$

where Z_{i1} includes x_{i1} and exogenous instruments. The likelihood function for a random sample is then:

$$L_i = \int \left(\phi[(z'_{i1}\lambda + \theta\alpha_i)(2y_{i1} - 1)] \prod_{t=2}^{T_i} \phi[(x'_{it}\beta + \gamma y_{it-1} + \alpha_i)(2y_{it} - 1)] \right) g(\alpha_i) d\alpha_i \tag{5}$$

where g(α) is the density probability function of unobserved heterogeneity specific to individuals, and in this standard case, α is taken to be normally distributed and the integral given in this last equation can be calculated using Gaussian-Hermite quadrature (Butler and Moffitt, 1982).

2.3. Wooldridge's cml estimator

In contrast to Heckman who approximates the joint probability of the full-observed y sequence, Wooldridge (2005) has proposed an alternative Conditional

[2] The distinction between true or structural and spurious state dependence in unemployment was clearly stressed by Heckman and Borjas (1980). Testing for true or spurious state dependence imply to test whether an individual's unemployment probability at a given point in time depends on his labour force status in the previous period in a causal way or is rather due to serially correlated explanatory variables and /or unobserved individual effects.

Maximum Likelihood (CML) estimator that considers the distribution conditional on the initial period value (and exogenous variables). Wooldridge suggests modelling the density of $(y_{i2}...y_{iT})$ conditional on (y_{i1}, x_i).

Specifying a model for yi1 given xi and αi is replaced by specifying one for α_i given y_{i1} and x_i. The model for α_i is specified in its simplest form as:

$$\alpha_i = \xi_0 + \xi_1 y_{i1} + z_i{'}\xi + a_i \quad (6)$$

Substituting into equation (3) gives:

$$Prob[y_{it} = 1 \backslash y_{it-1}, \mathrm{x}_{it}, \alpha_i] = \Phi(x'_{it}\beta + \gamma y_{it-1} + \xi_0 + \xi_1 y_{i1} + z_i\xi + a_i), t=2,...,Ti \quad (7)$$

2.4. Orme's two-step estimator

Orme's two-step estimator is used for addressing the issue of endogeneity. Orme (1997, 2001) uses an approximation to substitute αi with another unobservable component that is uncorrelated with the initial observation y_{i1}.

We can write: $\alpha_i = \delta\eta_i + \varpi_i$ (8)

where ϖ_i *is* orthogonal to η_i by construction and distributed as N(0,1). Substituting for α_i in (3) gives:

$$Prob[y_{it} = 1 \backslash y_{it-1}, \ldots, y_1, \mathrm{x}_{it}, \varpi_i] = \Phi(x'_{it}\beta + \gamma y_{it-1} + \delta\eta_i + \varpi_i), \text{ t=2,...,Ti} \quad (9)$$

This equation has two time-invariant unobserved components, η_i et ϖ_i. Since $E[\varpi_i \backslash y_{i1}] = 0$ by construction, the initial conditions problem will be addressed.

As Orme notes that under the assumption of bivariate normality for the joint distribution of (η_i, α_i), $E[\eta_i \backslash y_{i1}] = e_i$

where $e_i = (2y_{i1} - 1)\varphi(\lambda' z_{i1})/\Phi(\{2y_{i1} - 1\}\lambda' z_{i1})$

(9) is the generalized error from a first period probit equation, analogous to that used in Heckman's sample selection model estimator (equation 4), where φ and Φ are the Normal density and distribution functions respectively.

We can then estimate (equation 9) by a random-effects probit model with η_i replaced with an estimate of e_i after the estimation of (equation 4) using a simple probit.

2.5. Empirical specification

The model includes, as discussed previously, the usual set of exogenous control variables such as family variables (gender, level of parents' education, residence, mobility and number of employed brothers and sisters) and educational variables (Qualifications or graduate degree, level of fluency in French). The state dependence effect is accounted for by the inclusion of the lagged labor market status variable y_{it-1}, with the allowance for unobservable individual characteristics in the model.

The empirical specification for testing the effects of unemployment experience of Moroccan University Graduates on the probability of being unemployed later involves the following latent equation for the random-effects dynamic probit model:

$$\mathrm{chom}^*_{it} = \gamma \mathrm{chom}_{it-1} + \beta_1 Gender_i + \beta_2 French_i + \beta_3 Residence_i + \beta_4 Mobility_i + \beta_5 Nb\_emp\_broth_i + \beta_6 \mathrm{High\_parents\_Educ2}_i + \beta_7 \mathrm{High\_parents\_Educ3}_i + \beta_8 \mathrm{High\_parents\_Educ4}_i + \beta_9 Adv\_studies_i + \alpha_i + \varepsilon_{it}$$

(i=1,..., N, t=1,...,T)

where chom^*_{it} is the latent dependent variable for individual i in period t describing an individual's unemployment propensity, chom_{it} is the unemployment status of the individual i at time t, aggregated into the categories 'employed' and 'non-employed'. A value of 1 indicates an individual's unemployment status in period t.

$Gender_i$ is a dichotomous variable indicating if the graduate is female or male (1=female).

$French_i$: whether someone's level of fluency in French language is high or not (1=High or excellent level).

$Adv\_studies_i$ indicates whether the graduate has completed 5 years and more of higher education after having his baccalaureate which is equivalent to the secondary school diploma (1=5 years and more)

$Residence_i$: respondents are asked if they lived with their parents while studying (1=live with parents).

$Mobility_i$ indicates if the graduate moves from the region of origin to another region to study in university (1=mobile).

$Nb\_emp\_broth_i$ is a discrete variable indicating the number of employed brothers and sisters.

The highest education level of one of the parents: we distinguish between four categories:

High_parents_Educ2$_i$: Primary school level,

High_parents_Educ3$_i$: Secondary school level,

High_parents_Educ4$_i$: Tertiary school level or higher education.

β_i $(i = 1, \ldots, 10)$ are the parameters to estimate, α_i are unobserved individual-specific random effects, and the ε_{it} are assumed to be distributed $N(0, \sigma^2)$.

3. RESULTS AND DISCUSSION

Estimates of the random-effects probit model for the probability of unemployment are given in Table A1 of the appendix, using Heckman, Wooldridge and Orme estimators respectively. The lagged dependent variable is included to allow for state dependence in our models.

In the Heckman estimator, the exogeneity hypothesis of the initial conditions in the random-effects model is rejected after using a simple significance test under the nullity of θ $(\theta = 0)$. In Wooldridge and Orme estimators, the estimate of the coefficient on the initial value of unemployment status is statistically significant. This test confirms the existence of a considerable correlation between the initial condition and the unobserved heterogeneity, which must be taken into account.

The Pooled probit model does not allow any correlation across different periods and the parameters estimates are inefficient. In Table A1, column 2 gives the standard random-effects probit estimates, treating lagged unemployment as exogenous. The Heckman estimates for the same model are given in column 3. The Wooldridge and the Orme two-step estimates are presented in columns 4 and 5 respectively.

The null hypothesis under the likelihood-ratio test for ρ is rejected in all the estimated models, i.e. $\rho \neq 0$. This result implies that pooled probit estimates are rejected and the random-effects probit model is retained.

In all estimated models, the coefficient of the lagged dependent variable (unemployment status) is highly significant. Hence, the estimated coefficient on lagged unemployment status is 4.137 for the random-effects probit, coefficients are reduced to 3.912, 3.925 and 3.929 for Heckman, the Wooldridge and the Orme estimators respectively.

To interpret at which level each of the explanatory variables affect the probability of being in unemployment status, we have introduced marginal effects on probabilities in Table A2 of the Appendix. These results show that an individual's current unemployment status is strongly dependent on his state in the previous period. The unemployment probability for a graduate who has been unemployed at the previous period strongly increases by 92,4% in the random-effects probit estimation, by 88.5% in the Wooldridge specification and by 88.7% in the Orme estimation. That is, once the individual experiences an unemployment spell, he is really scarred by his experience.

Overall, estimated coefficients shown in the Appendix have the expected sign and are of reasonable magnitude in the structural reduced-form probit equation as in the Orme and Wooldridge estimators. As expected, men are less likely to be unemployed than women at a significant decreasing rate of 2.1% in the random-effects probit specification, and 2.7% and 1.8% respectively in the Orme and Wooldridge estimators.

In our model, the variable *age of the graduate* is not significant and has no effect on the probability of unemployment.

Marginal effects coefficients show that the probability of being in unemployment is significantly lower for graduates who have excellent or high level fluency in French language, at a decreasing rate of 2.4% % in the random-effects probit specification, and 3% and 1.7% in the Orme and the Wooldridge estimators.

We also conclude that the probability of being unemployed significantly decreases with the number of brothers and sisters who work at a decreasing rate of 0.4% in both the Orme and the Wooldridge estimators.

It is also interesting to notice that unemployment probability increases for graduates who lived with their parents while they were studying in the university compared to those who were not. Living with parents increases the unemployment probability to 3% in the Orme estimator and to 2.6% in the Wooldridge estimator.

Furthermore, the highest level of education of one of the parents has a significant impact on unemployment probability. In fact, graduates who have at least one of their parents with tertiary school level of education are less likely to be unemployed. Their probability of being in unemployment decreases at 3.4% in the Orme estimator and at 3.5% in the Wooldridge estimator.

Concerning educational qualification variable, we notice that individuals who spend 5 years and more in Higher Education are less likely to be unemployed. Their probability of unemployment decreases to 2.7% in the random-effects probit specification, to 2.3% and 0.7% in the Wooldridge and Orme estimators respect-tively.

After analyzing the regional mobility effect of our university graduates, we found an important association between mobility to study in university and the probability to be in unemployment. Thus, a graduate who move to study in university from his region of origin to another region is less likely to be unemployed after graduation: -1,4% in the random-effects probit specification, and -1.3% in the Orme and the Wooldridge estimators.

CONCLUSION

This paper consists on the examination of the effect of state dependence on unemployment probability. Although of considerable interest, this type of analyses has never been intended for university graduates in Morocco. We have particularly tested at which level an individual's current unemployment probability depends on his labor force status in the previous period. Our estimations confirm that, in the special case of the state dependence, accounting for unobserved heterogeneity is pertinent.

One avenue of research would be to inspect the effect of the time of occurrence of the unemployment spell on the probability to be unemployed and to see if this effect is always linear in the whole observation period. In other words, does an unemployment spell just after graduation have the same impact as an unemployment spell two or three years after graduation? Is the stigmatization effect immediate after leaving university or is it linked to the duration of unemployment? This fact suggests a hypothesis that opens up a new plausible line of inquiry.

The main finding is that state dependence in unemployment overestimates the risk to be in unemployment. The probability of unemployment increases at a rate of 92% if the graduate had experimented unemployment in the previous period. This rate is reduced to 89% when the unobserved heterogeneity and initial conditions are taken into account in both the Orme and the Wooldridge estimators meaning that individuals who experiment unemployment are more likely to be in unemployment in the future. One explanation to this finding is the existence of stigmatization effects which mean that individuals who are or who have been unemployed face difficulties finding a new job in the future and may have lower probabilities to be hired. Indeed, unemployment, especially long-term unemployment may be a negative signal to employers. This result has been also explained in the traditional literature by the depreciation of human capital as a result of a persistent situation of non-employment, thus, the graduate's human capital tends to deteriorate over time (Heckman and Borjas, 1980, p. 250). Many empirical studies explain the rise of stigmatization effect. Thus, Oberholzer-Gee (2007) suggest that employers are less likely to invite job searchers, who apply for a job interviews within their company, if they conclude through their CVs that applicants were unemployed or long-term unemployed.

In general, difficulties in accessing to employment may result from barriers at the entry of the labor market or from the discouragement during the job search process (Flinn and Heckman, 1983; Van den Berg, 1994). Moreover, in economies such as Morocco, where companies do not have enough developed a culture of training for their staff, young people find themselves vulnerable to entry into the labor market unlike experienced labor force (El Aynaoui and Ibourk, 2018).

In addition, many authors argue that the mismatch between demand and skill supply of young workers is a determining influencing factor of the situation of unemployment among young people in Morocco and the MENA region (Ibourk et al., 2014 ; Masood Ahmed, 2012 ; UNESCO, 2012 ; Assaf and Benhassine, 2003, cited in World Bank, 2004). Several studies about the MENA region show that employers confirm that the lack of skills represent an important constraint to hiring. Furthermore, the mismatch between acquired and required skills provides a plausible explanation for the difficulties of accessing to the labor market for young people. However, as stipulated in the human capital and job search theories, some of the young graduates prefer to wait longer in a situation of unemployment before accepting a convenient job for them extending the period between leaving the University and the first job held (El Aynaoui and Ibourk, 2018).

Our results about gender differences indicate that women are more likely to be in unemployment that men. This finding has been found in few studies.

Johnson (1983) suggests that the women unemployment rate is likely to be higher than the men's one. One explanation is that women who want to flow out from home production into employment are likely to experiment a period of intervening unemployment. In contrary, men who want to change jobs are likely to remain in employment. Tansel and Tasçi (2004) show that men are experiencing lower unemployment durations than women. Eusamio (2004) found that men had less difficulties to leave unemployment in the period 1994-1998. According to Havet (2006), having children may lead to decrease the probability of women to get a stable job. Gassab and Ben Ouada Jamoussi (2011) have studied unemployment among graduates of higher education in Tunisia and found that the rate of unemployed women outnumbers the men rate.

Our results about the effect of French language on the probability of being in unemployment indicate that graduates whose French ability is high are less likely to know a non-employment state. In Morocco, French language monopolizes the modern labor market and is the language of science, technology and new technologies (see for more details, Benzakour et al., 2000 and Benzakour, 2001, 2007 and 2010). In addition to that, in an extremely difficult labor market, having fluent oral and written French is an important asset (Bourdereau, 2006).

Regarding the effect of household structure on the probability of unemployment, it is captured by two variables: the number of employed siblings and the educational level of the parents. The negative effect of the number of employed siblings on the probability of unemployment is explained by the fact that this variable is likely to reinforce the social network of the graduate and to contribute to implement favorable attitudes to the activity within the household. This issue has been treated in some few studies such as the one of Rees and Gray (1982) who suggest the fact that siblings are able to help each other find jobs. O'Regan and Quigley (1993) show that youth are more likely to be employed if their mothers, fathers or siblings are employed. Recently, Rao and Chatterjee (2018) estimate the relationship between sibling gender and wage rates. Thus, brothers help to increase wages of men through social networks but the wages of women are insensitive to sibling gender.

We also examine whether the educational qualification reduces the risk of becoming unemployed. Several studies report this link between educational qualification and the incidence of unemployment such as Nickell (1979). Using UK data who demonstrates that acquiring qualifications at ordinary and high levels decreases the unemployment duration by 12 percent. Mincer (1991) found that one of the benefits of education is a lowered probabilitiy of unemployment. In the same way, Farber (2004) concludes that people who lose their jobs with high level of education have more chances to be re-employed full-time. Idiris Aden (2017) found, using data in the case of Canada's labor market, that individuals that have a relatively higher level of education have lower risk of unemployment.

The mobility to study in university from the region of origin to another region reduces the probability of unemployment after graduation. This finding was supported also by Bacci et al. (2008) who found that students who move away from their region of origin to study are much more likely to find employment in the region where they graduated.

REFERENCES

Aden I., 2017. Impact of education on unemployment evidence from Canada. Research paper. Department of Economics of the University of Ottawa.

Arulampalam W., 1999, Practitioners' corner - A note on estimated coefficients in random effects probit models. *Oxford Bulletin of Economics and Statistics*, 61(4), 597-602.

Bacci S., Chiandotto B., Di Francia A., 2008. Graduates Job Mobility: A Longitudinal Analysis, *Statistica*, 68(3), 255-279.

Benzakour F., Gaadi D., Queffélec A., 2000. *Le Français au Maroc. Lexique et contacts de langues*, Duculot, AUPELF-UREF, Bruxelles.

Benzakour F., 2001. Français de référence et français en usage au Maroc. Une adéquation illusoire : l'exemple de l'écart lexical, Actes du Colloque International « Le français de référence. Constructions et appropriations d'un concept », Louvain-La-Neuve, Novembre 1999, Cahiers de l'Institut de Linguistique de Louvain.

Benzakour F., 2007. Langue française et langues locales en terre marocaine: rapports de force et reconstructions identitaires, Géopolitique de la langue française, *revue Hérodote*, 126, éditions La Découverte, Paris.

Benzakour F., 2010. Le français au Maroc. Enjeux et réalité, in Le français en Afrique, Revue du Réseau des Observatoires du Français Contemporain en Afrique.

Blanchard O.J., Diamond P., 1994. Ranking, Unemployment Duration, and Wages. *Review of Economic Studies*, 61(3), 417-434.

Blasco S., Givord P., 2010. Les trajectoires professionnelles en début de vie active : quel impact des contrats temporaires ? INSEE working paper.

Bourdereau F., 2010. Politique linguistique, politique scolaire : la situation du Maroc, *Le français aujourd'hui*, 2006/3, n° 154.

Chamberlain G., 1984. Panel Data. In Griliches, Z. and Intriligator, MD. eds., *Handbook of Econometrics*, volume II, Elsevier Science Publishers BV, chapter 22.

Chrysanthou G.M., 2008. Determinants of trade union membership in Great Britain during 1991-2003, UC3M Working papers. Economics we082315, Universidad Carlos III de Madrid. Departamento de Economía.

Corcoran M., Hill M.S., 1985. Reoccurrence of Unemployment Among Adult Men, *Journal of Human Resources*, 20, 165-83.

Didier B., Hanchane S., Werquin P., 1996. Mobilité professionnelle initiale : éducation et expérience sur le marché du travail : un modèle Probit à effet aléatoire. *Economie et Statistique*, 299.

Doeringer P., Piore M.J., 1971. *Internal Labor Market and Manpower Analysis*. Lexiton (Mass.).

Doiron D., Gorgens T., 2008. State Dependence in Youth Labor Market Experiences, and the Evaluation of Policy Interventions. *Journal of Econometrics*, 145, 81-97.

El Aoufi N., Bensaid M., 2008. *Les jeunes mode d'emploi. Chômage et employabilité au Maroc*. Economie critique, Rabat.

El Aynaoui K., Ibourk A., 2018. Les enjeux du marché du travail au Maroc, OCP Policy Center.

Eusamio E., 2004. "El Diferencial de las Tasas de Paro de Hombres y Mujeres en España (1994-1998)" [The Difference between the Unemployment Rates of Men and Women in Spain (1994-1998)]. CEMFI, Thesis no. 0404.

Farber H.S., 2004. Job loss in the united states:1981-2001. Nber working paper series. Working paper 9707. National bureau of economic research.

Favereau O., Sollogoub M., Zighéra J.A., 1991. Une approche longitudinale de la segmentation du marché du travail. *Formation Emploi*, 33.

Flaig G., Licht G., Steiner V., 1993. Testing for State Dependence Effects in a Dynamic Model of Male Unemployment Behavior. In Bunzel, H. & al., *Panel Data and Labor Market Dynamics*, Amsterdam, North Holand.

Frijters P., Lindboom M., Van Den Berg G., 2000. Persistencies in the Labour Market, Working Paper, Free university Amsterdam.

Gassab M., Ben Ouada H. J., 2011. Determinants of Graduate Unemployment in Tunisia. Working Papers 16, AlmaLaurea Inter-University Consortium.

Guillotin Y., Sevestre P., 1994. Estimations de fonctions de gains sur données de panel : endogénéité du capital humain et effets de sélection. *Économie et Prévision*, 116.

Haan P., 2006. Slowly, But Changing: How Does Genuine State Dependence Affect Female Labor Supply On The Extensive And Intensive Margin? JEPS Working Papers (06-002).

Hansen J., Lofstrom M., 2009. The dynamics of immigrant welfare and labor market behavior. *Journal of Population Economics*, 22(4), 941-970.

Hansen J., Lofstrom M., Zhang X., 2006. State dependence in Canadian welfare participation: IZA Discussion Papers.

Havet N., 2006. L'insertion professionnelle des jeunes et mesures publiques, les trajectoires différenciées entre les hommes et les femmes. *Analyses d'économie et de statistique*, 81.

Heckman J., 1981. Heterogeneity and State Dependence. In Rose, S. ed., *Studies in Labor Markets*, Chicago Press, Chicago II.

Heckman J.J., Borjas G.J., 1980. Does unemployment cause future unemployment? Definitions, questions and answers from a continuous time model of heterogeneity and state dependence. *Economica*, 47(187), 247-283.

Hyslop D.R., 1999, State Dependence, Serial Correlation and Heterogeneity in Intertemporal Labor Force Participation of Married Women, *Econometrica*, 67, 55-94.

Islam N., 2006, Dynamic labour force participation of married women in Sweden. Working Papers in Economics 184, University of Gothenburg.

Kari H., 2003. Education and Unemployment: State Dependence in Unemployment Among Young People in the 1990s', Discussion Papers 312, VATT Institute for Economic Research.

Ibourk A., Bougroum M., Ouaghad A., Sahib H., 2014. Etude de diagnostic sur la situation de l'emploi au Maroc. Préalable à la formulation de la stratégie nationale de l'emploi, Rapport Global, BIT.

Laflamme C., Baby A., 1993. Integration of youth into the labor market: Some theoretical considerations on a structural/conjuncrural issue. *Alberta Journal of Educational Research*, XXXIXd, 97-109.

Le Maire D., Scheuer C., 2006. Determinants of Labour Force Participation for Selected Groups With Weak Labour Market Attachment: A panel Data Analysis For Denmark, Velfærdskommisionen.

Mansuy M., Couppié T., Fetsi A., Scatoli C., 2001. Transitions entre le système éducatif et la vie active : chiffres clés sur la formation professionnelle dans l'Union européenne, Luxembourg : Office des publications officielles des Communautés européennes.

Muhleisen M., Zimmermann K.F., 1994. A Panel Analysis of Job Changes and Unemployment, *European Economic Review*, 38, 793-801.

Nickell S., 1979. Education and lifetime patterns of unemployment. *Journal of Political Economy*, 87(5), 117-131.

Orme C.D., 1997. The Initial Condition Problem and Two-Step Estimation in Discrete Panel Data Models, Mimeo, University of Manchester.

O'Regan K.M., Quigley J.M., 1993. Family networks and youth access to jobs. *Journal of Urban Economics*, 34(2), 230-248.

Prowse V., 2005. State dependence in a multi-state model of employment dynamics: IZA Discussion Papers.

Rao N., Chatterjee T., 2018. Sibling gender and wage differences. *Applied Economics*, 50(15), 1725-1745.

Rees A., Gray W., 1982. "Family Effects in Youth Employment", NBER Chapters, in: *The Youth Labor Market Problem: Its Nature, Causes, and Consequences*, National Bureau of Economic Research, 453-474.

Stewart M.B., 2007. Inter-related dynamics of unemployment and low-wage employment, *Journal of Applied Econometrics*, 22, 511-531.

Stewart M.B., Swaffield J.K., 1999. Low Pay Dynamics and Transition Probabilities, *Economica*, 66(261), 23-42.

Tanguy L., 1986, L'introuvable relation formation et emploi. La Documentation Française.

Tansel A., Taşçi H.M., 2004. Determinants of Unemployment Duration for Men and Women in Turkey, IZA Discussion Papers, No. 1258, Institute for the Study of Labor (IZA).

UNESCO, 2012. Jeunes et compétences : l'éducation au travail, Rapport mondial de suivi sur l'EPT.

Wooldridge J., 2005, Simple solutions to the initial conditions problem in dynamic, nonlinear panel data models with unobserved heterogeneity, *Journal of Applied Econometrics*, 20, 39-54.

World Bank, 2004. *Unlocking the Employment Potential in the Middle East and North Africa, Toward a new social contract*, MENA Development Report.

APPENDIX

Table A1: Estimation results for Unemployment Probabilities of University Graduates

	Random effects Probit	Heckman Estimator	Wooldridge Estimator	Orme Estimator
Lagged dependent variable (Yt-1)	4.139*** (0.052)	3.911*** (0.067)	3.927*** (0.064)	3.932*** (0.065)
Initial condition (at t=1)	-	-	0.502*** (0.105)	0.305*** (0.065)
Gender	-0.165*** (0.051)	-0.255*** (0.066)	-0.163*** (0.059)	-0.246*** (0.062)
Residence with parents	0.196*** (0.065)	0.260*** (0.081)	0.217*** (0.076)	0.257*** (0.077)
French level	-0.185** (0.058)	-0.268*** (0.075)	-0.153** (0.068)	-0.258** (0.070)
Number of employed brothers and sisters	-0.028* (0.015)	-0.041** (0.019)	-0.035** (0.018)	-0.039* (0.018)
Mobility	-0.122* (0.072)	-0.133* (0.089)	-0.131* (0.084)	-0.128* (0.083)
Age	Non-sign.	Non-sign.	Non-sign.	Non-sign.
Highest level of education of one of the parents				
No schooling	Ref	Ref	Ref	Ref
Primary school level	-0.145* (0.081)	-0.171* (0.100)	-0.187** (0.095)	-0.166* (0.094)
Secondary school level	-0.197** (0.071)	-0.222*** (0.088)	-0.235** (0.083)	-0.217** (0.083)
Tertiary school level	-0.306*** (0.080)	-0.358*** (0.099)	-0.372*** (0.094)	-0.352*** (0.093)
Qualification degree				
Having less than 5 years in High Education	Ref	Ref	Ref	Ref
Having 5 years and more in High Education	-0.213*** (0.056)	-0.258*** (0.070)	-0.205*** (0.065)	-0.256*** (0.066)
ρ	0.033*** (0.024)	0.153*** (0.043)	0.102*** (0.031)	0.101*** (0.031)
σ_u	0.186*** (0.070)	-	0.337*** (0.057)	0.336*** (0.057)
θ	-	2.841*** (0.989)	-	-
Log likelihood	-1677.03	-2102.900	-1662.834	-1663.5298
Wald	6475.19 (0.000)	4231.92 (0.000)	5695.37 (0.000)	5708.75 (0.000)

*The table presents marginal effects and standard deviations in brackets. ***, **, * indicate thresholds of significance respectively of 1%, 5% and 10%. Sample size= 22518.*

Source: Author's calculation (A sample of 2009 year's graduates from 3 universities).

Table A2: Dynamic Probit Model results for Graduates' Unemployment Behavior (Marginal effects)

	Random effects probit	Wooldridge Estimator	Orme Estimator
Lagged dependent variable (Yt-1)	0.924*** (0.005)	0.885*** (0.012)	0.887*** (0.011)
Initial condition (at t=1)	-	0.051*** (0.009)	0.031*** (0.006)
Gender	-0.016*** (0.008)	-0.017*** (0.006)	-0.026*** (0.006)
Residence with parents	0.023*** (0.007)	0.022*** (0.007)	0.025*** (0.007)
French level	-0.024** (0.008)	-0.017** (0.008)	-0.031** (0.009)
Number of employed brothers and sisters	-0.003* (0.002)	-0.004* (0.002)	-0.004* (0.002)
Mobility	-0.014* (0.008)	-0.013* (0.008)	-0.013* (0.008)
Age	Non-sign.	Non-sign.	Non-sign.
Highest level of education of one of the parents			
No schooling	Ref	Ref	Ref
Primary school level	-0.016* (0.008)	-0.018** (0.008)	-0.016* (0.008)
Secondary school level 1	-0.022*** (0.008)	-0.023*** (0.008)	-0.022** (0.008)
Tertiary school level	-0.033*** (0.008)	-0.035*** (0.008)	-0.033*** (0.008)
Qualification degree			
Having less than 5 years in High Education	Ref	Ref	Ref
Having 5 years and more in High Education	-0.025*** (0.007)	-0.021*** (0.007)	-0.027*** (0.007)
ρ Unobserved heterogeneity	0.033*** (0.024)	0.102*** (0.031)	0.101*** (0.031)
Log likelihood	-1677.03	-1662.834	-1663.5298
Wald	6475.19 (0.000)	5695.37 (0.000)	5708.75 (0.000)

*The table presents marginal effects and standard deviations in brackets. ***, **, * indicate thresholds of significance respectively of 1%, 5% and 10%.*

Source: Author's calculation (A sample of 2009 year's graduates from 3 universities).

Les effets de la dépendance d'état sur le chômage des diplômés de l'université au Maroc : Une analyse utilisant un modèle probit dynamique

Résumé - Cet article examine la relation qui existe entre le passage d'un individu par une situation de chômage dans le passé et sa situation professionnelle actuelle. Dans la littérature, cette relation est appelée « dépendance d'état ». Les données de cette étude sont issues d'une enquête adressée à un échantillon représentatif des diplômés des facultés et des écoles de trois universités marocaines. Nous avons estimé un modèle probit dynamique à effets aléatoires pour tester l'effet de la dépendance d'état sur un panel des diplômés actifs lauréats des trois universités. La probabilité de chômage à l'instant t dépend principalement du statut du diplômé sur le marché du travail à l'instant t-1 et des caractéristiques personnelles de l'individu. Une fois que l'hétérogénéité individuelle observée et non observée est contrôlée, les résultats de la modélisation révèlent que le fait de tomber dans le chômage augmente la probabilité de chômage dans le futur, validant la théorie des « effets de retour négatifs » qui stipule que la transition par des périodes de chômage empêche l'accumulation de l'expérience dans le travail et peut contribuer à la dégradation du capital humain.

Mots clés

Capital humain
Marché du travail
Modèle probit dynamique à effets aléatoires
Données de panel
Effets de stigmatisation

Région et Développement
n° 49-2019
www.regionetdeveloppement.org

Chocs climatiques et migration saisonnière dans la région de Tahoua au Niger : une approche à partir d'un modèle dichotomique

Ibrahim MOHAMED BELLO*

Résumé - L'objectif de cet article est d'analyser empiriquement les déterminants de la migration saisonnière, qui est une pratique très répandue, dans la région sahélienne de Tahoua en mettant l'accent sur l'effet des chocs climatiques et la vulnérabilité alimentaire des ménages. Nous estimons un modèle probit basé sur les données de l'enquête sur la vulnérabilité à l'insécurité alimentaire des ménages (EVIAM-2015) réalisée par l'INS-Niger et *al.* en 2015. Nos résultats indiquent que le revenu par tête du ménage, le nombre des membres actifs dans le ménage ainsi que le sexe, le statut matrimonial et l'activité principale du chef de ménage déterminent sa probabilité de migrer. La baisse des récoltes résultant des chocs climatiques n'est pas statistiquement significative. Cependant, les chocs climatiques provoquent une hausse des prix alimentaires et la vulnérabilité alimentaire des ménages influence leur décision de migrer.

Classification JEL
C10, C25, Q18, Q54, R20

Mots-clés
Migration saisonnière
Chocs climatiques
Vulnérabilité alimentaire
Tahoua

L'auteur remercie le rapporteur anonyme et la rédaction de la revue pour leurs remarques et suggestions pertinentes. Il remercie également les participants au colloque international « Economie des migrations en Afrique sub-saharienne » tenu en Décembre 2018 à l'Université des Sciences Sociales et de Gestion de Bamako au Mali.

* LARADES, FADEG, Université de Tahoua (Niger) ; medbello2003@yahoo.fr

INTRODUCTION

Par définition, la migration fait référence au déplacement d'une ou plusieurs personnes d'un pays à un autre ou à l'intérieur d'un même pays impliquant un changement de lieu de résidence habituelle (OIM, 2007). La décision de migrer ou le projet migratoire s'inscrit selon la théorie néoclassique dans une logique individuelle. Toutefois, l'extension du cadre conceptuel par la nouvelle économie de la migration (NEM) propose de ramener l'unité décisionnelle de l'échelle individuelle à l'échelle du ménage avec la prise en compte de la structure familiale (Harbinson, 1981). La NEM considère la migration comme une stratégie collective de gestion du risque en l'absence des marchés de crédit et d'assurance (Stark et Levhari, 1982 ; Gubert, 2010). Dans cet esprit, on peut dire que la migration agit comme une forme d'assurance pour les ménages agricoles en zones rurales contre les aléas conjoncturels comme la sécheresse, les inondations, les catastrophes naturelles, etc. (Piguet, 2013).

Au Niger, comme dans la plupart des pays sahéliens, les effets des chocs climatiques de plus en plus récurrents et sévères induisent une vulnérabilité alimentaire chronique. Pour y faire face, et en réponse, les ménages ruraux majoritairement agricoles développent des stratégies informelles d'adaptation telle que la migration saisonnière. Dans la région de Tahoua selon INS-Niger et *al.* (2015) environ 6 villages sur 10 ont connu des problèmes alimentaires au cours des 12 derniers mois et près de 4 villages sur 10 ont estimé que leur situation alimentaire s'est dégradée par rapport au même mois de l'année précédente. Ainsi, le choix porté sur la région de Tahoua pour conduire cette étude se justifie car elle est non seulement la plus affectée par la sécheresse et la crise alimentaire ces dernières années (INS-Niger et *al.*, 2015) mais elle a aussi une forte tradition migratoire (Mounkaila, 2010).

L'objectif de cette étude est de déterminer les facteurs explicatifs de la migration saisonnière dans la région de Tahoua en mettant l'accent sur les variables relatives aux chocs climatiques et à la situation alimentaire des ménages. L'expérience et la répercussion des chocs climatiques ainsi que la vulnérabilité alimentaire influencent-elles la probabilité de migrer pour un ménage ? Telle est la principale interrogation autour de laquelle s'articule le présent article.

Nous exposons dans une première section la revue de la littérature qui analyse la migration comme une mesure d'adaptation face aux chocs climatiques en milieu rural sahélien. Notre source de données statistiques, l'enquête EVIAM-2015 et ses principaux enseignements sont présentés dans une deuxième section. Nous retenons dans une troisième section une approche empirique basée sur la spécification et l'estimation d'un modèle probit et discutons des résultats.

1. LA MIGRATION AU SAHEL : UNE MESURE D'ADAPTATION FACE AU CHANGEMENT CLIMATIQUE

La migration comme stratégie d'adaptation face aux chocs climatiques a fait l'objet d'une abondante littérature dans les pays en développement et plus particulièrement dans ceux du Sahel.

Dans une étude du Programme des Nations Unies pour l'Environnement (2011) consacrée à la sécurité des moyens d'existence des populations sahéliennes, la migration saisonnière apparaît comme une stratégie d'adaptation à la variabilité climatique. Le lien entre le changement climatique, les sécheresses et les migrations dans les pays du Sahel a fait l'objet de différentes études notamment au Niger, au Mali, au Burkina Faso, au Sénégal, au Tchad et en Ethiopie (Gervais, 1987 ; Jouve, 1991 ; Findley, 1994 ; Mounkaila, 2002 ; Henri et *al.*, 2004 ; Konseiga, 2007 ;

Dominique, 2010 ; Gray et *al.*, 2012 ; Fourissala et Gormo, 2013 ; Lalou et Delaunay, 2015 ; Hummel, 2016).

Au Niger, les pratiques migratoires sont temporaires car ne donnant pas lieu à une installation durable et définitive des migrants (Boyer et *al.*, 2010). La mobilité des hommes et la migration saisonnière au Sahel relèvent justement des stratégies paysannes de gestion des chocs liés à la sécheresse et à l'insécurité alimentaire (Jouve, 1991 ; Mounkaila, 2002). Une enquête auprès des ménages et des communautés sahéliennes a permis à Cissé et *al.* (2010) de considérer la migration comme une mesure d'adaptation à la variabilité climatique, et d'expliquer l'accélération du phénomène migratoire au Sahel par la dégradation environnementale et les conditions climatiques défavorables. Au Burkina Faso, toujours au Sahel, la migration apparait comme l'unique stratégie de survie dans les régions confrontées à une pénurie de ressources naturelles (Konseiga, 2007). Au Sénégal, la migration constitue également une réponse des paysans à la sécheresse (Dominique, 2010). Les travaux de Dominique (2010) montrent que dans les cinq dernières années précédant le Recensement Général de 1988, les régions sénégalaises les plus touchées par la sécheresse sont celles qui présentent un solde migratoire négatif. Dans la même logique, Gray et *al.* (2012) ont analysé les effets de la sécheresse sur la mobilité de la population rurale éthiopienne sur une période de dix ans. Il apparaît que la migration des hommes s'accentue avec la sécheresse et que les ménages exploitant des terres peu fertiles sont les plus vulnérables. Par ailleurs, Lalou et Delaunay (2015) remarquent que les migrations saisonnières des populations rurales du Bassin arachidier du Sénégal se sont généralisées et ont atteint une grande ampleur avec la crise agricole consécutive à l'arrêt des subventions aux paysans dans le cadre des programmes d'ajustement structurel. Notons que la vulnérabilité alimentaire a aussi joué un rôle important dans l'explication de la migration saisonnière des populations rurales sénégalaises (Chung et Guenard, 2013). Dans une autre étude portant sur le lien entre le changement climatique et la migration dans la bande sahélienne au Tchad, Fourissala et Gormo (2013) s'appuient sur les sources orales et autres documents historiques pour conclure que les épisodes de sécheresse des années 1973, 1984, 2000, 2009, et les vagues de famines qui en ont résultées, ont drainé un important flux migratoire parmi les agriculteurs et éleveurs du Sahel. Cela fait du changement climatique le premier facteur des migrations dans la bande sahélienne au Tchad.

Toute cette littérature dédiée aux pays du Sahel explique la migration comme une stratégie d'adaptation au changement climatique. Dans un tel contexte, marqué par des sécheresses répétitives, la persistance des crises alimentaires et des famines, la migration saisonnière répond à une question de survie des ménages ruraux agricoles.

2. L'ENQUÊTE EVIAM-2015 ET SES ENSEIGNEMENTS

2.1. L'enquête EVIAM-2015

Notre analyse empirique mobilise les données de l'enquête nationale sur la vulnérabilité à l'insécurité alimentaire des ménages ruraux (EVIAM) réalisée sur toute l'étendue du territoire national en décembre 2014 et janvier 2015 par l'Institut National de la Statistique (INS-Niger) avec l'appui des partenaires au développement. Le « questionnaire ménage » administré lors de cette enquête renseigne notamment sur les caractéristiques socio-économiques du ménage, les sources de revenus du ménage, les difficultés ou chocs, les stratégies de résilience face aux chocs, la migration, etc. L'échantillonnage est effectué de façon aléatoire et à deux degrés. 1472 zones de dénombrement ont d'abord été tirées. 15 ménages ont été ensuite systématiquement tirés dans chaque zone de dénombrement avec probabilité égale. Au total, l'enquête a porté sur un échantillon de 21668 ménages ruraux sur l'ensemble du territoire national.

Pour la région de Tahoua en particulier, l'enquête EVIAM (INS-Niger et *al.*, 2015) a concerné un échantillon de 4866 ménages ruraux répartis dans les différents départements de la région comme suit : Abalak (373 ménages), Bagaroua (501 ménages), Birni N'Konni (161 ménages), Bouza (550 ménages), Illéla (503 ménages), Keita (533 ménages), Madaoua (551 ménages), Malbaza (165 ménages), Tahoua département (507 ménages), Tassara (337 ménages), Tchintabaraden (343 ménages) et Tillia (341 ménages). De cette base de données, nous avons rigoureusement extrait les ménages qui ont effectivement répondu au « Point XII » du questionnaire portant sur la migration saisonnière, soit un total de 3501 ménages. Ainsi, l'exploitation de ces données nous permet d'appréhender le profil de la migration saisonnière dans la région de Tahoua ainsi que son lien avec les chocs climatiques et la vulnérabilité alimentaire des ménages ruraux.

2.2. Les chocs climatiques et leurs effets dans la région de Tahoua

Par définition, un choc désigne ici la matérialisation d'un événement aléatoire et imprévisible dont l'occurrence est susceptible d'affecter le bien-être des ménages (Mohamed Bello, 2016). Notre mesure des chocs repose sur la perception et l'expérience des chocs par les ménages enquêtés car ces derniers rapportent eux-mêmes avoir subi ces chocs ou pas au cours de douze derniers mois (INS-Niger et *al.*, 2015).

Les chocs liés au climat (ou *chocs climatiques*) produisent des effets directs (ou *effets-chocs climatiques*) sur les ménages. Les chocs climatiques (*sécheresse, inondations, catastrophes naturelles*) et les effets-chocs climatiques (*baisse des récoltes, hausse des prix alimentaires*) sont d'une ampleur variable dans la région de Tahoua. D'après le graphique 1, la sécheresse a affecté 39,9% des ménages ruraux interrogés lors de l'EVIAM-2015. La baisse des récoltes est la difficulté qui a touché le plus grand nombre de ménages ruraux (56,8%). La hausse des prix alimentaires vient en troisième position (31,2%). Les catastrophes naturelles (7,6%) et les inondations (9,5%) apparaissent comme les chocs climatiques les moins cités par les ménages.

La prévalence de la sécheresse et ses corollaires comme la baisse des récoltes et/ou la hausse des prix alimentaires peuvent aggraver davantage la situation alimentaire et nutritionnelle des ménages ruraux. Dans de telles situations, ils ont souvent recours à la migration saisonnière comme mesure d'adaptation et de résilience.

Graphique 1. Proportion des chocs et effets-chocs climatiques dans la région de Tahoua

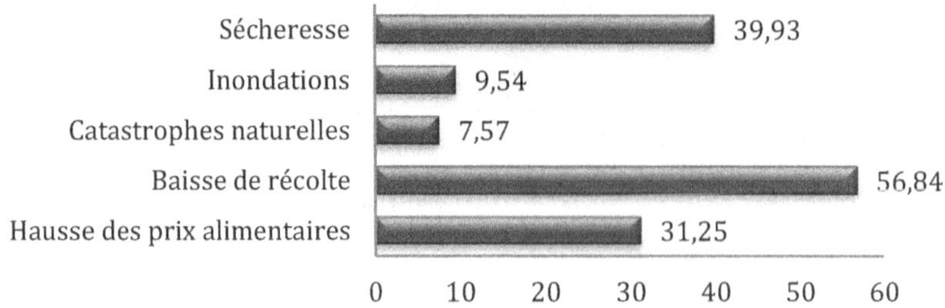

Source : Auteur, à partir de l'enquête auprès des ménages EVIAM-2015.

2.3. Caractéristiques de la migration saisonnière dans la région de Tahoua

La migration des individus induite par les effets du changement climatique peut être définitive ou temporaire (saisonnière ou circulaire). L'INS-Niger (2013) distingue la migration de courte durée (moins de 12 mois) et celle de longue durée (plus de 12 mois). Toutefois, la migration temporaire la plus fréquente reste la migration saisonnière (Dumont, 1995). En zones rurales sahéliennes, cette forme de mobilité constitue un rempart contre les effets liés aux chocs climatiques en permettant une diversification des sources de revenu. Il s'agit d'une stratégie de court terme visant à assurer les moyens de subsistance des ménages en cherchant des revenus complémentaires ailleurs tout en évitant la rupture avec leur terroir (Delaunay et *al.*, 2017). Notons que la migration saisonnière comme stratégie d'adaptation aux effets du changement climatique peut se faire au sein du pays ou à l'international.

Au Niger, le phénomène migratoire est largement dominé par des mouvements saisonniers de courte durée (moins de 6 mois) avec une préférence marquée pour les destinations africaines (63,3% des migrants pour l'ensemble du Niger).

Dans la région de Tahoua, la proportion des migrants saisonniers dont la durée de séjour est supérieure à 9 mois est de 18,9%. Par contre ceux qui n'y restent pas plus de 6 mois sont d'environ 63,5% parmi lesquels 26,9% reviennent au bout de 3 mois et 36,5% séjournent entre 3 et 6 mois (tableau 1). Ces données confirment le caractère saisonnier du phénomène migratoire dans la région de Tahoua.

Tableau 1. Proportion des migrants par durée de séjour

Moins de 3 mois	Entre 3 et 6 mois	Entre 6 et 9 mois	Plus de 9 mois	Total
26,94 %	36,53 %	17,60 %	18,93 %	100 %

Source : Auteur, à partir des données EVIAM-2015.

Une autre particularité de la migration saisonnière dans la région de Tahoua se rapporte au choix des destinations africaines par rapport aux autres villes du Niger (migration interne), d'Europe ou d'Amérique. En effet, près de 17,3% des migrants saisonniers de la région de Tahoua restent au Niger, environ 1,4% quittent l'Afrique, et jusqu'à 81,3% choisissent de rester en Afrique (voir tableau 2). La migration saisonnière intra-continentale est donc de loin la plus fréquente dans la région (soit 98,6% des migrants). Cela s'explique par l'objectif principalement attribué à cette forme de migration qui est celui de gestion des chocs et des effets-chocs climatiques. Ainsi, la proportion des migrants saisonniers de la région qui optent pour les destinations africaines est largement au-dessus de la moyenne nationale (soit 81,3% à Tahoua contre 63,3% au plan national). Les principales destinations africaines de ces migrants saisonniers sont la Côte d'Ivoire, le Nigéria, le Bénin, le Cameroun, le Gabon, la Libye et l'Algérie.

Tableau 2. Proportion des migrants saisonniers par destination

	A l'intérieur du Niger	En Afrique	Hors d'Afrique	Total
Tahoua	17,3 %	81,3 %	1,4 %	100 %
National	35,1 %	63,3 %	1,6 %	100 %

Source : Auteur, à partir des données EVIAM-2015.

Il existe un lien entre la vulnérabilité alimentaire des ménages et la migration saisonnière. Les ménages vulnérables appartiennent à la catégorie des ménages qui ne sont pas en situation d'insécurité alimentaire mais qui sont susceptibles de l'être dans le futur si aucune mesure n'est envisagée. La migration saisonnière est justement appréhendée comme une mesure qui permet aux ménages vulnérables d'échapper au risque d'insécurité alimentaire (Jouve, 1991 ; Mounkaila, 2002). Nous avons calculé la proportion des migrants selon les effets des chocs climatiques ressentis par les ménages. Nous avons retenu deux effets découlant directement de l'occurrence des chocs climatiques que nous avons appelé des *effets-chocs climatiques*. Il s'agit notamment de la *baisse des récoltes* (1er effet-choc climatique) et de la *hausse des prix alimentaires* (2ème effet-choc climatique). Ces effets des chocs climatiques, combinés ou non, sont des facteurs évidents de la vulnérabilité alimentaire des ménages ruraux, et donc susceptibles de les contraindre à la migration saisonnière.

Parmi les ménages ayant rapporté avoir subi la baisse de récolte, près de 27,1% ont enregistré la migration d'au moins un membre du ménage. Cette proportion est de 26,1% pour les ménages frappés par la hausse des prix alimentaires. De plus, en s'intéressant à la situation alimentaire des ménages, l'on remarque que la plus forte proportion des ménages ayant déclaré des migrants se situe dans la catégorie des ménages vulnérables (soit 28,6%) et la plus faible proportion se trouve parmi les ménages en sécurité alimentaire (soit 22,3%). Il apparaît que dans la région de Tahoua, des proportions relativement non négligeables des migrants saisonniers ressortent des ménages ayant enregistré la baisse des récoltes ou ayant été éprouvés par la hausse des prix alimentaires ou même des ménages déclarés vulnérables à l'insécurité alimentaire. Ces résultats indiquent que dans la région de Tahoua, la migration saisonnière est une pratique utilisée par les ménages vulnérables et ceux confrontés aux effets néfastes des chocs climatiques.

Tableau 3. Proportion des migrants saisonniers par effet-choc climatique et par classe d'insécurité alimentaire dans la région de Tahoua

	Migration d'au moins un membre du ménage au cours des 12 derniers mois		
	Oui (%)	Non (%)	Total (%)
Effets-Chocs climatiques subis par le ménage			
Effet-choc climatique 1 -- *Baisse de récoltes*	**27,09**	72,91	100
Effet-choc climatique 2 -- *Hausse des prix alimentaires*	**26,14**	73,96	100
Classes d'insécurité alimentaire du ménage			
Ménages en insécurité alimentaire (*sévère ou modérée*)	**25,21**	74,79	100
Ménages vulnérables (*à risque d'insécurité alimentaire*)	**28,65**	71,35	100
Ménages en sécurité alimentaire	**22,30**	77,70	100

Source : Auteur, à partir des données EVIAM-2015.

3. LES DÉTERMINANTS DE LA DÉCISION DE MIGRER ET LE RÔLE DES FACTEURS CLIMATIQUES : UN MODÈLE PROBIT

3.1. Spécification du modèle probit

La modélisation d'une variable dépendante binaire se fait principalement à l'aide soit d'un modèle de probabilité linéaire soit d'un modèle logit ou probit. Cependant, on reproche un certain nombre de problèmes à la spécification linéaire pour modéliser et estimer une variable binaire (Maddala, 1983 ; Aldrich et Nelson,

1984 ; Davidson et Mckinnon, 1999 ; Grenne, 2002 ; Hurlin, 2003). En effet, la régression de variable binaire par les moindres carrés ordinaires (MCO) ignore le caractère discret de la variable dépendante et ne contraint pas les probabilités prédites à être comprises entre 0 et 1. Ainsi, la valeur prédite de la probabilité peut donc être soit inférieure à 0, soit supérieure à 1. De plus, comme la variable dépendante ne prend que deux valeurs (0 ou 1), le terme d'erreur doit nécessairement admettre une loi binomiale discrète qui exclut en particulier l'hypothèse de normalité des résidus. C'est pourquoi une manière appropriée d'appréhender ici la décision de migrer est d'utiliser un modèle dichotomique de type logit ou probit.

Nous considérons dans la lignée de la nouvelle économie de la migration que la décision de migrer relève d'un choix collectif du ménage. On définit donc une variable binaire Y (migration) qui prend la valeur 1 si le ménage (ou au moins un membre du ménage) a migré au cours des douze derniers mois, et 0 sinon.

La décision de migrer renvoie à une variable latente non observable Y^* (comme l'utilité tirée de la migration) qui est supposée être une fonction linéaire des variables explicatives X et du terme d'erreurs ε. Soit :

$$Y_i^* = \beta_1 X_1 + \beta_2 X_2 + \cdots + \beta_k X_k + \cdots + \beta_N X_N + \varepsilon_i \, , i = 1, \dots, \mathrm{N}$$

Ce qui peut simplement s'écrire :

$$Y_i^* = X_i'\beta + \varepsilon_i \ \ , i = 1, \dots, \mathrm{N}$$

avec X_i un vecteur des variables explicatives, β un vecteur des coefficients à estimer et ε_i le terme d'erreurs normalement distribué c'est-à dire $\varepsilon_i \sim N(0,1)$.

La formulation mathématique du modèle correspond alors à :

$$Y_i = \begin{cases} 0 \ \ si \ \ Y_i^* = X_i'\beta + \varepsilon_i < 0 \\ 1 \ \ si \ \ Y_i^* = X_i'\beta + \varepsilon_i \geq 0 \end{cases}$$

La formulation en termes de probabilités équivaut à :

$$\Pr(Y_i = 1) = \Pr(Y_i^* \geq 0) = \Pr(X_i'\beta + \varepsilon_i \geq 0) = \Pr(\varepsilon_i \geq -X_i'\beta)$$

Or le modèle probit suppose pour les termes d'erreurs une loi normale centrée réduite ; $\varepsilon_i \sim N(0,1)$.

Posons Φ la fonction de répartition de la loi normale centrée réduite. On a alors :

$$\Pr(Y_i = 1) = \Pr(\varepsilon_i \geq -X_i'\beta) = \ 1 - \Phi(-X_i'\beta) = \Phi(X_i'\beta)$$

Finalement, la probabilité associée à la décision de migrer s'écrit :

$$p_i = \Pr(Y_i = 1) = \Phi(X_i'\beta) = \int_{-\infty}^{X_i'\beta} \frac{1}{\sqrt{2\pi}} e^{-\frac{z^2}{2}} dz \, , \forall \, i = 1, \dots, \mathrm{N}$$

Puisque $\Pr(Y_i = 0) = 1 - \Pr(Y_i = 1) = 1 - \Phi(X_i'\beta)$ on a alors $\Pr(Y_i = 0) = \Phi(-X_i'\beta)$.

Le vecteur des paramètres β est estimé par la méthode de maximum de vraisemblance. La fonction de vraisemblance s'écrit :

$$L(\beta) = \prod_{i=1}^{N} p(Y_i) = \left(\prod_{i=1}^{m} P(Y_i = 0)\right)\left(\prod_{i=m+1}^{N} P(Y_i = 1)\right)$$

$$L(\beta) = \left(\prod_{i=1}^{m} \Phi(-X_i'\beta)\right)\left(\prod_{i=m+1}^{N} \Phi(X_i'\beta)\right) = \left(\prod_{i=1}^{m} 1 - \Phi(X_i'\beta)\right)\left(\prod_{i=m+1}^{N} \Phi(X_i'\beta)\right)$$

$$L(\beta) = \prod_{i=1}^{N} \{[\Phi(X_i'\beta)^{Y_i}][\Phi(-X_i'\beta)^{1-Y_i}]\} = \prod_{i=1}^{N} \{[\Phi(X_i'\beta)^{Y_i}][1 - \Phi(X_i'\beta)]^{1-Y_i}\}$$

L'expression de la log-vraisemblance est :

$$l(\beta) = \ln L(\beta) = \ln\left(\prod_{i=1}^{N} \{[\Phi(X_i'\beta)^{Y_i}][1 - \Phi(X_i'\beta)]^{1-Y_i}\}\right)$$

$$l(\beta) = \ln L(\beta) = \sum_{i=1}^{N} Y_i . \ln[\Phi(X_i'\beta)] + \sum_{i=1}^{N} (1 - Y_i) . \ln[1 - \Phi(X_i'\beta)]$$

Les conditions de maximisation de la log-vraisemblance $l(\beta)$ est que sa dérivée première est égale à zéro et sa dérivée seconde négative. Le vecteur des estimateurs $\hat{\beta}$ est alors celui pour lequel : $\frac{\partial l(\beta)}{\partial \beta} = 0$ et $\frac{\partial^2 l(\beta)}{\partial \beta^2} < 0$.

Notons que ces coefficients $\hat{\beta}$ ne sont pas interprétables, puisqu'ils sont issus de la régression d'une variable latente non observable Y^*. Par contre, les signes de ces coefficients fournissent des informations utilement interprétables.

3.2. Les variables explicatives du modèle

Les chocs climatiques et/ou leurs répercussions (directes et/ou indirectes) sont susceptibles d'influencer la décision de migrer des ménages ruraux. Toutefois, comparativement à la littérature existante qui s'intéresse aux chocs climatiques (sécheresse, inondation, catastrophe naturelle, etc.) comme facteurs de migration saisonnière, notre étude présente la particularité de se focaliser non pas sur les chocs, mais plutôt sur les conséquences (effets directs et indirects) de ces chocs au sein des ménages ruraux, notamment la baisse des récoltes ou la hausse des prix alimentaires. C'est pourquoi, dans l'ensemble des chocs identifiés dans l'EVIAM-2015 (INS-Niger et *al.*, 2015), nous retenons ceux relatifs à la baisse des récoltes et à la hausse des prix alimentaires, particulièrement observées au Niger (Mohamed Bello, 2016). Ces chocs sont introduits dans le modèle sous forme des variables muettes. Elles prennent les valeurs 1 si le ménage a subi l'effet d'un choc climatique et 0 sinon. Les chocs climatiques peuvent aussi avoir des répercussions sur la vulnérabilité alimentaire des ménages ruraux agricoles (effets indirects). Ainsi, la situation alimentaire des ménages, comme facteur influençant la décision de migrer, est aussi introduite dans le modèle sous forme de variable qualitative à trois modalités.

En parallèle des facteurs climatiques, les caractéristiques démographiques et socio-économiques du ménage peuvent influencer sa décision de migrer : le revenu par tête du ménage, la taille du ménage, le nombre des membres actifs dans le ménage, le sexe du chef de ménage, le statut matrimonial du chef de ménage, l'activité principale du chef de ménage, la possession du bétail et la zone agro-écologique de résidence du ménage.

Les définitions, la mesure et les signes attendus des variables explicatives du modèle sont consignés dans le tableau 4.

3.3. Présentation et interprétation des résultats du modèle économétrique

Le tableau 5 présente les résultats de l'estimation du modèle probit. La statistique de Wald montre que le modèle est globalement significatif à 1%. La qualité de l'ajustement est de 76,46% même si le Pseudo-R^2 est de 0,088 (justifié par la nature transversale des données). Mais il faut rappeler que sur le plan méthodologique l'ajustement importe moins que la significativité statistique des coefficients.

Dans l'interprétation des signes des coefficients, seules les variables significatives retiendront notre attention.

Tableau 4. Définitions et mesures des variables explicatives du modèle

Variables explicatives	Nature, description et mesure des variables explicatives du modèle	Signes attendus
Revenu par tête du ménage	Variable quantitative calculée par le montant du revenu mensuel du ménage divisé par la taille du ménage.	(-)
Taille du ménage	Variable quantitative qui donne le nombre total des membres du ménage.	(+)
Membres actifs dans le ménage	Variable quantitative indiquant le nombre des membres actifs dans le ménage.	(+)
Sexe du chef de ménage	Variable dummy qui renvoie au sexe du chef de ménage. Elle prend la valeur 0 si le ménage est dirigé par un homme, et 1 si c'est une femme (*la modalité de référence est : Homme*)	(+)
Statut matrimonial du chef de ménage	Variable qualitative qui renseigne sur la situation matrimoniale du chef de ménage. Elle prend les valeurs : 1 = marié(e) monogame, 2 = marié(e) polygame, 3 = Célibataire(e)/Divorcé(e), et 4 = veuf (ve). (*la modalité de référence : Marié(e) monogame*)	(+/-)
Activité principale du chef de ménage	Variable qualitative qui indique la principale activité du chef de ménage. Elle prend les valeurs : 1 = agriculture, 2 = élevage, 3 = autres, et 0 = inactif. (*la modalité de référence est : Inactif*)	(+/-)
Effet-choc climatique 1 : *Baisse des récoltes*	Variable dummy qui renseigne sur l'expérience de cet effet-choc climatique par le ménage enquêté. Elle prend la valeur 1 si le ménage rapporte avoir subi une baisse de récolte au cours des 12 derniers mois, et 0 sinon.	(+)
Effet-choc climatique 2 : *Hausse des prix alimentaires*	Variable dummy qui renseigne sur l'expérience de cet effet-choc climatique par le ménage enquêté. Elle prend la valeur 1 si le ménage rapporte avoir fait face à une hausse des prix alimentaires au cours des 12 derniers mois, et 0 sinon.	(+)
Situation alimentaire du ménage	Variable qualitative à trois modalités reflétant la situation alimentaire du ménage. Elle prend les valeurs : 1 = ménage en sécurité alimentaire, 2 = ménage vulnérable à l'insécurité alimentaire, et 3 = ménage en insécurité alimentaire. (*la modalité de référence : Sécurité alimentaire*)	(+)
Zone agro-écologique de résidence du ménage	Variable qualitative à trois modalités qui renvoie à la zone agro-écologique de résidence du ménage. Cette variable prend les valeurs : 1 = zone agricole, 2 = zone agropastorale et 3 = zone pastorale. (*la modalité de référence est: Zone agricole*)	(+/-)
Petits ruminants	Variable quantitative qui renseigne sur la possession d'animaux notamment le nombre des petits ruminants dont dispose le ménage (ovins + caprins)	(-)
Gros ruminants	Variable quantitative qui renseigne sur la possession d'animaux notamment le nombre des gros ruminants dont dispose le ménage (bovins + camelins)	(-)
Asins	Variable quantitative qui renseigne sur la possession d'animaux notamment le nombre d'asins dont dispose le ménage (ânes + ânesses)	(+/-)

Source : Auteur.

Tableau 5. Déterminants de la décision de migrer dans la région de Tahoua

Variable dépendante : Migration (*décision de migrer*)

Variables explicatives	Coefficients	Ecarts-types robustes	P-value
Caractéristiques socio-économiques et démographiques du ménage et chef de ménage			
Revenu par tête du ménage	$-3{,}06.10^{-6}$**	$1{,}52.10^{-6}$	0,044
Taille du ménage	0,0001	0,0076	0,988
Nombre de membres actifs dans le ménage	0,0200**	0,0095	0,035
Sexe du chef de ménage (*Référence : homme*)	0,8729***	0,0919	0,000
Statut matrimonial du chef de ménage (*Référence : marié (e) monogame*)			
Marié (e) polygame	- 0,0533	0,0701	0,447
Célibataire / divorcé (e)	- 0,5817***	0,1938	0,003
Veuf (ve)	- 0,9804***	0,1197	0,000
Activité principale du chef de ménage (*Référence : inactif*)			
Agriculture	- 0,6578***	0,1524	0,000
Elevage	- 0,7820***	0,1837	0,000
Autres	- 0,5788***	0,1558	0,000
Expérience de chocs climatiques par le ménage (Effets-chocs climatiques subis)			
Baisse des récoltes	0,0290	0,0524	0,580
Hausse des prix alimentaires	0,1095**	0,0527	0,038
Situation alimentaire du ménage (*Référence : ménage en sécurité alimentaire*)			
Ménage en vulnérabilité alimentaire	0,1234**	0,0571	0,031
Ménage en insécurité alimentaire	0,0528	0,0681	0,438
Zone agro-écologique de résidence du ménage (Référence : zone agricole)			
Zone agropastorale	0,0442	0,0570	0,438
Zone pastorale	- 0,6881***	0,0732	0,000
Possession du bétail par le ménage			
Petits ruminants (ovins + caprins)	- 0,0061*	0,0036	0,090
Gros ruminants (bovins + camelins)	- 0,0019	0,0094	0,836
Asins (ânes + ânesses)	0,1097***	0,0276	0,000
Constante	- 0,1243	0,1679	0,459

Nombre d'observations : 3501.
Test de significativité globale de Wald chi2 (19) = 305,94 Prob > chi2 = 0,000
Pseudo-R^2 = 0,0877
Taux de prédictions correctes : 76,46%
(***), (**) et (*) : significatifs respectivement à 1%, 5% et 10%.

Source : Auteur, à partir du logiciel Stata.

Le revenu par tête du ménage influence significativement la décision de migrer du ménage : plus le ménage dispose d'un revenu par tête élevé moins il décide de migrer. La migration saisonnière est donc contrainte par la faiblesse de revenu et la vulnérabilité à la pauvreté.

Nos résultats indiquent également que la propension à migrer est beaucoup plus élevée chez les ménages dirigés par des femmes comparativement à ceux dirigés par des hommes. Les ménages dirigés par des femmes sont relativement plus vulnérables à l'insécurité alimentaire car elles dépendent souvent d'exploitations agricoles à faible productivité (Adjamagbo et *al.*, 2006), et sont donc plus enclines à la migration pour survivre.

La décision de migrer est aussi influencée par le nombre d'actifs dans le ménage. Plus le nombre de travailleurs au sein du ménage est grand plus la probabilité de migration de l'un au moins des membres du ménage est importante. Ainsi, la présence de « sureffectifs » impose que certains bras valides peuvent migrer alors que d'autres peuvent choisir de rester pour subvenir aux besoins urgents du ménage.

Le statut matrimonial et l'activité principale du chef du ménage influencent significativement la probabilité de migrer. Par rapport au marié (e) monogame, le statut de célibataire/divorcé et de veuf du chef de ménage encourage moins la décision de migrer. L'inactivité du chef de ménage est un facteur de vulnérabilité et de pauvreté qui oblige le ménage à migrer. Ainsi, comparativement à un ménage dirigé par un chef inactif, les ménages dont les chefs travaillent dans l'agriculture, l'élevage ou d'autres secteurs sont moins contraints à la migration saisonnière.

La décision de migrer est aussi en lien avec la possession du bétail par le ménage. La possession des petits ruminants (ovins et caprins) influence négativement la probabilité de migrer car ces animaux sont facilement liquidables sur les marchés locaux et permettent aux ménages ruraux d'obtenir un certain revenu. Par contre, lorsque le ménage dispose des asins (ânes et ânesses), il est plus enclin à migrer car les asins sont des moyens qui facilitent le déplacement et le déménagement des ménages ruraux.

Par ailleurs, concernant les facteurs climatiques et leurs corollaires, ce n'est pas en soi la baisse des récoltes sur une année (effet statistiquement non significatif) qui peut provoquer la migration saisonnière. Il apparaît que c'est d'abord la hausse des prix alimentaires et la vulnérabilité alimentaire qui augmentent la probabilité de migrer dans le ménage. Dans cette logique, la migration saisonnière peut être comprise comme une stratégie du ménage pour contrecarrer les effets néfastes des chocs climatiques.

CONCLUSION

La migration saisonnière est une pratique répandue au Niger et dans la région de Tahoua. Il existe une préférence marquée pour les destinations africaines des migrants de la région. En outre, le mouvement saisonnier des ménages dans cette région est largement dominé par des séjours de courte durée, généralement de moins de six mois.

Les ménages ruraux de la région de Tahoua frappés par les effets des chocs climatiques connaissent une proportion de plus en plus importante de migrants saisonniers. Les ménages vulnérables choisissent de migrer afin d'éviter les crises alimentaires et la famine.

Dans cet article, nous avons mis en exergue les déterminants de la décision de migrer au sein des ménages de la région à l'aide de l'estimation d'un modèle probit. Il ressort que les variables socioéconomiques comme le revenu par tête du ménage, le nombre de membres actifs dans le ménage, les femmes chefs de ménage, le statut matrimonial et l'inactivité du chef de ménage jouent un rôle important sur la décision de migrer. La possession des animaux par le ménage notamment les petits ruminants et les asins influe également sur la décision de migrer.

Quant aux variables relatives aux effets des chocs climatiques dans la région sahélienne surtout agropastorale de Tahoua, il faut retenir que c'est particulièrement la hausse des prix alimentaires et l'état de vulnérabilité alimentaire qui augmentent la probabilité de migrer.

Comme prolongement à cette étude, une analyse mériterait d'être menée sur plusieurs années et de confronter nos résultats aux comportements de migration définitive et d'arbitrage avec la migration saisonnière.

REFERENCES

Adjamagbo, A., Delaunay, V., Lévi, P., et Ndiaye, O., 2006, Comment les ménages d'une zone rurale du Sénégal gèrent-ils leurs ressources ?, *Études rurales,* n° 177, pp. 69-90.

Aldrich, J. and Nelson, F., 1984, *Linear probability, logit and probit models*, Beverly Hills, Sage Publications.

Boyer, F., et Mounkaila, H., 2010, Partir pour aider ceux qui restent ou la dépendance face aux migrations. L'exemple des paysans sahéliens, *Hommes et Migrations,* n°1286-1287, pp. 212-220.

Chung, E. H.-C., et Guénard C., 2013, Mobilité en milieu rural sénégalais : une exploration de la relation avec la vulnérabilité alimentaire et le réseau social. *In* Duchêne-Lacroix C., Mader P., (Eds.) : *Ici et là : ressources et vulnérabilités dans la vie multilocale,* Itinera, 34, Basel, Société suisse d'histoire, pp. 161-184.

Cissé, P., Malicki, Z., Barbier, B., et Maïga, A., 2010, Les migrations, une stratégie d'adaptation à la variabilité climatique en zones sahéliennes, *Revue de Géographie du Laboratoire Leïdi,* n° 8, pp. 184-196.

Davidson, R. and Mackinnon, J. G., 2004, *Econometric theory and methods*, Foxit Software Company 2004.

Delaunay V., Sauvain C., Franzetti R., Golay G., Moulay A., Engeli E., 2017, La migration temporaire des jeunes au Sénégal. Un facteur de résilience des sociétés rurales sahéliennes ?, *Afrique Contemporaine,* n° 259, pp. 75-94.

Dominique, R., 2010, Partir pour mieux durer : la migration comme réponse à la sécheresse au Sénégal ?, *Espace Populations Sociétés*, pp. 37-53.

Dumont, G-F., 1995, *Les migrations internationales. Les nouvelles logiques migratoires*, Collection Mobilité spatiale, Sedes, Paris, France, 224 p.

Findley, S., 1994, Does drought increase migration? A study of migration from Rural Mali during the 1983-1985 drought, *International Migration Review,* 28 (3), pp. 539-553.

Fourissala, R. H., et Gormo, J., 2013, Changement climatique et migration dans la bande sahélienne du Tchad, *Locus : revista de história, Juiz de Fora,* 18 (2), pp. 163-180.

Gervais, R., 1987, Pour une problématique démographique des catastrophes dites naturelles. L'exemple du Niger 1969-1974. *In* D. Gauvreau, J. Gregory, M. Kempeneers, V. Piché (Eds.), *Démographie et sous-développement dans le Tiers-monde,* Université de Montréal et Mc Gill University, 316 p.

Gray, C. and Mueller, V., 2012, Drougth and population mobility in rural Ethiopia, *World development*, vol. 40, 1, pp. 134-145.

Greene, W. H. (2002) *Econometric Analysis*, 5th Edition, Prentice Hall, New Jersey.

Gubert, F. (2010) Pourquoi migrer ? Le regard de la théorie économique, *Regards croisés sur l'économie,* vol. 2, n° 8, pp. 96-105.

Harbinson, S., 1981, Family structure and family strategy in migration decision making, *In* Gordon, F.D.J. and Robert, W.G. (Eds.): *Migration decision making. Multidisciplinary approaches to microlevel studies in developed and developing countries,* New York, Pergamon Press, pp. 225-251.

Hummel, D., 2015, Climate change, land degradation and migration in Mali and Senegal. Some policy implications, *Migration and Development*, 5(2), pp. 211-233.

Hurlin, C., 2003, Econométrie des variables qualitatives. Modèles dichotomiques univariés, Polycopié du cours, Master ESA, Université d'Orléans, 57 p.

INS-Niger, 2013, Manuel des concepts et définitions, Direction de la coordination et de développement de la statistique, Institut National de la Statistique, Niger.

INS-Niger et SAP, 2015, Enquête conjointe sur la vulnérabilité à l'insécurité alimentaire des ménages au Niger, Rapport d'enquête EVIAM, Avril.

Jouve, P., 1991, Sécheresse au Sahel et stratégies paysannes, *Sécheresse*, 2 (1), pp. 61-69.

Konseiga, A., 2007, Household migration decisions as survival strategy: the case of Burkina Faso, *Journal of African Economies*, vol. 16, 2, pp. 198-233.

Lalou, R. et Delaunay, V., 2015, Migrations saisonnières et changement climatique en milieu rural sénégalais : forme ou échec de l'adaptation ? *In* Sultan, B. et *al.* (Eds.) : *Les sociétés rurales face aux changements environnementaux en Afrique de l'Ouest*, IRD Editions, pp. 287-313.

Maddala, G. S., 1983, *Limited-dependent and qualitative variables in Econometrics*, Cambridge University Press.

Mohamed Bello, I., 2016, Les stratégies de gestion de risques agricoles au Niger : évidence empirique et implication pour les ménages agricoles, *Economie Rurale*, n° 351, pp. 67-78.

Mounkaïla, H., 2002, De la migration circulaire à l'abandon du territoire local dans le Zarmaganda (Niger), *Revue Européenne des Migrations Internationales*, vol. 18, n° 2, pp. 161-187.

Mounkaila, H., 2010, Circulations migratoires et envoi de fonds dans la région de Tahoua (Niger), *In* Hocine, L., Eddine, H. N., Chantel, C-J. et Sassi, S. (Eds), *Les migrations africaines : Economie, Société et Développement*, pp. 125-148.

OIM, 2007, *Glossaire de la migration*, Droit international de la migration n°9 (Rédaction de R. Perruchoud), Organisation Internationale pour les Migrations, Genève, Suisse.

Piguet, E., 2013, Les théories des migrations. Synthèse de la prise de décision individuelle, *Revue Européenne des Migrations Internationales*, vol. 29, n°3, pp. 141-161.

Programme des Nations Unies pour l'Environnement, 2011, *Sécurité des moyens d'existence. Changements climatiques, migrations et conflits au Sahel*, Programme des Nations Unies pour l'Environnement, Genève.

Stark, O. et Levhari, D., 1982, On migration and risk in LDC, *Economic Development and Cultural Change*, vol. 31, n°1, pp. 191-196.

Stojanov, R., Kelman, I., Martin, M., Vikhrov, D., Kniveton, D., and Duzi, B., 2014, *Migration as adaptation? Population dynamics in the age of climate variability*, Global Change Research Centre, The Academy of Sciences of the Czech Republic.

Climate shocks and seasonal migration in the region of Tahoua in Niger: an approach with a dichotomous model

Abstract - The main objective of this article is to analyze empirically the determinants of seasonal migration in the Sahel region of Tahoua with a focus on variables related to the effects of climate shocks and household food vulnerability. Indeed, we estimate a probit model using data from the Household Vulnerability to Food Insecurity Survey (EVIAM-2015) realized by INS-Niger et al. (2015). Our results indicate that the household per capita income, the number of active members in the household as well as the sex, marital status and main activity of the head of the household determine the probability to migrate. The fall in harvests resulting from climate shocks is not statistically significant. However, climatic shocks cause a rise in food prices and households' food vulnerability influences the households' decision to migrate.

Key-words

Seasonal migration
Climate shocks
Food vulnerability
Tahoua

Région et Développement

n° 49-2019

www.regionetdeveloppement.org

Transferts de fonds des migrants et sécurité alimentaire dans les pays de l'Afrique de l'Ouest

Michel NAMÉ*

Résumé - Cette étude vise à mieux comprendre les conditions de l'impact des transferts de fonds des migrants sur la sécurité alimentaire et la réduction de la pauvreté suite à un choc climatique. Nous utilisons pour ce faire un modèle spécifié en VAR (à vecteur autorégressif) sur des données de panel comprenant 7 pays de l'Union Economique et Monétaire Ouest Africaine (UEMOA) classés en 3 groupes selon leur pluviométrie, et collectées sur la période 1990-2010. Les résultats obtenus font ressortir un effet positif des transferts de fonds sur la réduction de la prévalence de la sous-alimentation et des écarts de pauvreté dans les pays moins pourvus en quantité de pluie, dont le secteur agricole est largement dépendant des cultures vivrières et les émigrés majoritairement d'origine rurale.

Classification JEL

Q54, F24, Q18, I32

Mots-clés

Choc climatique
Transferts des migrants
Sécurité alimentaire
Pauvreté
Afrique de l'Ouest

* Université de Liège, jmname@doct.ulg.ac.be; name_juste2009@yahoo.fr

INTRODUCTION

Selon les estimations de l'Organisation des Nations Unies pour l'alimentation et l'agriculture (FAO, 2012, p. 5), plus de 868 millions[1] de personnes seraient encore sous-alimentées et quelque deux milliards de personnes continueraient de souffrir des séquelles de carences en micronutriments. La plupart des personnes touchées se trouveraient en grande partie dans les pays en développement et notamment dans les zones rurales (Banque mondiale, 2008, p. 112). Elles ne disposeraient pas de ressources leur permettant de produire une quantité suffisante de denrées alimentaires ou de les acheter sur les marchés et n'auraient souvent pas accès à l'eau potable, à l'assainissement et aux services de santé encore moins à l'éducation. Or, une bonne nutrition reste le moteur essentiel d'une croissance économique durable (FAO, 2012, p. 2). Si les aides accordées aux Etats, dans le cadre de l'Aide Publique au Développement (APD)[2], ont pour rôle de contribuer à leur développement, elles doivent en parallèle permettre de garantir à leurs populations, dans la durée, en qualité et en quantité suffisante, l'accès aux produits alimentaires (FAO, 1996). L'APD accompagnerait la mise en place de politiques économiques permettant de favoriser la croissance des pays bénéficiaires (Burnside et Dollar, 1997, p. 33 ; 2000, p. 864) et ainsi de lutter contre la pauvreté (Ravaillon et Chen, 1997, p. 378 ; Dollar et Kraay, 2001, p. 9).

Les objectifs de croissance économique et de lutte contre la pauvreté devraient conduire à une allocation plus importante de l'APD dans le secteur agricole des pays en développement (Banque mondiale, 2008, p. 311). En plaçant ce secteur au centre des interventions extérieures, l'objectif premier de développement durable à savoir éliminer l'extrême pauvreté et la faim de moitié d'ici 2030 pourrait être atteint. Le secteur agricole et le milieu rural sont pourtant négligés et ne bénéficieraient pas toujours d'investissements suffisants de la part des pouvoirs publics et des bailleurs de fonds (Banque mondiale, 2008, p. 2). Alors que 75 % de la population pauvre mondiale vit dans les espaces ruraux, seulement 4 % de l'APD serait consacré au développement de l'agriculture en Afrique (Banque mondiale, 2008, p. 277). Le constat est que le taux de prévalence de la sous-alimentation reste très important en Afrique subsaharienne et surtout dans la zone sahélienne. Cela serait dû pour l'essentiel, à la vulnérabilité des populations aux changements climatiques (Generoso, 2012, p. 6), mais aussi à l'instabilité politique et aux fluctuations des prix des denrées alimentaires (Barrios et *al.*, 2008, p. 287, 289).

Une part importante des phénomènes migratoires concerne les localités rurales pauvres (Banque mondiale, 2006, p. 130 ; BAD[3], 2007, p. 23). La migration dans ce cas, est considérée comme une alternative saisie par les ménages afin de répondre au déficit de ressources et de crédit ou d'atténuer leur vulnérabilité aux chocs climatiques (Stark, 1991, p. 14). Les transferts de fonds des migrants[4] peuvent servir à lisser la consommation des familles bénéficiaires (Gubert, 2008, p. 52) qui les utiliseraient comme assurance face aux chocs exogènes au Botswana (Lucas et Stark, 1985) et aux Philippines (Yang et Choi, 2005). Clarke et Wallsten (2003, p.

---

[1] Le rapport (FAO, 2014, p. 2) indique 805 millions de personnes sous-alimentées. Il note donc une petite amélioration, mais 75 % de la population reste sous-alimentée en Afrique subsaharienne.

[2] L'aide publique au développement peut être définie comme le transfert de ressources publiques par les pays les plus industrialisés, réunis au sein du Comité d'Aide au Développement, vers les pays pauvres en vue de contribuer à leur développement (Charnoz et Severino, 2007, p. 3).

[3] Banque Africaine de Développement.

[4] 80% des ménages bénéficiaires des transferts de fonds des migrants sont proches de la limite du seuil de pauvreté (BAD, 2007).

21) relèvent aussi une augmentation des envois de fonds des migrants en période de dérives climatiques extrêmes en Jamaïque. Ratha (2007, p. 3) note également une hausse du volume des transferts de fonds lors de catastrophes naturelles en Amérique Centrale. Plus de la moitié des revenus des ménages touchés par une perturbation pluviométrique serait compensée par les transferts de fonds des migrants dans l'optique de maintenir leur niveau de dépenses habituelles aux Philippines (Yan et Choi, 2005, p. 14). Ce serait un contrat implicite d'assurance entre le migrant et sa famille d'origine pour De La Brière et *al.* (1997, p. 3). Selon Gubert (2002, p. 199), dans ce contrat implicite, les migrants maliens s'engageraient à subvenir aux besoins de leurs familles en leur versant systématiquement une sorte de prime d'assurance en cas de faibles récoltes. En permettant de lisser la consommation, les transferts de fonds des migrants seraient un important moyen de résilience des ménages lors d'un choc climatique, même s'ils peuvent parfois conduire à de moindres efforts sur le plan productif Gubert (2008, p. 53).

Ainsi, l'occurrence d'un choc climatique à un moment précis, dans une région donnée, entraîne-t-il en réponse une augmentation des transferts de fonds ? Si tel est le cas, est-ce qu'on peut dire que les chocs climatiques (sécheresse, inondation...) sont le principal motif des phénomènes migratoires observés ? Par ailleurs, comment les transferts de fonds deviennent-ils un moyen de résilience (sécurité alimentaire) pour les ménages bénéficiaires subissant des aléas climatiques ? Et quelles en sont les implications économiques ?

Cette étude vise à mieux comprendre les conditions de l'impact supposé positif des transferts de fonds des migrants sur la sécurité alimentaire et la réduction de la pauvreté suite à un choc climatique simultanément subi par un ensemble de pays. L'étude porte sur 7 pays de l'Union Economique et Monétaire Ouest Africaine (UEMOA) sur la période 1990-2010.

Une première section donne une revue sélective de la littérature sur les transferts des migrants et leur impact sur la croissance économique et la réduction de la pauvreté dans les pays récipiendaires. Nous utilisons pour ce faire un modèle VAR (à vecteur autorégressif) en panel dont la spécification est donnée dans une deuxième section ; cette spécification est suivie de tests de recherche d'une (ou plusieurs) racine(s) unitaire(s) dans un souci de vérification de la robustesse de nos estimations. Les résultats sont présentés et discutés dans une troisième section.

1. UNE REVUE DE LA LITTÉRATURE

D'après les Nations Unies (ONU, 1998, p. 10), les transferts de fonds proviennent des natifs étrangers ayant au moins une année de présence ou d'intention de présence dans les pays d'immigration. Ces montants regrouperaient ceux des naturalisés, leur descendance et des travailleurs saisonniers (Lerch et Wanner, 2008, p. 4). Ces transferts seraient aujourd'hui bien loin devant l'APD en volume[5] et viendraient juste après les investissements directs étrangers (IDE) comme moyen de financement extérieur (Generoso, 2012, p. 12-13 ; Faini, 2007, p. 168). Ils constitueraient une allocation directe et stable (Buch et Kuckulenz, 2004, p. 12 ; Gupta et *al.*, 2007, p. 41 ; Rocher et Pelletier, 2008, p. 27 ; Ebeke, 2010, p. 5) et ne seraient soumis à aucune(s) conditionnalité(s) (Kapur et Singer, 2006, cité par Ebeke, 2010, p. 4). Cependant, leur relation positive et significative sur la croissance économique des pays bénéficiaires n'est pas toujours évidente. Les transferts de fonds des migrants auraient un caractère contracyclique par rapport aux indicateurs économiques des pays bénéficiaires (Sayan, 2006, p. 10-11 ; Gupta et *al.*, 2009, p. 107-109 ; Neagu et Schiff, 2009, p. 17). Leur augmentation (diminution) serait

[5] Trois fois l'APD en 2009, selon la Banque mondiale (2011, p. 3).

fonction de l'évolution négative (positive) du Produit Intérieur Brut (PIB). Ils posséderaient avant tout une propriété d'atténuation de la volatilité du taux de croissance du PIB des pays récepteurs (Chami et *al.*, 2008, p. 66). Mais, d'un autre côté, de bons indicateurs économiques pourraient stimuler les envois de fonds des migrants ayant pour but l'investissement (Ebeke, 2010, p. 5). Pour Edwards et Ureta (2003, p. 456), les transferts de fonds des migrants favorisent le développement par l'accumulation du capital humain. Il a été constaté que les fonds des migrants, s'ils sont utilisés en grande partie pour des dépenses de consommation alimentaire, servent également à d'autres dépenses telles que la santé, l'éducation et le logement (BAD, 2007, p. 23). Toutefois, Baldwin (1970) et Miyagiwa (1991) notent une diminution du capital humain lorsque la migration concerne les personnes les plus qualifiées (fuite des cerveaux), qui peut avoir pour effet de ralentir la croissance des pays touchés par ce type d'émigration. Selon Chami et *al.* (2005, p. 77), les transferts de fonds des migrants réduiraient la participation au marché du travail des ménages bénéficiaires dans le cas où le montant transféré serait nettement supérieur à leurs revenus – ce qui entrainerait une moindre croissance et stimulerait moins l'esprit d'entrepreneuriat de ces ménages selon la BAD (2007, p. 46). Cette relation de dépendance des ménages vis-à-vis des transferts reste limitée selon Medenou (2010, p. 29), qui trouve que les fonds auraient un impact positif sur la croissance du Bénin à long terme *via* la consommation. Plus le ménage recevra des fonds et plus il cherchera à gagner son autonomie financière à travers la réalisation d'investissements productifs. Woodruff et Zenteno (2007, p. 525) montrent également une relation positive et significative des envois de fonds sur la croissance via l'investissement productif. Mais selon les enquêtes de la BAD (2007, p. 44-45), l'investissement productif ne représenterait qu'une part marginale dans l'utilisation des fonds reçus. Par ailleurs, Amuedo et Pozo (2004, p. 1414-1415) et Bourdet et Falk (2006, p. 281) trouvent un impact négatif et significatif des envois de fonds sur la croissance en astreignant les économies des pays bénéficiaires au « malaise hollandais » par leur effet sur le taux de change réel. Mais Faini (2007, p. 173-174) n'a pu trouver un quelconque impact significatif entre le taux de change réel et les transferts de fonds. Pour lui, le taux de change réel ne pourrait constituer un levier par lequel les envois de fonds impacteraient significativement la croissance. L'impact peut dépendre aussi de la qualité des institutions et de la stabilité politique des pays (Faini, 2007 ; Ahouré, 2008). Au final, l'existence d'une relation entre transferts et potentiel de croissance serait fonction de l'utilisation des fonds par les ménages bénéficiaires (Generoso, 2012, p. 16 ; Gupta et *al.*, 2007, p. 42).

Le constat est moins nuancé s'agissant du rôle que joueraient les transferts de fonds des migrants sur le maintien ou la hausse du revenu des ménages et donc dans la lutte contre la pauvreté et la réduction des inégalités (Lachaud, 2004 ; Banque mondiale, 2006 ; Gupta et *al.*, 2007 ; Lerch et Wanner, 2008 ; Gubert et *al.*, 2010 ; Generoso, 2012 ; Sambo, 2018). Pour Ebeke et Goff (2010), les transferts de fonds réduiraient les inégalités de revenus dans les pays à revenu par habitant sensiblement élevé, dans les pays d'émigration de main-d'œuvre peu qualifiée et dans les pays présentant des coûts de mobilité faibles. Mansuri (2008, p. 9) montre également que les transferts de fonds permettraient aux enfants des ménages du Pakistan, comptant en leur sein au moins un migrant, de rester plus longtemps dans le cursus scolaire. Néanmoins, Stark et *al.* (1988, p. 310-311) indiquent que l'impact des transferts sur la réduction de la pauvreté et des inégalités est forcément lié à la manière dont ceux-ci sont redistribués. Cela peut dépendre du type de migration (interne ou externe) et des périodes migratoires. Nonobstant ces effets positifs sur la pauvreté et les inégalités, les transferts de fonds pourraient intensifier la demande de produits importés aussi bien dans les zones rurales qu'urbaines, entraînant ainsi une élévation du coût de la vie et une baisse de la capacité à consommer des ménages (Generoso, 2012, p. 17 ; Ahouré, 2008, p. 5). Azam et Gubert (2005, p. 1335) présentent également le risque de consommation ostentatoire que pourraient avoir les ménages bénéficiaires des transferts de fonds et les tensions dues aux inégalités que cela pourrait susciter.

En somme, l'effet positif des transferts des migrants sur la croissance économique des pays d'émigration semble difficile à montrer et fait débat, mais leur impact positif sur la réduction de la pauvreté et des inégalités dans certaines conditions préalables ressort plus nettement dans la littérature.

2. DONNÉES ET MÉTHODOLOGIE

2.1. Les données

Notre but est d'analyser sur la période 1990-2010 l'impact des transferts de fonds des migrants sur la sécurité alimentaire face à un choc climatique dans 7 pays de l'UEMOA : Burkina-Faso, Bénin, Côte d'Ivoire, Mali, Niger, Sénégal et Togo, excepté la Guinée-Bissau par manque de données disponibles sur les transferts de fonds et les importations alimentaires. On mesure la sécurité alimentaire (variable expliquée) par le nombre de personnes sous-alimentées. Pour les variables explicatives, les transferts de fonds des migrants sont mesurés par les transferts personnels et la rémunération des employés saisonniers ; un choc climatique est capté par les quantités de précipitations annuelles. Sont prises comme variables de contrôle la valeur ajoutée agricole (en % de PIB) et les importations alimentaires (en % des importations de marchandises).

2.1.1. La mesure de la pauvreté par la sécurité alimentaire

D'après la loi d'Engel (1895), la part des dépenses alimentaires dans le budget des ménages diminue avec l'augmentation du revenu. De ce fait, les ménages les plus exposés aux risques de sous-alimentation sont ceux ayant les revenus les plus faibles (Yabilé, 2013, p. 211). L'indicateur de pauvreté le plus pertinent dans ce cas est la prévalence de la sous-alimentation[6], indicateur quantitatif de sécurité alimentaire proposé par l'Organisation des Nations Unies pour l'alimentation et l'agriculture (FAO). C'est un indicateur qui paraît robuste. Par exemple, Kaboré et Taondyande (2009) ont montré la convergence de cet indicateur avec une mesure qualitative de la sous-alimentation au Burkina-Faso.

Selon la FAO (1996), « La sécurité alimentaire existe lorsque tous les êtres humains ont, à tout moment, un accès physique et économique à une nourriture suffisante, saine et nutritive leur permettant de satisfaire leurs besoins énergétiques et leurs préférences alimentaires pour mener une vie saine et active ». La FAO définit la « sous-alimentation » comme la situation des individus incapables de maintenir une vie saine et active parce qu'ayant un apport énergétique alimentaire insuffisant. C'est un indicateur qui détermine la proportion (en pourcentage) de personnes sous-alimentées dans le monde. Il est obtenu en fonction du nombre de kilocalories (kcal) disponibles par hectare de culture et par an, de la prévalence de la pauvreté mesurée par rapport au PIB annuel et du prix des denrées alimentaires. Si cette proportion est inférieure à 5 %, on conclut qu'il y a une insécurité alimentaire faible (cas général des pays industrialisés), lorsqu'elle dépasse 35 %, on dit que l'insécurité alimentaire est forte. Cet indicateur fournit une représentation certes partielle (seulement l'accès économique et physique) mais qui paraît non négligeable de l'état de la sécurité alimentaire. La FAO propose comme pallia-

[6] FAO (2014).

tif un grand nombre d'indicateurs par famille de dimensions, permettant d'obtenir une évaluation un peu plus large de l'insécurité alimentaire, mais ne fournit aucun indicateur unique prenant en compte la sécurité alimentaire dans tous ses aspects. Il existe cependant un indicateur composite proposé par l'International Food Production Research Institute (IFPRI), mais il est très peu fourni.

2.1.2. Les transferts de fonds des migrants : les transferts personnels et la rémunération des employés

Les transferts personnels sont des transferts courants[7] (en espèces ou en nature) réalisés par des individus résidents dans un pays à destination d'autres individus non-résidents et inversement. Ces données sont obtenues grâce à un système international de communication des transactions financières mis en place auprès des banques (commerciales), des réseaux postaux et des sociétés de transferts d'argent (Western Union, Money Gram…). Ils ne prennent pas en compte les dépenses d'éducation (sommes perçues par un étudiant étranger par exemple).

La rémunération des employés représente l'ensemble des rémunérations obtenues par les travailleurs frontaliers et saisonniers et autres travailleurs de courte durée qui sont employés dans une économie autre que celle dont ils sont résidents, et des résidents employés par des entités non-résidentes. Ces rémunérations sont pondérées par un coefficient représentant le coût de la vie en pourcentage du salaire minimum dans chaque pays d'accueil des travailleurs.

La somme de ces deux composantes (transferts personnels + rémunération des employés) permet d'avoir une estimation assez précise des transferts de fonds des migrants. Cependant, les données obtenues ne prennent pas en compte les transactions financières utilisant les canaux informels dont l'apport, variable selon les pays, pourrait être important. Le Fonds Monétaire International (FMI, 2009, p. 5) et tacitement la Banque mondiale, selon un rapport conjoint, reconnaissent que les statistiques sur les envois de fonds ne sont pas d'excellente qualité. Les transferts, de par leur nature hétérogène, sont très difficiles à mesurer. Les enquêtes directes auprès des migrants et/ou des familles d'origine au niveau microéconomique et ensuite agrégées au niveau macroéconomique pourraient permettre d'avoir des estimations plus complètes sur les transferts et de mieux cerner les flux migratoires. Toutefois, elles sont très coûteuses et complexes dans leur mise en œuvre.

2.1.3. Les chocs climatiques : les précipitations annuelles

Les données sur les précipitations proviennent de la base de données du Climatic Research Unit (CRU)[8]. Cette base est composée de données brutes mensuelles allant de janvier 1901 à décembre 2012 et concernent la version 3.21. C'est une version offrant une haute résolution (0.5°) de données maillées présentant les variations mois par mois du climat (précipitations et évaporation potentielle) à l'échelle mondiale. Une version plus récente (CRU TS3.24) est également disponible (1901-2015). C'est la base de données la plus fournie et la plus complète existante sur les données climatiques. Elle est aussi régulièrement mise à jour.

Les données sont d'abord recueillies par quadrillage constitué de carreaux de 0,5° latitude/longitude. Un carreau délimite ainsi chaque terre émergée (excepté l'Antarctique). Ce qui fait un total de 67 420 grilles de données pour les précipitations. Ensuite, elles sont pondérées doublement afin de prendre en compte la variabilité du degré de latitude (valeur angulaire très instable) et les frontières des

[7] World Development Indicators (WDI, World Bank, 2014).
[8] University of East Anglia, Norwich.

différents pays. Cette pondération se fait à l'aide d'une programmation spécifique[9]. On obtient au final des précipitations mensuelles et annuelles pour chaque pays.

Selon la typologie de L'hôte et *al.* (1996) et en fonction des données de précipitations obtenues sur notre panel, nous avons classé les pays en 3 groupes climatiques distincts. Le groupe **A** comprenant le *Mali* et le *Niger*. C'est dans ce groupe qu'on enregistre les plus faibles précipitations annuelles. Le climat caractéristique est de type semi-aride ou subdésertique. Les hauteurs moyennes annuelles dans ce climat n'excèdent pas 400 mm de pluie mais sont généralement supérieures à 100 mm. Le *Burkina-Faso* et le *Sénégal* possèdent respectivement un climat tropical pur (hauteurs de pluies comprises entre 700 et 1000 mm) et un climat de type tropical semi-aride caractérisé par une pluviométrie annuelle inférieure à 700 mm. Ils constituent le groupe climatique intermédiaire **B**. Le dernier groupe **C** constitué du *Bénin*, de la *Côte d'Ivoire* et du *Togo*, regroupe les précipitations les plus importantes enregistrées (supérieures à 1000 mm de pluie par an en moyenne). Ces pays connaissent un climat favorable de type tropical de transition.

2.1.4. Les importations alimentaires (en % des importations de marchandises)

La base de données sur les importations alimentaires est extraite des statistiques mensuelles du commerce international (Comtrade) des Nations Unies. Elle est régulièrement renseignée par plus de 140 pays (y compris notre panel de pays) sur les données annuelles de produits (importées et exportées). Ces données (en millions de dollars $ US courants) sont classées par la Division des Statistiques de l'ONU par section de la classification type pour le commerce international version révisée n°3 (CTCI Rév. 3), chaque section comprenant à son tour un nombre déterminé de divisions.

Selon cette classification, nos données comprennent les produits des sections 0 (nourriture et animaux vivants), 1 (boissons et tabacs), 4 (huiles et graisses végétales et animales) et la division 22 (oléagineux, huile de noix et huile d'amande) de la section 2 (Matières brutes non comestibles à l'exception des carburants).

2.1.5. La valeur ajoutée agricole (% de PIB)

Les statistiques sur la valeur ajoutée agricole[10] concernent les données agrégées des divisions 1 à 5 de la CTCI et comprennent également les chiffres sur la foresterie, la chasse, la pêche ainsi que les cultures et la production animale. La valeur ajoutée agricole est calculée par addition de toutes les productions agricoles des secteurs constitutifs des divisions retenues auxquelles on retire les inputs (facteurs de production) intermédiaires. Le produit net (en pourcentage de PIB) est obtenu en retirant la dépréciation des biens fabriqués, la perte de valeur ou la dégradation des ressources naturelles. Cependant, pour les pays où les données sur la valeur ajoutée sont continuellement renseignées et actualisées, c'est le PIB calculé sans prise en compte des impôts indirects ou des subventions d'exploitation (divers aides aux agriculteurs) qui sert de dénominateur pour la pondération.

2.2. Spécification du modèle

Nous optons pour un modèle en panel VAR afin de mieux cerner l'effet des transferts de fonds des migrants sur la pauvreté et les implications économiques qui en découlent à la suite d'un choc exogène. La modélisation en panel VAR pos-

[9] Réalisée et disponible au CERDI, Université d'Auvergne.

[10] World Development Indicators (WDI, World Bank, 2014).

sède les avantages qui sont (i) de résoudre le problème d'endogénéité des variables du modèle (Love et Zicchino[11], 2006, p. 193), (ii) de contourner le souci de la faible taille des séries en combinant les dimensions spatiale (pays) et temporelle (année), ce qui permet d'obtenir des résultats d'estimation plus robustes et (iii) de prendre en compte l'hétérogénéité inobservée des individus (pays) captée par les effets spécifiques individuels. Le modèle en panel VAR découle de la jonction de la modélisation VAR traditionnelle (Sims, 1980) et de l'économétrie des données en panel. Les fonctions de réponses impulsionnelles ainsi que la décomposition de la variance obtenues par l'estimation du modèle permettent d'analyser les interactions entre les variables. On peut toutefois noter que cette méthode est moins utilisée que d'autres pour traiter ces questions car elle peut connaître quelques limites sur le plan économétrique (données non-cylindrées et transformées, endogénéité de certaines variables).

Notre modèle VAR prend en compte l'hétérogénéité difficilement observable entre les pays à travers l'introduction dans la forme fonctionnelle d'une constante individuelle captant les effets spécifiques (fixes) à chaque pays. La forme réduite de notre modèle s'écrit comme suit :

$$Y_{it} = \alpha_i + \Gamma(L)Y_{it} + \varepsilon_{it} \qquad (1)$$

avec Y_{it} un vecteur de variables stationnaires, $\Gamma(L)$ le polynôme matriciel défini sur un opérateur de retard L et ayant la forme fonctionnelle suivante :

$$\Gamma(\mathrm{L}) = \Gamma_1 L_1 + \Gamma_2 L_2 + \dots\dots\dots + \Gamma_p L_p \qquad (2)$$

où α_i est la constante individuelle, ε_{it} un vecteur d'erreurs idiosyncratiques de moyenne nulle, à variance constante et non autocorrélé. Les paramètres i (i = 1,...., N) et t (t = 1,...., T) représentent respectivement les pays et les pas de temps sur la période choisie (1990-2010). Le vecteur Y_{it} renferme nos 5 variables exprimées en logarithme (log) :

$$[\ Lprec, Lrem, Lund, Lagri, Lfim\ ] \qquad (3)$$

Lprec désigne le logarithme des précipitations annuelles en mm de pluie, *Lrem* les transferts des migrants exprimés en logarithme, *Lund* le log de la prévalence de la sous-alimentation, *Lagri* la valeur ajoutée agricole (en % du PIB) exprimée aussi en logarithme et *Lfim* le log des importations alimentaires (en % des importations de marchandises).

Opter pour un modèle en panel VAR suggère une structure commune pour chacun des individus du panel. Aussi, la prise en compte des effets fixes dans la spécification donne des estimateurs biaisés puisqu'il y a corrélation entre la constante individuelle (perturbation ou aléa inobservable) et au moins l'une des variables endogènes retardées selon que la forme fonctionnelle du modèle soit en niveau, en différence première ou en écart aux moyennes individuelles (Sevestre, 2002).

Pour contourner cette difficulté, Love et Zicchino (2006, p. 195) proposent l'utilisation d'une procédure de différenciation des variables du modèle en écart à la moyenne des observations futures (procédure de transformation de Helmert) afin de réduire les perturbations. La procédure se présente comme suit.

Soit $Y_{it} = (y_{it}^1, y_{it}^2, \dots, y_{it}^M)'$ le vecteur des variables stationnaires du modèle et $\varepsilon_{it} = (\varepsilon_{it}^1, \varepsilon_{it}^2, \dots, \varepsilon_{it}^M)'$ le vecteur des erreurs idiosyncratiques, y_{it}^m et ε_{it}^m les valeurs quelconques respectives des vecteurs Y_{it} et ε_{it}, T étant l'horizon temporel.

[11] En mars 2017, Love et Zicchino (2006) a été cité 774 fois. Nombreux sont les articles ayant utilisé la spécification en panel VAR redéveloppée par les auteurs.

Soit également $\bar{y}_{it}^{m} = \sum_{s=t+1}^{T} \frac{y_{is}^{m}}{T-t}$ et $\bar{\varepsilon}_{it}^{m} = \sum_{s=t+1}^{T} \frac{\varepsilon_{is}^{m}}{T-t}$ les moyennes des observations futures $\bar{y}_{it}^{m}$ et $\bar{\varepsilon}_{it}^{m}$.

Les variables sont transformées de la manière suivante :

$$\tilde{y}_{it}^{m} = \delta_{it} (y_{it}^{m} - \bar{y}_{it}^{m}) \quad (4)$$

$$\tilde{\varepsilon}_{it}^{m} = \delta_{it} (\varepsilon_{it}^{m} - \bar{\varepsilon}_{it}^{m}) \quad (5)$$

avec $\delta_{it} = \sqrt{\frac{T-t}{T-t+1}}$, ce qui donne le modèle transformé qui suit :

$$Y_{it} = \alpha_i + \Gamma(L)Y_{it} + \tilde{\varepsilon}_{it} \quad (6)$$

où $Y_{it} = (\tilde{y}_{it}^{1}, \tilde{y}_{it}^{2}, \ldots, \tilde{y}_{it}^{M})'$ et $\tilde{\varepsilon}_{it} = (\tilde{\varepsilon}_{it}^{1}, \tilde{\varepsilon}_{it}^{2}, \ldots, \tilde{\varepsilon}_{it}^{M})'$.

Selon Arellano et Bover (1995, p. 41-42), cette transformation préserve l'homoscédasticité et n'entraîne pas d'autocorrélation des erreurs. L'utilisation de ce type de spécification repose exclusivement sur l'analyse des fonctions de réponses impulsionnelles calculées à partir des coefficients estimés en VAR et de la décomposition de la variance.

Les fonctions de réponses impulsionnelles ou fonctions impulsion-réponse sont généralement utilisées pour appréhender les interactions pouvant exister entre les variables d'un modèle VAR. Elles retranscrivent la dynamique d'une variable y_t^{A} suite à un choc exogène (une impulsion) subi par une autre variable y_t^{B} à une date *T*. Les autres variables du modèle sont supposées constantes aux périodes antérieures ou égales à ($t \leq T$). Cela veut dire que si on donne une impulsion à la variable y_T^{B} ($\varepsilon_T^{B} = +1$), on s'attend à avoir la réponse de la variable y_{T+h}^{A}, (*h* étant l'horizon postérieur à *T*) ayant pour innovation ε_T^{A} stable à l'instant *T* du choc, de même que pour les autres variables du modèle. Mais vouloir obtenir un tel résultat suppose une corrélation entre les innovations[12] (ε_T^{B} , ε_T^{A}) des deux variables. Dans ce cas, un choc exogène sur y_t^{B} influençant y_t^{A}, subira à son retour la réponse de y_t^{A}. Ainsi, afin d'extraire l'information attendue et singulière à la variable y_t^{A} suite à l'impulsion sur y_t^{B} , il convient de décomposer les résidus de sorte à les rendre orthogonaux. C'est la décomposition de Cholesky (*cf.* les premiers travaux de Sims, 1980). Cette décomposition permet d'avoir une matrice triangulaire des innovations. Cependant, la disposition des variables dans le modèle conditionne la direction de propagation du choc sur les innovations rendues pures. L'hypothèse à la base de la décomposition de Cholesky stipule que les variables figurant en première position (plus exogènes) affecteront les variables suivantes instantanément et aussi de façon retardée alors que les variables disposées antérieurement (plus endogènes) affecteront les variables précédentes seulement avec un retard (Love et Zicchino, 2006, p. 194). Ainsi, la variable *Lprec*, la plus exogène au modèle, occupe le premier rang (Generoso, 2012, p. 23-24), suivront respectivement les variables *Ltranf* et *Lund* pour appréhender la réponse des transferts des migrants après un choc sur les précipitations et saisir l'effet de cette réponse sur la proportion des personnes sous-alimentées, et ensuite sur la valeur ajoutée agricole *Lagri* et les importations alimentaires *Lfim* plus endogènes au modèle (*cf.* équation (3))[13].

[12] Dans un modèle VAR ou en panel VAR, le processus vectoriel des innovations ε_{it} peut être non corrélé mais avoir des innovations corrélées entre elles.

[13] Cette disposition a été retenue après des permutations entre les variables du modèle et en fonction de la littérature existante.

L'analyse des fonctions de réponses passe ensuite par l'estimation d'intervalles de confiance encadrant les dynamiques des variables. Ceux-ci sont générés par simulation Monte Carlo. Cette simulation produit de nouvelles matrices de coefficients (Γ) et permet de calculer les fonctions de réponses à partir des matrices de variance-covariance des résidus des nouveaux coefficients estimés. Le processus renouvelé plusieurs fois permet d'avoir des intervalles de confiance. L'étape finale dans l'analyse des fonctions impulsion-réponse est la décomposition de la variance. Elle décèle la contribution en pourcentage de chaque innovation pure à la variance totale de l'erreur de prévision cumulée à un horizon de temps ($T + h$). Car, à la suite des réponses aux impulsions, on peut exprimer la matrice de variance-covariance triangulaire de l'erreur sous la forme d'une combinaison linéaire des variances de chaque innovation. La décomposition de la variance exprime le rapport en pourcentage de la variance de chacune de ces innovations sur la variance totale de l'erreur de prévision.

2.3. Tests de racines unitaires

Pour le descriptif des tests retenus, on peut consulter l'annexe 1. On peut conclure des tableaux 1, 2 et 3 que la série de données sur les précipitations (*Lprec*) est stationnaire sans transformation en différence première. Les transferts de fonds (*Lrem*), la valeur ajoutée (*Lagri*) et les importations des denrées alimentations (*Lfim*) sont intégrées d'ordre (1), c'est-à-dire stationnaire après transformation en différence première I (1). Par contre, les résultats des tests sur la prévalence de la sous-alimentation (*Lund*) sont mitigés. La série est partiellement stationnaire en I (1), option : sans tendance pour le test de Im, Pesaran et Shin (2003). Pour les tests de Maddala et Wu (1999) et de Pesaran (2003), elle est stationnaire sans transformation et avec un retard. Par contre, les tests MW (1999) et Pesaran (2003) sur sa différence première indiquent une présence de racine unitaire. Toutefois en suivant le tableau 4 nous pouvons remarquer que la série est parfaitement stationnaire en I (5) pour les tests IPS, MW et Pesaran (2003).

Au final, l'équation (3) se réécrit comme suit :

[*Lprec, DLrem,* D^5 *Lund, DLagri, DLfim*]

Tableau 1: Résultats du test de Im, Pesaran et Shin (2003), IPS

	Niveau (N=7 ; T=21)	Différence première (N=7 ; T=20)	
Lprec	P value	P value	Décision
Constante	0.0000	-	Stationnaire
Constante et tendance	0.0000	-	Stationnaire
Lrem			
Constante	0.7740	0.0000	Racine unitaire
Constante et tendance	0.0669	0.0000	Racine unitaire
Lund			
Constante	0.9999	0.0402	Racine unitaire
Constante et tendance	0.4658	0.1547	Racine unitaire
Lagri			
Constante	0.0022	0.0000	Stationnaire
Constante et tendance	0.0010	0.0000	Stationnaire
Lfim			
Constante	0.2478	0.0000	Racine unitaire
Constante et tendance	0.0053	0.0000	Stationnaire

H0 : Présence de racine unitaire après transformation en différence première.
Source : Extrait du logiciel Stata version 11.

Tableau 2 : Résultats du test de Maddala et Wu (1999), MW

	Niveau (N=7 ; T=21)		Différence première (N=7 ; T=20)		
Lprec	Chi_sq	P value	Chi_sq	P value	Décision
Constante (K=0)	113.5237	0.0000	-	-	Stationnaire
Constante (K=1)	67.2629	0.0000	-	-	Stationnaire
Constante et tendance (k=0)	105.3347	0.0000	-	-	Stationnaire
Constante et tendance (K=1)	51.6340	0.0000	-	-	Stationnaire
Lrem					
Constante (k=0)	6.5278	0.9514	83.2322	0.0000	Racine unitaire
Constante (k=1)	11.5344	0.6436	58.0523	0.0000	Racine unitaire
Constante et tendance (k=0)	8.2670	0.8750	56.0321	0.0000	Racine unitaire
Constante et tendance (k=1)	24.6599	0.0381	36.1613	0.0010	Stationnaire
Lund					
Constante (k=0)	3.7424	0.9968	20.4392	0.1169	Racine unitaire
Constante (k=1)	43.3101	0.0001	24.2257	0.0430	Stationnaire
Constante et tendance (k=0)	14.1359	0.4396	7.8417	0.8974	Racine unitaire
Constante et tendance (k=1)	50.0916	0.0000	12.4699	0.5686	Stationnaire
Lagri					
Constante (k=0)	32.9293	0.0029	144.6160	0.0000	Stationnaire
Constante (k=1)	35.6196	0.0012	98.0228	0.0000	Stationnaire
Constante et tendance (k=0)	19.7030	0.1398	118.4798	0.0000	Racine unitaire
Constante et tendance (k=1)	27.7795	0.0152	79.7177	0.0000	Stationnaire
Lfim					
Constante (k=0)	26.4105	0.0229	99.3108	0.0000	Stationnaire
Constante (k=1)	23.1390	0.0580	62.5193	0.0000	Racine unitaire
Constante et tendance (k=0)	21.3210	0.0937	71.9503	0.0000	Racine unitaire
Constante et tendance (k=1)	16.0342	0.3113	44.8657	0.0000	Racine unitaire

H0 : Présence de racine unitaire après transformation en différence première.
Source : Extrait du logiciel Stata version 11.

Tableau 3: Résultats du test de Pesaran (2007)

Ce test nécessite des données en panel très cylindrées ce qui n'est pas le cas des données sur les importations alimentaires (*Lfim*).

	Niveau (N=7 ; T=21)		Différence première (N=7 ; T=20)		
Lprec	Z[t-bar]	P value	Z[t-bar]	P value	Décision
Constante (K=0)	-6.079	0.000	-	-	Stationnaire
Constante (K=1)	-4.548	0.000	-	-	Stationnaire
Constante et tendance (k=0)	-5.196	0.000	-	-	Stationnaire
Constante et tendance (K=1)	-3.126	0.001	-	-	Stationnaire
Lrem					
Constante (k=0)	1.364	0.914	-4.771	0.000	Racine unitaire
Constante (k=1)	-0.141	0.444	-2.532	0.006	Racine unitaire
Constante et tendance (k=0)	1.541	0.938	-3.042	0.001	Racine unitaire
Constante et tendance (k=1)	-0.259	0.398	-1.339	0.090	Racine unitaire
Lund					
Constante (k=0)	3.102	0.999	-1.236	0.108	Racine unitaire
Constante (k=1)	-3.293	0.000	-0.749	0.227	Stationnaire
Constante et tendance (k=0)	0.390	0.652	0.813	0.792	Racine unitaire
Constante et tendance (k=1)	-2.879	0.002	2.300	0.989	Stationnaire
Lagri					
Constante (k=0)	-2.137	0.016	-6.639	0.000	Stationnaire
Constante (k=1)	-3.897	0.000	-4.960	0.000	Stationnaire
Constante et tendance (k=0)	-0.460	0.323	-5.500	0.000	Racine unitaire
Constante et tendance (k=1)	-2.336	0.010	-4.026	0.000	Stationnaire

H0 : Présence de racine unitaire après transformation en différence première.
Source : Extrait du logiciel Stata version 11.

Tableau 4: Résultats des tests sur la variable Lund

		Test de IPS			
Lund	P value		P value		
Constante	0.9999		0.0000	Racine unitaire	
Constante et tendance	0.4658		0.0000	Racine unitaire	
		Test de MW			
Lund	Chi_sq	P value	Chi_sq	P value	
Constante (k=0)	3.7424	0.9968	504.6111	0.0000	Racine unitaire
Constante (k=1)	43.3101	0.0001	134.6444	0.0000	Stationnaire
Constante et tendance (k=0)	14.1359	0.4396	490.5102	0.0000	Racine unitaire
Constante et tendance (k=1)	50.0916	0.0000	98.2323	0.0000	Stationnaire
		Test de deuxième génération Pesaran (2003)			
Lund	Z[t-bar]	P value	Z[t-bar]	P value	
Constante (k=0)	3.102	0.999	-11.456	0.000	Racine unitaire
Constante (k=1)	-3.293	0.000	-5.390	0.000	Stationnaire
Constante et tendance (k=0)	0.390	0.652	-10.845	0.000	Racine unitaire
Constante et tendance (k=1)	-2.879	0.002	-3.298	0.000	Stationnaire

H0 : Présence de racine unitaire après transformation en différence première.
Source : Extrait du logiciel Stata version 11.

3. RÉSULTATS DU MODÈLE ET DISCUSSIONS

L'impact des transferts de fonds des migrants sur la sécurité alimentaire après un choc climatique a été observé grâce aux fonctions de réponses obtenues sur des intervalles de confiance générés par simulation Monte Carlo (200 répétitions) suite à l'estimation du vecteur autorégressif (avec prise en compte de l'hétérogénéité inobservée) sur un horizon de temps (10 années). Les informations pures (signe, ampleur et persistance) décrivant les réponses des variables après impulsion ont été extraites par la décomposition de la variance de l'erreur de prévision. Elle a permis d'avoir (en pourcentage) le pouvoir explicatif du choc (instantané ou retardé) subi par une variable sur le comportement d'une autre.

Rappelons que nous avons regroupé notre panel de pays en trois groupes distincts selon leurs quantités de précipitations annuelles. Des plus faiblement pourvus que sont le Mali et le Niger (groupe A) aux pays mieux dotés en précipitations, le Bénin, la Côte d'Ivoire et le Togo (groupe C). Le Burkina-Faso et le Sénégal constituant le groupe intermédiaire B. On peut constater que des pays frontaliers peuvent ne pas être pareillement dotés en précipitations et de ce fait, ne pas appartenir au même groupe climatique. Toutefois, ils pourraient partager des zones enregistrant de faibles ou de fortes précipitations annuelles puisque les données pluviométriques disponibles sont des moyennes agrégées annuellement par pays sans prise en compte des spécificités intra et/ou inter-régionales. On ne pourrait donc pas rejeter l'hypothèse d'une corrélation des innovations des précipitations entre pays et entre groupes de pays dans notre estimation étant donné qu'une perturbation sur ceux-ci se mesure sur une année. Ce qui a conduit à considérer pour ces pays un choc négatif de façon simultanée. Cette simultanéité prenant en compte l'étendu du choc et ses répercussions dans le temps considéré. On s'attend globalement à une incidence plus importante à la suite d'une répartition annuelle inhabituelle des chutes de pluies dans les zones et pays faiblement pourvus en volume. De ce fait, les réponses sur la sécurité alimentaire obtenues devraient théoriquement être différentes d'un groupe de pays à l'autre. Car les dynamiques migratoires intra et/ou internationales qui en découleraient feraient probablement varier différemment les transferts de fonds en aval. La valeur ajoutée agricole (par l'afflux ou la baisse de main-d'œuvre) et les importations ne pourraient que suivre des trajectoires tout aussi différentes.

Ainsi, on a essayé de prévoir à l'aune de ces flux migratoires, pour ces trois groupes de pays, les effets d'un choc négatif (+1 écart-type[14] sur les innovations des précipitations) sur la quantité des transferts de fonds des migrants et leur résonnance sur la proportion de personnes sous-alimentées, la valeur ajoutée agricole et le niveau des importations de marchandises.

3.1. L'impact des transferts de fonds des migrants sur la sécurité alimentaire après un choc climatique

Dans le groupe A (Mali et Niger) caractérisé par une faible pluviométrie, un choc négatif sur les précipitations stimule les transferts de fonds des migrants à hauteur de 16,1 %[15]) la première année de l'occurrence du choc (figure 1) et explique 22,1 % de ce comportement. Les montants perçus diminuent progressivement au fur et à mesure que le choc se dilue jusqu'à atteindre des valeurs négatives (- 4,3 % et -3,4 % respectivement pour h=2 et h=3).

L'irrégularité des précipitations, les sécheresses, la dégradation des terres cultivables, les déficits hydriques et l'avancée du désert perturbent lourdement les activités agricoles dominées par les cultures vivrières (mil, sorgho et maïs) et l'élevage domestique (OIM, 2009a, p. 60 ; OIM, 2009b, p. 47). De ce fait, les changements climatiques extrêmes accentueront la migration (interne et externe) des populations les plus touchées qui seront à la recherche de nouvelles terres cultivables, de nouveaux pâturages ou d'emplois saisonniers. Les nouveaux migrants solliciteront logiquement les réseaux existants afin de réduire les coûts et aléas migratoires, mais surtout pour trouver plus rapidement un emploi (agricole saisonnier ou informel) et un logement (OCDE/CIRES, 2017, p. 53). Les Nigériens iront probablement au Burkina Faso, en Côte d'Ivoire ou au Nigéria (OIM, 2009b, p. 47) et les Maliens partiront pour la Côte d'Ivoire, le Burkina Faso ou la Guinée (OIM, 2009a, p. 52). Ces corridors sont historiquement empruntés par des ruraux pauvres. On suppose dans un premier temps qu'ils mobiliseront des fonds plus importants qu'auparavant à destination de leurs familles d'origine plus vulnérables afin de compenser la faiblesse accrue des récoltes mais aussi pour financer d'éventuels nouveaux départs. La baisse des montants transférés à la deuxième année pourrait s'expliquer par la réduction du nombre d'individus bénéficiaires[16] due au nombre croissant des migrants, au soutien financier des nouveaux arrivants et peut-être aussi à une tendance à la hausse du coût de la vie dans les pays d'accueil (la Côte d'Ivoire en l'occurrence). Les montants redeviendront plus importants au fur et à mesure de la dilution du choc et des vagues partielles de retour des migrants dans l'optique de revaloriser les terres cultivables abandonnées.

Le groupe B avec des précipitations moyennes (Burkina Faso et Sénégal) enregistre une baisse des transferts de -1,2 % la première année du choc et une accentuation de -6,4 % la deuxième année avant de se stabiliser à partir de la quatrième année. Les précipitations contribuant à hauteur de 15,65 % dans l'évolution des montants.

---

[14] Toute chose étant égale par ailleurs, nous retenons que les pratiques agricoles (traditionnelles) des pays considérés sont fonction de leur environnement et surtout des précipitations moyennes enregistrées. De ce fait, un choc négatif, c'est-à-dire une perturbation pluviométrique, peut représenter une abondance anormale ou une faiblesse globale des précipitations sur une année donnée.

[15] Cette augmentation pourrait-être encore plus importante dans la mesure où une grande partie (entre 25 et 80%) des envois de fonds des migrants passe par le secteur informel (BAD, 2007, p. 6).

[16] On formule l'hypothèse qu'il n'y a pas d'asymétrie d'information. Le migrant reste régulièrement au courant de la situation économique et des mouvements d'individus au sein de sa famille d'origine.

Figure 1: Réponses des transferts de fonds des migrants suite à un choc sur les précipitations

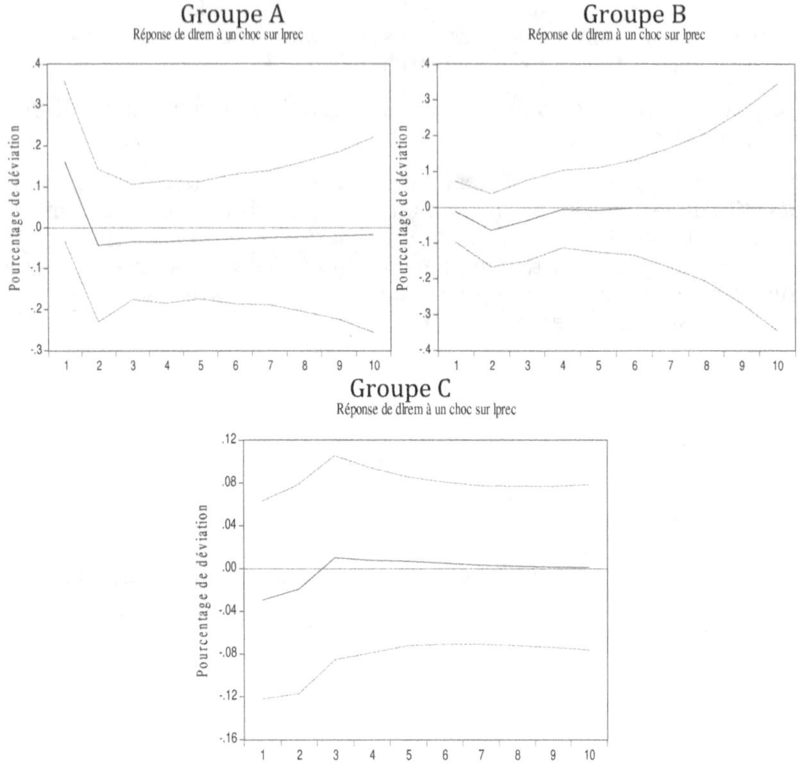

Source : Extrait du logiciel Eviews version 7.

La Côte d'Ivoire reste la destination privilégiée loin devant le Ghana et le Gabon des Burkinabè quand ils peuvent émigrer (OIM, 2016, p. 3). Les migrants burkinabè comme ceux d'origine sénégalaise sont principalement d'origine rurale et aussi dépendants des cultures vivrières et de l'élevage domestique (OIM, 2016, p. 21 ; OIM, 2009c, p. 65). Cependant, une perturbation pluviométrique avec son corollaire d'érosion, d'appauvrissement des sols additionnés au manque d'infrastructures de développement et d'emploi pousse les Sénégalais vers les grandes villes (OIM, 2009c, p. 35-36). Les éventuelles migrations internationales concerneront davantage l'Europe que les pays frontaliers (la Guinée-Bissau et le Mali, pays aussi vulnérables). Le financement des départs sera plus élevé et les transferts espérés mettront plus de temps à être perçus. La nécessité de subvenir aux besoins urgents des populations pourrait prendre le dessus sur tout nouveau projet de migration internationale. Au Burkina Faso également quand habituellement la pluviométrie baisse, on constate dans un premier temps un déplacement des populations du plateau-central surpeuplé et aride vers le sud et le sud-ouest moins peuplé et ayant un climat plus favorable aux activités agricoles (OIM, 2016). Les transferts internationaux déclineraient en fonction des individus bénéficiaires dont le nombre se réduit au fur et à mesure de nouvelles migrations interrégionales au sein du pays. La quatrième année de l'occurrence du choc peut être marquée par des migrations internes de retour et la recomposition partielle de la famille d'origine.

On constate également une réduction globale des transferts pour le groupe C (Côte d'Ivoire, Bénin et Togo) pourvu d'une pluviométrie plus favorable. Elle est de -2,9 % et de -1,9 % les deux premières années, suivie d'une hausse de 1 % la troisième année et d'une stabilisation des montants à partir de la neuvième année après le choc. Cependant les précipitations n'expliquent que 1,76 % de la variation des envois de fonds.

L'émigration en Côte d'Ivoire s'est accentuée avec la longue crise sociopolitique que le pays a traversée (OCDE/CIRES, 2017, p. 49). Globalement, les émigrés ivoiriens (autour de 5% de la population totale) s'établissent en France et au Burkina Faso et de façon plus permanente (OIM, 2009d, p. 52-54 ; OCDE/CIRES, 2017, p. 51). La France, comme premier pays de destination, reçoit une migration plutôt urbaine et relativement aisée au regard des contraintes et dépenses importantes qu'elle suppose. Par contre, les Ivoiriens au Burkina Faso seraient pour la grande majorité des descendants de migrants ruraux burkinabè (OCDE/CIRES, 2017, p. 50). Les Togolais et les Béninois quant à eux, se déplacent principalement et plus ou moins temporairement vers le Nigéria pour la recherche d'emploi, la poursuite des études ou l'apprentissage (OIM, 2015, p. 35 ; OIM, 2011, p. 48). Il s'agit aussi de migrants qualifiés et d'origine urbaine pour la plupart. Un choc climatique dans ces pays dont la pluviométrie est plus abondante n'aura peut-être pas d'influence majeure sur les comportements migratoires internationaux. Cependant, le Burkina Faso subissant lui aussi et plus intensément les effets de la même dérive climatique, on peut s'attendre à un retour systématique des émigrés du Burkina Faso vers la Côte d'Ivoire plus développée économiquement (OIM, 2016). Cela conduirait automatiquement à une baisse des transferts de fonds. La hausse progressive des montants traduirait dans ce cas l'amorce d'une reprise de l'émigration jusqu'à la troisième année. Par ailleurs, on peut également envisager des déplacements internes de jeunes ruraux vers les zones urbaines. L'exode rural et le délaissement à moyen-long terme des terres cultivables des ruraux âgés pourraient pousser les émigrés à des tentatives d'appropriation ou d'extension de leurs surfaces d'exploitation des cultures pérennes (cacao, café, coton) au détriment de certaines cultures vivrières (légumes, tubercules). Ce qui ne pourrait se faire sans dépenses conséquentes d'où la légère hausse des transferts de la troisième jusqu'à la neuvième année de l'occurrence du choc.

3.2. Les effets des transferts des migrants sur la proportion des personnes touchées par la sous-alimentation

La stimulation des envois de fonds des migrants après des niveaux de précipitation très instables présente un effet notable sur le nombre de personnes sous-alimentées dans les différents groupes de pays.

L'augmentation constatée des transferts de fonds suite à un choc négatif sur les précipitations permet de réduire la proportion des personnes sous-alimentées de -0,2 % dans le groupe A et d'environ 1% dans le groupe B malgré la diminution des montants transférés la première année du choc (tableau 5). Cependant, la persistance dans la réduction des envois de fonds au cours de la deuxième année entraine alors une augmentation de 1,4% des personnes sous-alimentées avant une relative stabilité à partir de la troisième année ; tandis qu'on observe une augmentation du nombre de sous-alimentés (+0,42%) dans le groupe C.

Les transferts des fonds contribuent faiblement (0,29%) à la réduction de la sous-alimentation dans le groupe A. Cette contribution pourrait être plus importante si les transferts informels étaient aussi pris en compte. Néanmoins, cet apport même modeste améliorerait vraisemblablement le pouvoir d'achat des ménages bénéficiaires en leur permettant l'accès aux aliments importés quand les rendements de production locale sont en baisse. Dans le groupe B cependant, malgré la réduction des transferts de fonds, la proportion des personnes sous-alimentées diminue la première année du choc. Les décisions d'émigration vers d'autres espaces agricoles moins touchés, le changement des habitudes de consommation (accès en plus grande quantité aux aliments locaux disponibles) dû à ces déplacements ainsi que la réduction du nombre de bénéficiaires des transferts pourraient expliquer cette réduction. Toutefois, l'augmentation de la population sous-alimentée la deuxième année laisserait entrevoir à la fois une pression graduelle sur les ressources naturelles disponibles dans les régions d'accueil et une précarité accentuée dans les zones urbaines. Cette précarité pourrait expliquer aussi l'augmentation du nombre de personnes souffrant de sous-alimentation (+0,42%) dans les pays du groupe C. Ces personnes pauvres et dépendantes des cultures vivrières plus vulnérables aux changements climatiques et se déplaçant globalement vers les villes subiront la hausse des prix des produits importés liée à leur forte demande.

Tableau 5: Contribution des envois de fonds dans l'évolution de la prévalence de la sous-alimentation

Groupes	Réponses	Contribution
Groupe A	-0.21%	0.29%
Groupe B	-0.97%	12.66%
Groupe C	+0.42%	0.77%

Source : Extrait du logiciel Eviews version 7.

3.3. Les implications économiques de l'évolution des transferts des migrants

Nous analysons ici les implications sur la valeur ajoutée agricole et le niveau des importations suite aux envois de fonds en cas de perturbation de la pluviométrie.

L'augmentation du montant des envois de fonds entraine une diminution de la valeur ajoutée agricole de -4,35 % et occasionne une hausse des importations des denrées alimentaires de +1,36 % la première année de l'apparition du choc sur les précipitations dans le groupe A (tableau 6). Cependant dans le groupe B, la diminution des transferts provoque une augmentation de 0,38 % de la valeur ajoutée agricole et une réduction du niveau des importations de -2,98 %. On note par contre une augmentation du niveau des importations des denrées alimentaires de 6,09 % malgré une hausse du niveau de production agricole de 1,66 % dans le groupe C.

Tableau 6: Contribution des envois de fonds dans l'évolution de la valeur ajoutée agricole et des importations

	Valeur ajoutée agricole		Importations des marchandises	
Groupes	Réponses	Contribution	Réponses	Contribution
A	-4.35%	4.28%	+1.36	0.74%
B	+0.38%	3.62%	-2.98%	5.77%
C	+1.66%	2.83%	+6.09%	18.00%

Source : Extrait du logiciel Eviews version 7.

Selon Generoso (2012), la hausse du niveau des importations de denrées alimentaires serait la résultante de la faible production agricole causée par le choc négatif sur les précipitations dans le groupe A plus vulnérable. Cependant pour Gubert (2008), l'accroissement du montant des transferts de fonds aurait un impact négatif sur la production agricole et entrainerait une relation de dépendance des ménages bénéficiaires vis-à-vis de ceux-ci. Ces derniers s'en remettraient directement aux envois de fonds et réduiraient les efforts de production, d'autant qu'ils sont plus importants en période de dérèglement climatique. Dans le groupe B moins vulnérable aux changements climatiques, la légère hausse de la production agricole s'expliquerait par l'augmentation de la main-d'œuvre agricole dans les zones moins impactées par un choc sur les précipitations. L'augmentation des rendements agricoles provenant plus des cultures vivrières (et directement consommées) que pérennes, réduirait le niveau des importations en denrées alimentaires. Par ailleurs, l'afflux de migrants ruraux maliens, nigériens et burkinabè aurait un fort impact sur la valeur ajoutée agricole en Côte d'Ivoire, dans le groupe C. L'apport de main-d'œuvre induit pourrait avoir un impact sensible sur les rendements de production de ces pays plus orientés vers des cultures agricoles d'exportation (café, cacao, hévéa, coton, anacarde...). A cela s'ajoute la baisse des rendements de production des cultures vivrières due aussi au détournement de certaines terres cultivables pour des plantations pérennes et à l'exode massif des jeunes vers les villes, expliquant ainsi l'élévation du niveau des importations de denrées en forte demande surtout en milieu urbain.

CONCLUSION

En utilisant la méthodologie d'estimation en panel VAR, nous avons pu analyser, en considérant la période 1990-2010, la prévalence de la sous-alimentation suite à l'envoi de fonds des migrants après un choc sur le niveau des précipitations dans 7 pays de l'Afrique de l'Ouest (UEMOA) regroupés en trois catégories (A, B et C) en fonction de leurs caractéristiques pluviométriques.

Ainsi, l'occurrence d'un choc climatique entraîne une élévation des montants transférés par les migrants originaires des pays de l'UEMOA les moins pourvus en quantités de pluie (groupe A). Ces transferts proviennent généralement des agriculteurs ou éleveurs ayant choisi d'émigrer précédemment vers des pays frontaliers moins vulnérables climatiquement. L'augmentation des transferts de fonds de ces migrants permet de réduire la proportion des personnes sous-alimentées en leur permettant l'accès en quantité suffisante aux aliments importés à cause de la faiblesse des récoltes. Dans ces conditions, la migration internationale reste la principale alternative pour cette population rurale fortement dépendante des cultures vivrières.

Dans les pays moyennement dotés en précipitations (groupe B), les envois de fonds des migrants n'augmentent pas forcément après un choc climatique. Mais, la prévalence de la sous-alimentation diminue quand même lorsque les cultures vivrières dominent l'essentiel du secteur agricole. On peut même enregistrer une hausse des rendements agricoles due à l'augmentation de la main-d'œuvre. L'émigration est ici plus inter-régionale qu'internationale et s'effectue vers des zones plus favorables aux cultures. La hausse de la valeur ajoutée agricole conduit alors à réduire la consommation de denrées importées.

Dans les pays plus favorisés en précipitations (groupe C), les transferts n'augmentent pas non plus après un choc. On y dénombre plus de personnes sous-alimentées qu'à l'ordinaire à cause de la hausse des prix des aliments importés. L'espace agricole dans ces pays est plus consacré à des cultures pérennes. L'émigration également interne se fait des zones dominées par les cultures vivrières (en faible production) vers les villes les plus proches. Par contre, l'accueil éventuel de migrants frontaliers augmente la main-d'œuvre agricole et a un impact positif sur la valeur ajoutée agricole.

Au final, on pourrait dire dans le contexte de l'Afrique de l'Ouest que l'occurrence d'un choc climatique à un moment précis subi par un ensemble de pays dans une région donnée n'entraîne pas systématiquement une augmentation des transferts de fonds. Ceux-ci augmentent et deviennent un véritable moyen de lutte contre la pauvreté et les inégalités dans les pays les plus fortement touchés par ce choc et où la vulnérabilité aux aléas climatiques reste le principal motif de migration en amont des transferts reçus. Toutefois, cette réaction des migrants en termes de transfert pourrait représenter une source complémentaire de financement menant à une résilience durable dans ces pays.

REFERENCES

Ahoure, A. E., 2008, Migrations, transferts, gouvernance et croissance dans les pays d'Afrique Sub-saharienne : une analyse à partir de données de panel, IMI workshop, Rabat.

Amuedo-Dorantes, C., Pozo S., 2004, Workers'remittances and the real exchange rate: a paradox of gifts, *World Development*, Vol. 32(8), pp. 1407-1417.

Arellano, J., O. Bover, 1995, Another Look at the Instrumental Variable Estimation of Error-Components Model, *Journal of Econometrics*, Vol. 68(1), pp. 29-51.

Azam, J.-P., Gubert, F., 2005, Those in Kayes. The impact of remittances on their recipients in Africa, *Revue économique*, Vol. 56(6), pp. 1331-1358.

BAD, 2007, *Les transferts des fonds des migrants, un enjeu de développement*, Tunis.

Bai, J., Ng, S., 2004, A PANIC Attack on Unit Roots and Cointegration, *Econometrica*, Vol. 72(4), pp. 1127-1178.

Baldwin, G. B., 1970, Brain Drain or Overflow, *Foreign Affairs*, n°48, pp. 358-372.

Banerjee, A., Marcellino M., Osbat C., 2004, Some Cautions on the Use of Panel Methods for Integrated Series of Macro-economic Data, *Econometrics Journal*, Vol. 7, pp. 322-340.

Banque mondiale, 2006, *Global Economic Prospects 2006: Economic Implications of Remittances and Migrations*, n°34320, The World Bank.

Banque mondiale, 2008, *Rapport sur le développement dans le monde : l'Agriculture au service du développement*, Washington DC.

Banque mondiale, 2011, *Recueil de statistiques sur les migrations et les envois de fonds, 2ème ed.*, Unité Migration et envois de fonds, Washington DC.

Barrett C. B., 2010, Measuring food insecurity, *Science*, 327(5967), pp. 825-828.

Barrios, S., Ouattara, B., Strobl, E. A., 2008, The impact of climatic change on agricultural production: Is it different for Africa ?, *Food Policy*, Vol. 33(4), pp. 287-298.

Bourdet, Y., Falck, H., 2006, Emigrants Remittances and Dutch Disease in Cape Verde, *International Economic Journal*, Vol. 20 (3), pp. 267-284.

Breitung, J., 2000, The local power of some unit root tests for panel data, in: B. Baltagi (ed.), *Nonstationary Panels, Panel Cointegration, and Dynamic Panels, Advances in Econometrics*, Vol. 15, Amsterdam, pp. 161-178.

Buch, C. M., Kuckulenz, A., 2004, Worker Remittances and Capital Flows to Developing Countries, *Discussion Paper* n° 04-031, Centre for European Economic Research (ZEW), Mannheim.

Burnside, C., D. Dollar, 1997, Aid, Policies and Growth, *Policy Research Working Paper* 1777, World Bank Development Research Group, Washington DC.

Burnside, C., Dollar, D., 2000, Aid, Policies and Growth, *American Economic Review paper 90*, n°4, pp. 847-868.

Chami, R., Barajas, A., Cosimano, T., Fullenkamp, C., Gapen, M., Montiel, P., 2008, Macroeconomic consequences of remittances, *Occasional Paper*, n° 259, IMF, Washington DC.

Chami, R., Fullenkamp, C., Jahjah, S., 2005, Are immigrant remittance flows a source of capital for development ?, *IMF Staff Papers*, Vol. 52(1), pp. 55–81.

Charnoz, O., Severino, J-M., 2007, *L'aide publique au développemen*t, Ed. La Découverte, coll. Repères, Paris.

Choi, I., 1999, Testing the Random Walk Hypothesis for Real Exchanges Rates, *Journal of Applied Econometrics*, Vol. 14(3), pp. 293-308.

Choi, I., 2002, *Combination Unit Root Tests for Cross-Sectionally Correlated Panels*, Mimeo, Hong Kong University of Science and Technology.

Clarke, G., Wallsten, S., 2003, *Do Remittances Act Like Insurance? Evidence from a Natural Disaster in Jamaica*, Development Research Group, World Bank, Washington, DC.

De La Briere, B., De Janvry, A., Lambert, S., E. Sadoulet, 1997, Why do migrants' remit ? An analysis for Dominican Sierra, *FCND Discussion Paper*, n°37, IFPRI.

Dickey, D. A., Fuller, W. A., 1979, Distribution of the Estimators for Autoregressive Time Series with a Unit Root, *Journal of the American Statistical Association*, n°74, pp. 417-431.

Dollar, D., Kraay, A., 2001, Growth Is Good for the Poor, *Policy research working paper 2587*, Vol. 1, Development Research Group, World Bank,Washington D.C.

Ebeke, C., Golf, M., 2010, Impact des envois de fonds des migrants sur les inégalités de revenu dans les pays en développement, *Revue économique*, Vol. 61(6), Paris, pp. 1051-1074.

Ebeke, C., 2010, Transferts des migrants, ouverture sur l'extérieur et dépenses publiques dans les pays en développement, Working Paper 201011, CERDI.

Edwards, A. C., Ureta, M., 2003, International migration, remittances, and schooling: evidence from el Salvador, *Journal of Development Economics*, Vol. 72(2), pp. 429-461.

Elliott, G., Rothenberg T., Stock J., 1996, Efficient Tests for an AutoRegressive Unit Root, *Econometrica*, Vol. 64(4), pp. 813-836.

Engel, E., 1895, Die Lebenskosten belgischer Arbeiterfamilien frueher und jetzt: Ermittelt aus Familienhaushaltsrechnungen und vergleichend zusammengestellt, *Bulletin of the International Institute of Statistics*, Vol. 9.

Faini, R., 2007, Migrations et transferts de fonds : Impact sur les pays d'origine, *Revue d'économie du développement*, Vol. 21, pp. 153-182.

FAO, 1996, *Sommet mondial de l'alimentation*, Rome.

FAO, 2012, *L'Etat de l'insécurité alimentaire dans le monde La croissance économique est nécessaire mais elle n'est pas suffisante pour accélérer la réduction de la faim et de la malnutrition*, Rome.

FAO, 2014, *L'état de l'insécurité alimentaire dans le monde : Créer un environnement plus propice à la sécurité alimentaire et à la nutrition*, Rome.

Findley, S. E., 1994, Does drought increase migration? A study of migration from rural Mali during the 1983-1985, *International Migration Review*, 25 (3), pp. 539-553.

FMI, 2009, *Transactions internationales liées aux envois de fonds : guide pour les statisticiens et les utilisateurs*, Guide.

Generoso, R., 2012, *Transferts de fonds et résilience des pays d'Afrique de l'Ouest face à la variabilité des précipitations : une perspective macroéconomique*, Cahier du CEMOTEV n°2012-03.

Gubert, F., 2002, Le comportement de transfert des migrants est-il guidé par un motif d'assurance ? L'exemple des Maliens de Kayes, *Cahier du GEMDEV*, n° 28, Paris, pp. 197-220.

Gubert, F., 2008, (In)cohérence des politiques migratoires et de codéveloppement françaises - Illustrations maliennes, *Politique africaine*, Vol. 1, n° 109, pp. 42-55.

Gubert, F., Lassourd, T., Mesple-Somps, S., 2010, Transferts de fonds des migrants, pauvreté et inégalités au Mali : Analyse à partir de trois scénarios contrefactuels, *Revue économique*, Vol. 61(6), Paris, pp. 1023-1050.

Gupta, S., Patillo, C., Wagh, S., 2007, L'impact bénéfique des envois de fonds sur l'Afrique, *Finances & Développement*, pp. 40-43.

Gupta, S., Pattillo, C. A., Wagh, S., 2009, Effect of remittances on poverty and financial development in sub-saharan Africa, *World Development*, Vol. 37(1), pp. 104-115.

Henry, S., Schoumaker, B., Beauchemin, C., 2004, The impact of rainfall on the first out-migration, a multi-level event-history analysis in Burkina Faso, *Population and Environment 25*, pp. 423-460.

Hurlin, C., Mignon, V., 2005, Une synthèse des tests de racine unitaire sur données de panel, *Economie et prévision*, n°169-170, pp. 253-294.

Im, K. S., Pesaran, M. H., Shin, Y., 2003, Testing for Unit Roots in Heterogeneous Panels, *Journal of Econometrics*, Vol. 115(1), pp. 53-74.

Jovičić, M., Mitrović, R.D., 2006, *Macroeconomic Analysis of Causes and Effects of Remittances: A Panel Model of the SEE Countries and a Case Study of Serbia, The wiiw Balkan Observatory Working Papers 063*, The Vienna Institute for International Economic Studies (WIIW).

Kabore, M., Taondyande, M., 2009, *Mesure de la sous-alimentation : une comparaison de l'approche paramétrique et non-paramétrique à partir des données de l'enquête permanente* *agricole 2006 au Burkina Faso*, Version provisoire, Wye City Group, Second Meeting, FAO, Rome.

Kapur, D., Singer, D., 2006, *Remittances and Government Spending, and the Global Economy*, In Annual Meeting, Draft, San Diego, CA.

Kniveton, D., K. Schmid-Verkerk, C. Smith, R. Black, 2008, *Climate Change and Migration: Improving methodologies to estimate flows*, Migration Research Series 33, International Organization for Migration (IOM), Geneva.

L'hote, Y., Dubreuil, P., Lerique, J., 1996, Carte des types de climats en Afrique noire à l'ouest du Congo : rappels et extension aux régimes hydrologiques, *In* Chevallier P., Pouyaud B. (éds.), *L'hydrologie tropicale : géosciences et outil pour le développement : mélanges à la mémoire de Jean Rodier.* Wallingford : AISH, pp. 55-65.

Lachaud, J-P., 2004, *Transferts privés de Côte d'Ivoire et pauvreté durable et transitoire au Burkina-Faso : Une analyse spatio-temporelle*, Document de travail n°93, Centre d'économie du développement, Université Montesquieu-Bordeaux IV.

Lerch, M., Wanner, P., 2008, *La mesure des transferts de fonds Nord – Sud : Nouvelles approches dans les pays d'immigration*, Communication écrite, Chaire Quetelet, Louvain-la-Neuve.

Levin, A., Lin, C. F., 1992, Unit Root Test in Panel Data: Asymptotic and Finite Sample Properties, Discussion Paper n° 92-93, University of California, San Diego.

Levin, A., Lin, C. F., Chu, C. S. J., 2002, Unit Root Test in Panel Data: Asymptotic and Finite Sample Properties, *Journal of Econometrics*, Vol. 108(1), pp. 1-24.

Love, I., Zicchino, L., 2006, Financial Development and Dynamic Investment Behavior: Evidence for a Panel VAR, *The Quarterly Review of Economics and Finance*, Vol. 46, pp. 190-210.

Lucas, R., Stark, O., 1985, Motivations to remit: evidence from Botswana, *Journal of Political Economy*, Vol. 93(5), pp. 901-918.

Maddala, G. S., Wu, S., 1999, A Comparative Study of Unit Root Tests with Panel Data and a New Simple Test, *Oxford Bulletin of Economics and Statistics*, special issue, pp. 631-652.

Mansuri, G., 2008, *Migration, School Attainment and Child Labor: Evidence from Rural Pakistan*, Working Paper S3945, Development Research Group, World bank, Washington, DC.

Medenou, A. T., 2010, *Analyse des canaux de transmission des transferts de fonds sur l'économie béninoise*, CAPOD, Bénin.

Miyagiwa, K., 1991, Scale economies in education and the brain drain problem, *International Economic Review*, Vol. 32 (3), pp. 743-59.

Moon, H. R., Perron, B., 2004, Testing for a Unit Root in Panels with Dynamic Factors, *Journal of Econometrics*, Vol. 122(1), pp. 81-126.

Neagu, I. C., Schiff, M., 2009, *Remittance stability, cyclicality and stabilizing impact in developing countries, Policy Research Working Paper Series* 5077, The World Bank.

OCDE, 1991, Commerce extérieur par produit, série C : Classification type pour le commerce international version Rev.3, *Direction statistique*, vol. 12, pp. 9-10.

OCDE/CIRES, 2017 : *Interactions entre politiques publiques, migrations et développement en Côte d'Ivoire, Les voies du développement*, Edition OCDE, Paris.

OIM, 2009a, *Migration au Mali : Profil national.*

OIM, 2009b, *Migration au Niger : Profil national.*

OIM, 2009c, *Migration au Sénégal : Profil national.*

OIM, 2009d, *Migration en Côte d'Ivoire : Profil national.*

OIM, 2011, *Migration au Bénin : Profil national.*

OIM, 2015, *Migration au Togo : Profil national.*

OIM, 2016, *Migration au Burkina Faso : Profil national.*

Pesaran, M. H., 2003, *A Simple Panel Unit Root Test in the Presence of Cross Section Dependence*, Mimeo, University of Southern California.

Phillips, P. C. B., Sul, D., 2003, Dynamic Panel Estimation and Homogeneity Testing Under Cross Section Dependence, *Econometrics Journal*, Vol. 6(1), pp. 217-259.

Ratha, D., 2007, *Leveraging remittances for development*, Development Prospects Group, World Bank, Washington, DC.

Ravaillon, M., S. Chen, 1997, What Can New Survey Data Tell Us About Recent Changes in Distribution and Poverty ?, *World Bank Economic Review* 11 (2), pp. 357-382.

Rocher, E., Pelletier, A., 2008, Les transferts de revenus des migrants : quel impact sur le développement économique et financier des pays de l'Afrique Sub-saharienne ?, *Bulletin de la Banque de France* n° 173, pp. 27-38.

Sambo, H., 2018, Understanding the effect of international remittances on undernourishment in Sub-Saharan Africa: A spatial model approach, *Région et Développement*, 47, pp. 43-61.

Sayan, S., 2006, *Business Cycles and Workers Remittances: How Do Migrant Workers Respond to Cyclical Movements of GDP at Home?*, Working Papers 06/52, International Monetary Fund.

Sevestre, P., 2002, *Économétrie des données de panel*, Dunod, Paris.

Sims, C. A., 1980, Macroeconomics and reality, *Econometrica*, Vol. 48(1), pp. 1-48.

Stark, O., 1991, *The migration of labor*, Cambridge & Oxford: Blackwell.

Stark, O., J. E. Taylor, Yitzhaki, S., 1988, Migration, remittances and inequality: a sensitivity analysis using the extended Gini index, *Journal of Development Economics*, Vol. 28 (3), pp. 309-322.

United Nations, 1998, Recommendation on Statistics of International Migration, *Statistical Papers Series M*, n° 58, Rev.1, New York.

Woodruff, C., Zenteno, R., 2007, Migration networks and microenterprises in Mexico, *Journal of Development Economics*, Vol. 82(2), pp. 509-528.

Yabile, K. R., 2013, Déterminants de la sous-alimentation des ménages en Côte d'Ivoire : Cas des régions Centre et Centre-Est, *European Scientific Journal*, Vol. 9 n° 14, pp. 207-228.

Yang, D., Choi, H., 2005, *Are Remittances Insurance? Evidence from Rainfall Shocks in the Philippines*, Working Papers 535, Research Seminar in International Economics, University of Michigan.

ANNEXES

Annexe 1 : Descriptif des tests de racine unitaire

L'analyse de la stationnarité des variables est indispensable pour estimer notre modèle et avoir des résultats robustes. Les premiers tests de stationnarité (présence ou absence de racine unitaire) sur les données de panel ont été élaborés par Levin et Lin (1992). Ils se sont basés sur les tests de racines unitaires de Dickey et Fuller (1979) en tenant compte de la possibilité d'autocorrélation des résidus et ont connu des versions modifiées appelées tests de Dickey-Fuller augmentés (ADF). Depuis lors, il en existe deux grands groupes : les tests de première génération et de deuxième génération.

Les tests de première génération plus communément utilisés sont ceux de Levin, Lin et Chu (2002), Breitung (2000), Im, Pesaran et Shin (2003), Maddala et Wu (1999). Pour ces tests, l'absence ou la présence d'une racine unitaire dans l'un ou l'autre des sous-groupes (individus d'une même série) ne peut s'obtenir que par séquence de tests. Un tel procédé pourrait avoir comme effet une mauvaise interprétation des résultats des tests selon Hurlin et Mignon (2005, p. 273-274). En plus, les tests de première génération formulent tous l'hypothèse d'indépendance interindividuelle des termes d'erreurs et considèrent les éventuelles corrélations transversales comme des paramètres de nuisance. Cependant, ces corrélations pourraient avoir un intérêt immédiat au niveau macroéconomique si le panel de données considéré couvre une région spécifique. Dans ce cas, l'utilisation des tests de première génération mènerait à des distorsions de taille et affaiblirait leur puissance selon Banerjee, Marcellino et Osbat (2004, p. 337). Les tests de deuxième génération sous l'hypothèse nulle de racine unitaire prennent explicitement en compte la présence d'une corrélation interindividuelle. Les méthodes utilisées pour traiter la dépendance entre les individus diffèrent cependant selon les auteurs : Bai et Ng (2004), Philips et Sul (2003), Moon et Perron (2004), Pesaran (2003).

On combine généralement les deux types de tests de stationnarité. On retiendra les résultats[17] des tests de Im, Pesaran et Shin (IPS) (2003) et de Maddala et Wu (MW) (1999) (tableaux 1 et 2) pour la première génération. Ce sont des tests qui prennent en compte l'hétérogénéité interindividuelle en cas de rejet de l'hypothèse nulle de racine unitaire. Ces deux tests paraissent ainsi plus puissants que le test de Levin, Lin et Chu (2002) – très similaire à celui de Breitung (2000) –

[17] Les tests de première génération ainsi que celui de deuxième génération de Pesaran (2003) ont été effectués sur le logiciel de statistiques et d'économétrie Stata version11.

selon Maddala et Wu (1999). Par ailleurs, le test de Maddala et Wu (1999) donnerait de meilleurs résultats que le test de Im, Pesaran et Shin (2003) par simulation Monte Carlo opérée par Maddala et Wu (1999) et confirmé globalement par Choi (1999). Pour la seconde génération, celui de Pesaran (2003) (tableau 3) semble le plus intéressant puisque son modèle ne subit pas de transformation dans la prise en compte des corrélations interindividuelles. En conservant les séries telles quelles, il y ajoute les moyennes individuelles (termes avancés) et les différences premières (termes retardés). Il obtient un modèle augmenté de type CADF (Cross Sectionaly Augmented Dickey-Fuller). De ce modèle CADF dans lequel est intégrée une composante commune, il en résulte des statistiques individuelles indépendantes de tout paramètre de nuisance. Une statistique moyenne de type CIPS (Cross sectionaly augmented Im, Pesaran et Shin, 2003) est tirée de la somme de ces statistiques individuelles.

Annexe 2 : Fonctions de réponses impulsionnelles

Fonctions de réponses impulsionnelles du Groupe A

			Response of LPREC :		
Period	LPREC	DLREM	DLUND	DLAGRI	DLFIM
1	0.165599	0.000000	0.000000	0.000000	0.000000
	(0.03110)	(0.00000)	(0.00000)	(0.00000)	(0.00000)
2	0.136647	0.000676	-0.078015	-0.020035	-0.016747
	(0.04818)	(0.04440)	(0.04233)	(0.04203)	(0.03075)
3	0.127306	-0.003801	-0.008402	-0.013022	-0.011738
	(0.05155)	(0.04042)	(0.03658)	(0.04274)	(0.03011)
4	0.111745	-0.000220	-0.052210	-0.009550	-0.012250
	(0.06441)	(0.04362)	(0.04466)	(0.04006)	(0.02501)
5	0.101492	-0.002156	-0.016771	-0.010969	-0.009292
	(0.07566)	(0.04404)	(0.04144)	(0.03988)	(0.02853)
6	0.089956	-0.000706	-0.034664	-0.008359	-0.009635
	(0.08834)	(0.04532)	(0.05274)	(0.04184)	(0.02627)
7	0.081239	-0.001433	-0.018164	-0.008334	-0.007747
	(0.10042)	(0.04944)	(0.05112)	(0.04328)	(0.02861)
8	0.072335	-0.000752	-0.024777	-0.006934	-0.007513
	(0.11432)	(0.05260)	(0.06485)	(0.04572)	(0.03013)
9	0.065086	-0.001027	-0.016569	-0.006564	-0.006356
	(0.12844)	(0.05987)	(0.06524)	(0.04934)	(0.03235)
10	0.058113	-0.000686	-0.018564	-0.005644	-0.005940
	(0.14498)	(0.06381)	(0.08303)	(0.05348)	(0.03506)

			Response of DLREM :		
Period	LPREC	DLREM	DLUND	DLAGRI	DLFIM
1	0.160944*	0.341034	0.000000	0.000000	0.000000
	(0.08729)	(0.05771)	(0.00000)	(0.00000)	(0.00000)
2	-0.043106*	-0.001219	0.029093	-0.008247	-0.025363
	(0.08132)	(0.10570)	(0.08659)	(0.09571)	(0.08093)
3	-0.034790*	0.001776	0.002091	0.020325	0.006691
	(0.06764)	(0.06614)	(0.07517)	(0.06496)	(0.04084)
4	-0.034920*	0.001007	0.009227	-0.000289	0.004699
	(0.06332)	(0.05234)	(0.07723)	(0.04621)	(0.03102)
5	-0.030681*	7.35E-05	0.011264	0.002723	0.002536
	(0.06090)	(0.04236)	(0.07328)	(0.03555)	(0.02570)
6	-0.027475*	0.000487	0.006491	0.003166	0.002760
	(0.06100)	(0.04075)	(0.07079)	(0.03437)	(0.02121)
7	-0.024594*	0.000288	0.008050	0.002279	0.002551
	(0.06111)	(0.03881)	(0.06601)	(0.03264)	(0.02124)
8	-0.022084*	0.000326	0.005911	0.002211	0.002160
	(0.06137)	(0.04108)	(0.06561)	(0.03516)	(0.02152)
9	-0.019737*	0.000246	0.006111	0.001936	0.002007
	(0.06254)	(0.04212)	(0.06762)	(0.03665)	(0.02205)
10	-0.017710*	0.000254	0.004933	0.001759	0.001760
	(0.06452)	(0.04728)	(0.07551)	(0.04037)	(0.02432)

Response of DLUND :					
Period	LPREC	DLREM	DLUND	DLAGRI	DLFIM
1	0.006302	-0.002191**	0.052111	0.000000	0.000000
	(0.01200)	(0.01336)	(0.00851)	(0.00000)	(0.00000)
2	0.000166	0.002542**	-0.037208	0.003227	-0.001777
	(0.01275)	(0.01646)	(0.01518)	(0.01321)	(0.01033)
3	0.002619	-0.001511**	0.023448	-0.002210	0.001411
	(0.01124)	(0.01393)	(0.01773)	(0.01381)	(0.01148)
4	0.000570	0.000938**	-0.015951	0.000939	-0.001232
	(0.00906)	(0.01279)	(0.02012)	(0.01234)	(0.01044)
5	0.001745	-0.000654**	0.009886	-0.000753	0.000580
	(0.00886)	(0.01270)	(0.02228)	(0.01162)	(0.00889)
6	0.000739	0.000411**	-0.007094	0.000312	-0.000561
	(0.00779)	(0.01318)	(0.02545)	(0.01141)	(0.00851)
7	0.001205	-0.000295**	0.004200	-0.000380	0.000199
	(0.00800)	(0.01479)	(0.02852)	(0.01215)	(0.00893)
8	0.000722	0.000175**	-0.003221	0.000103	-0.000284
	(0.00792)	(0.01653)	(0.03327)	(0.01346)	(0.00990)
9	0.000882	-0.000134**	0.001732	-0.000202	5.19E-05
	(0.00875)	(0.01948)	(0.03825)	(0.01553)	(0.01091)
10	0.000634	7.19E-05**	-0.001501	1.35E-05	-0.000156
	(0.00938)	(0.02241)	(0.04562)	(0.01811)	(0.01256)

Response of DLAGRI :					
Period	LPREC	DLREM	DLUND	DLAGRI	DLFIM
1	0.001905	-0.043534*	-0.080639	0.185525	0.000000
	(0.05490)	(0.05681)	(0.04620)	(0.03271)	(0.00000)
2	-0.008346	0.008671*	-0.024967	-0.021450	0.023870
	(0.04142)	(0.05742)	(0.05626)	(0.05624)	(0.04449)
3	-0.005187	-0.003733**	0.031695	-0.010649	-0.004921
	(0.03569)	(0.03233)	(0.04858)	(0.04317)	(0.02703)
4	-0.003363	0.001029**	-0.015891	0.006133	-0.000556
	(0.02848)	(0.02465)	(0.04376)	(0.03063)	(0.01913)
5	-0.002774	-0.000353**	0.010025	-0.000975	0.001459
	(0.02762)	(0.02150)	(0.04370)	(0.02766)	(0.01494)
6	-0.003172	0.000345**	-0.004822	0.000470	-0.000276
	(0.02769)	(0.02335)	(0.04331)	(0.02442)	(0.01439)
7	-0.002312	-0.000204**	0.004527	0.000119	0.000518
	(0.02841)	(0.02434)	(0.04790)	(0.02743)	(0.01316)
8	-0.002401	0.000195**	-0.001891	0.000366	6.89E-05
	(0.03000)	(0.02615)	(0.05525)	(0.03101)	(0.01322)
9	-0.001945	-8.04E-05**	0.002290	8.95E-05	0.000312
	(0.03315)	(0.02847)	(0.06739)	(0.03608)	(0.01305)
10	-0.001876	9.50E-05**	-0.000590	0.000254	0.000108
	(0.03681)	(0.03464)	(0.08009)	(0.04406)	(0.01336)

Response of DLFIM :					
Period	LPREC	DLREM	DLUND	DLAGRI	DLFIM
1	0.003983	0.013655**	-0.024063	0.001352	0.159174
	(0.04260)	(0.04210)	(0.03724)	(0.03603)	(0.02343)
2	-0.012065	-0.007993**	0.029203	-0.079088	-0.024561
	(0.04131)	(0.04757)	(0.04508)	(0.04639)	(0.03269)
3	0.010254	-0.002785**	0.009282	0.021122	-0.004431
	(0.03188)	(0.03620)	(0.04622)	(0.03566)	(0.02993)
4	0.004330	0.002095**	-0.019124	-3.34E-07	0.001902
	(0.02604)	(0.02554)	(0.04350)	(0.02990)	(0.02487)
5	0.004625	-0.000995**	0.011064	-0.002867	-0.000347
	(0.02380)	(0.02236)	(0.04450)	(0.02264)	(0.02106)
6	0.003692	0.000381**	-0.008670	0.000647	-0.000967
	(0.02447)	(0.02092)	(0.04525)	(0.02221)	(0.01683)
7	0.003796	-0.000319**	0.003672	-0.000688	3.81E-05
	(0.02217)	(0.02204)	(0.04649)	(0.01943)	(0.01817)
8	0.003015	0.000146**	-0.004016	-0.000152	-0.000544
	(0.02174)	(0.02329)	(0.04797)	(0.02124)	(0.01955)
9	0.002959	-0.000168**	0.001222	-0.000399	-0.000150

	(0.02230)	(0.02610)	(0.05128)	(0.02330)	(0.02166)
10	0.002484	5.18E-05**	-0.002110	-0.000167	-0.000345
	(0.02269)	(0.02924)	(0.05670)	(0.02642)	(0.02474)

Cholesky Ordering: LPREC DLREM DLUND DLAGRI DLFIM
Standard Errors: Monte Carlo (200 repetitions)

Fonctions de réponses impulsionnelles du Groupe B

			Response of LPREC :		
Period	LPREC	DLREM	DLUND	DLAGRI	DLFIM
1	0.141664	0.000000	0.000000	0.000000	0.000000
	(0.02566)	(0.00000)	(0.00000)	(0.00000)	(0.00000)
2	0.020372	-0.039705	0.032661	0.011529	-0.014035
	(0.04602)	(0.04154)	(0.02737)	(0.03579)	(0.03186)
3	0.007440	0.005826	-0.025416	-0.000746	0.003056
	(0.04170)	(0.03350)	(0.02169)	(0.02348)	(0.02470)
4	0.007846	-0.013425	0.020112	0.004650	-0.007170
	(0.04144)	(0.02732)	(0.02212)	(0.01792)	(0.02019)
5	-0.000170	0.006408	-0.014797	-0.002122	0.004354
	(0.04145)	(0.03539)	(0.02289)	(0.01835)	(0.02096)
6	0.002230	-0.006624	0.011466	0.002290	-0.004178
	(0.04532)	(0.03481)	(0.02783)	(0.01879)	(0.02120)
7	-0.000661	0.004448	-0.008765	-0.001492	0.002995
	(0.05125)	(0.04528)	(0.03124)	(0.02109)	(0.02538)
8	0.000891	-0.003744	0.006808	0.001267	-0.002451
	(0.06157)	(0.05316)	(0.03861)	(0.02354)	(0.02729)
9	-0.000509	0.002782	-0.005262	-0.000932	0.001853
	(0.07463)	(0.07159)	(0.04647)	(0.02901)	(0.03288)
10	0.000465	-0.002209	0.004085	0.000742	-0.001458
	(0.09685)	(0.09201)	(0.05997)	(0.03492)	(0.03722)

			Response of DLREM :		
Period	LPREC	DLREM	DLUND	DLAGRI	DLFIM
1	-0.012221**	0.162183	0.000000	0.000000	0.000000
	(0.04015)	(0.03233)	(0.00000)	(0.00000)	(0.00000)
2	-0.064584**	0.033054	0.019115	-0.028329	0.040886
	(0.04976)	(0.04619)	(0.03085)	(0.04137)	(0.03921)
3	-0.037449*	0.022996	-0.017079	-0.006812	0.000482
	(0.05454)	(0.04731)	(0.02557)	(0.03097)	(0.02727)
4	-0.005464**	0.005973	0.007179	-0.002260	0.004723
	(0.04904)	(0.04967)	(0.02352)	(0.02707)	(0.02447)
5	-0.007180*	0.004904	-0.004765	-0.002133	0.001656
	(0.05631)	(0.05382)	(0.02386)	(0.02223)	(0.02238)
6	-0.001031*	0.000187	0.002666	-2.50E-06	-7.13E-05
	(0.06854)	(0.06838)	(0.02820)	(0.02406)	(0.02636)
7	-0.001246*	0.001573	-0.002034	-0.000616	0.000858
	(0.08842)	(0.08899)	(0.03425)	(0.02663)	(0.02627)
8	-0.000139	-0.000520	0.001450	0.000178	-0.000405
	(0.11702)	(0.12230)	(0.04559)	(0.03206)	(0.03368)
9	-0.000282	0.000705	-0.001139	-0.000248	0.000441
	(0.16214)	(0.16946)	(0.06123)	(0.03885)	(0.03731)
10	3.46E-05	-0.000423	0.000868	0.000141	-0.000292
	(0.22440)	(0.23940)	(0.08425)	(0.05195)	(0.04864)

			Response of DLUND :		
Period	LPREC	DLREM	DLUND	DLAGRI	DLFIM
1	0.008488	-0.009702***	0.039682	0.000000	0.000000
	(0.01102)	(0.00947)	(0.00626)	(0.00000)	(0.00000)
2	-0.010745	0.014270**	-0.026426	-0.005093	0.006870
	(0.01560)	(0.01402)	(0.00850)	(0.01103)	(0.00887)
3	0.002201	-0.008367**	0.018602	0.003007	-0.005331
	(0.01583)	(0.01232)	(0.01170)	(0.01214)	(0.01224)
4	-0.002570	0.007724**	-0.014042	-0.002732	0.004916

	(0.01408)	(0.01257)	(0.01448)	(0.01186)	(0.01281)
5	0.001042	-0.005521**	0.010697	0.001883	-0.003687
	(0.01459)	(0.01353)	(0.01765)	(0.01290)	(0.01383)
6	-0.001025	0.004498**	-0.008278	-0.001526	0.002960
	(0.01410)	(0.01509)	(0.02160)	(0.01514)	(0.01528)
7	0.000652	-0.003404**	0.006402	0.001143	-0.002263
	(0.01546)	(0.01691)	(0.02706)	(0.01897)	(0.01752)
8	-0.000552	0.002677**	-0.004966	-0.000900	0.001770
	(0.01646)	(0.01933)	(0.03462)	(0.02491)	(0.02035)
9	0.000406	-0.002061**	0.003850	0.000691	-0.001366
	(0.01964)	(0.02223)	(0.04552)	(0.03370)	(0.02447)
10	-0.000324	0.001605**	-0.002986	-0.000538	0.001062
	(0.02271)	(0.02612)	(0.06087)	(0.04650)	(0.03010)

Response of DLAGRI :					
Period	LPREC	DLREM	DLUND	DLAGRI	DLFIM
1	0.046777	0.003839**	-0.009782	0.055097	0.000000
	(0.01606)	(0.01255)	(0.01417)	(0.00825)	(0.00000)
2	-0.009204	-0.011186**	0.009666	-0.006758	-0.005760
	(0.02174)	(0.02044)	(0.01189)	(0.01860)	(0.01704)
3	0.003850	0.005310**	-0.009506	0.000552	0.003207
	(0.01632)	(0.01230)	(0.01221)	(0.01374)	(0.01402)
4	0.000731	-0.005018**	0.008173	0.001200	-0.002956
	(0.01551)	(0.01203)	(0.01289)	(0.01114)	(0.01170)
5	-0.000345	0.003308**	-0.006419	-0.000991	0.002134
	(0.01418)	(0.01203)	(0.01314)	(0.01124)	(0.01129)
6	0.000644	-0.002751**	0.005006	0.000906	-0.001769
	(0.01451)	(0.01175)	(0.01448)	(0.01198)	(0.01195)
7	-0.000383	0.002041**	-0.003867	-0.000680	0.001349
	(0.01500)	(0.01301)	(0.01714)	(0.01424)	(0.01345)
8	0.000345	-0.001619**	0.002998	0.000544	-0.001066
	(0.01614)	(0.01398)	(0.02199)	(0.01839)	(0.01547)
9	-0.000244	0.001240**	-0.002321	-0.000416	0.000822
	(0.01788)	(0.01643)	(0.02904)	(0.02398)	(0.01831)
10	0.000197	-0.000968**	0.001800	0.000325	-0.000640
	(0.02138)	(0.01847)	(0.03934)	(0.03259)	(0.02205)

Response of DLFIM :					
Period	LPREC	DLREM	DLUND	DLAGRI	DLFIM
1	-0.025918	-0.029816**	0.008387	0.029047	0.153286
	(0.04244)	(0.03959)	(0.03745)	(0.03708)	(0.02408)
2	-0.069651	-0.017697**	-0.012209	0.000963	-0.072271
	(0.05046)	(0.04746)	(0.03300)	(0.04737)	(0.04130)
3	0.031763	0.023190**	-0.013993	-0.003347	0.032431
	(0.05216)	(0.04195)	(0.03866)	(0.04223)	(0.04541)
4	-0.011403	-0.017107**	0.022182	0.003235	-0.015843
	(0.04499)	(0.04109)	(0.04238)	(0.03233)	(0.04837)
5	0.001788	0.013440**	-0.021379	-0.003482	0.009831
	(0.04468)	(0.03974)	(0.04820)	(0.02844)	(0.05032)
6	0.000544	-0.010031**	0.017846	0.002992	-0.006832
	(0.04329)	(0.04765)	(0.05582)	(0.02860)	(0.05475)
7	-0.001228	0.007791*	-0.014209	-0.002498	0.005165
	(0.04455)	(0.05188)	(0.06859)	(0.03257)	(0.06181)
8	0.001093	-0.005981*	0.011107	0.001972	-0.003958
	(0.04870)	(0.06344)	(0.08361)	(0.03741)	(0.07142)
9	-0.000917	0.004646*	-0.008635	-0.001550	0.003071
	(0.05554)	(0.07238)	(0.10336)	(0.04462)	(0.08278)
10	0.000713	-0.003595*	0.006700	0.001203	-0.002379
	(0.06459)	(0.09029)	(0.12699)	(0.05434)	(0.09685)

Cholesky Ordering: LPREC DLREM DLUND DLAGRI DLFIM
Standard Errors: Monte Carlo (200 repetitions)

Fonctions de réponses impulsionnelles du Groupe C

			Response of LPREC :		
Period	LPREC	DLREM	DLUND	DLAGRI	DLFIM
1	0.123518	0.000000	0.000000	0.000000	0.000000
	(0.01593)	(0.00000)	(0.00000)	(0.00000)	(0.00000)
2	0.083330	0.006997	0.000764	0.004129	0.004601
	(0.02586)	(0.02069)	(0.01346)	(0.01954)	(0.01899)
3	0.054562	0.005466	0.000577	-8.22E-05	0.002688
	(0.03347)	(0.02129)	(0.00525)	(0.01233)	(0.01323)
4	0.036557	0.004057	6.66E-05	0.000323	0.001930
	(0.03700)	(0.01973)	(0.00670)	(0.00989)	(0.00951)
5	0.024342	0.002796	0.000315	8.00E-05	0.001285
	(0.03922)	(0.01799)	(0.00377)	(0.00876)	(0.00808)
6	0.016272	0.001899	1.68E-05	3.94E-06	0.000854
	(0.04094)	(0.01746)	(0.00433)	(0.00783)	(0.00724)
7	0.010874	0.001281	0.000138	4.41E-05	0.000581
	(0.04303)	(0.01748)	(0.00323)	(0.00760)	(0.00684)
8	0.007265	0.000857	1.18E-05	-8.72E-06	0.000381
	(0.04556)	(0.01824)	(0.00350)	(0.00757)	(0.00668)
9	0.004858	0.000575	5.79E-05	1.88E-05	0.000260
	(0.04875)	(0.01945)	(0.00313)	(0.00781)	(0.00667)
10	0.003246	0.000384	7.74E-06	-3.76E-06	0.000171
	(0.05263)	(0.02114)	(0.00330)	(0.00822)	(0.00678)

			Response of DLREM :		
Period	LPREC	DLREM	DLUND	DLAGRI	DLFIM
1	-0.029540**	0.259653	0.000000	0.000000	0.000000
	(0.04850)	(0.03539)	(0.00000)	(0.00000)	(0.00000)
2	-0.019221**	0.085673	0.012183	-0.079059	0.004004
	(0.04879)	(0.05005)	(0.02885)	(0.04676)	(0.04048)
3	0.010034**	0.028624	-0.013449	-0.008985	0.003989
	(0.04705)	(0.04160)	(0.01435)	(0.02422)	(0.02073)
4	0.007597**	0.009011	0.009246	-0.003007	0.001567
	(0.04045)	(0.02936)	(0.01145)	(0.02004)	(0.01275)
5	0.006655**	0.003110	-0.006163	-0.003427	0.000154
	(0.03587)	(0.02473)	(0.00842)	(0.01473)	(0.00890)
6	0.004863**	0.001409	0.003935	0.001380	0.000685
	(0.03277)	(0.02243)	(0.00635)	(0.01437)	(0.00732)
7	0.003177**	0.000524	-0.002426	-0.001329	-4.91E-05
	(0.03137)	(0.02233)	(0.00578)	(0.01403)	(0.00631)
8	0.002297**	0.000386	0.001527	0.000758	0.000284
	(0.03011)	(0.02309)	(0.00494)	(0.01485)	(0.00624)
9	0.001445**	0.000161	-0.000922	-0.000507	-1.87E-05
	(0.02994)	(0.02459)	(0.00493)	(0.01577)	(0.00632)
10	0.001033**	0.000147	0.000579	0.000308	0.000116
	(0.03005)	(0.02651)	(0.00464)	(0.01712)	(0.00670)

			Response of DLUND :		
Period	LPREC	DLREM	DLUND	DLAGRI	DLFIM
1	-0.001929	0.004234***	0.039037	0.000000	0.000000
	(0.00739)	(0.00757)	(0.00497)	(0.00000)	(0.00000)
2	0.002356	0.001659**	-0.026062	-0.009156	-0.001410
	(0.00904)	(0.01044)	(0.00561)	(0.00705)	(0.00643)
3	0.001905	0.001166***	0.016645	0.006933	0.001605
	(0.00565)	(0.00752)	(0.00633)	(0.00778)	(0.00558)
4	0.000695	-6.20E-05***	-0.010415	-0.005189	-0.000956
	(0.00547)	(0.00606)	(0.00626)	(0.00640)	(0.00416)
5	0.001072	0.000377***	0.006461	0.003323	0.000719
	(0.00378)	(0.00426)	(0.00587)	(0.00521)	(0.00305)
6	0.000305	-7.87E-05***	-0.003977	-0.002128	-0.000397
	(0.00399)	(0.00346)	(0.00542)	(0.00410)	(0.00220)
7	0.000481	0.000142***	0.002449	0.001320	0.000284
	(0.00311)	(0.00254)	(0.00491)	(0.00337)	(0.00169)

8	0.000147	-3.13E-05***	-0.001501	-0.000818	-0.000152
	(0.00349)	(0.00226)	(0.00444)	(0.00282)	(0.00132)
9	0.000208	5.58E-05***	0.000923	0.000503	0.000109
	(0.00318)	(0.00189)	(0.00398)	(0.00246)	(0.00113)
10	7.15E-05	-1.04E-05***	-0.000565	-0.000309	-5.65E-05
	(0.00362)	(0.00189)	(0.00361)	(0.00216)	(0.00094)

Response of DLAGRI :					
Period	LPREC	DLREM	DLUND	DLAGRI	DLFIM
1	0.004538	0.016652**	0.019518	0.090699	0.000000
	(0.01610)	(0.01776)	(0.01629)	(0.01223)	(0.00000)
2	-0.020475	0.003627**	-0.001958	-0.031138	-0.004518
	(0.01760)	(0.01945)	(0.01139)	(0.01909)	(0.01482)
3	-0.004685	0.002347***	-0.001965	0.005898	0.001182
	(0.01030)	(0.00959)	(0.01050)	(0.01428)	(0.00826)
4	-0.005141	-3.62E-05***	0.002018	-0.001819	-0.000421
	(0.00873)	(0.00596)	(0.00818)	(0.00932)	(0.00348)
5	-0.002717	-9.95E-05***	-0.001577	-0.000154	-0.000149
	(0.00715)	(0.00434)	(0.00659)	(0.00727)	(0.00239)
6	-0.001918	-0.000148***	0.001029	0.000280	-2.77E-05
	(0.00634)	(0.00339)	(0.00500)	(0.00582)	(0.00177)
7	-0.001273	-0.000148***	-0.000678	-0.000297	-0.000123
	(0.00583)	(0.00291)	(0.00406)	(0.00469)	(0.00135)
8	-0.000824	-7.97E-05***	0.000413	0.000200	-2.73E-06
	(0.00568)	(0.00266)	(0.00331)	(0.00386)	(0.00122)
9	-0.000573	-7.42E-05***	-0.000264	-0.000136	-5.66E-05
	(0.00564)	(0.00256)	(0.00290)	(0.00323)	(0.00101)
10	-0.000366	-3.76E-05***	0.000158	8.45E-05	-2.70E-06
	(0.00577)	(0.00259)	(0.00255)	(0.00280)	(0.00100)

Response of DLFIM :					
Period	LPREC	DLREM	DLUND	DLAGRI	DLFIM
1	0.013318	0.060953**	-0.006675	0.047430	0.123756
	(0.02618)	(0.02472)	(0.02141)	(0.02024)	(0.01401)
2	-0.020628	-0.020554**	0.006730	-0.017279	-0.009190
	(0.02616)	(0.02884)	(0.01564)	(0.02651)	(0.02138)
3	-0.007325	-0.004558**	-0.007147	0.007591	6.15E-05
	(0.01778)	(0.01449)	(0.01323)	(0.01711)	(0.01089)
4	-0.007756	-0.002233***	0.005406	0.000690	-0.000467
	(0.01515)	(0.00863)	(0.00910)	(0.01050)	(0.00570)
5	-0.004867	-0.001008***	-0.003688	-0.000882	-0.000529
	(0.01340)	(0.00599)	(0.00685)	(0.00782)	(0.00398)
6	-0.003316	-0.000451***	0.002328	0.001050	1.30E-05
	(0.01250)	(0.00494)	(0.00492)	(0.00599)	(0.00277)
7	-0.002316	-0.000351***	-0.001488	-0.000699	-0.000268
	(0.01202)	(0.00440)	(0.00381)	(0.00479)	(0.00219)
8	-0.001473	-0.000156***	0.000903	0.000475	1.34E-05
	(0.01218)	(0.00418)	(0.00301)	(0.00399)	(0.00187)
9	-0.001044	-0.000145***	-0.000570	-0.000299	-0.000114
	(0.01227)	(0.00419)	(0.00252)	(0.00338)	(0.00183)
10	-0.000660	-6.76E-05***	0.000342	0.000187	1.42E-06
	(0.01276)	(0.00426)	(0.00215)	(0.00299)	(0.00174)

Cholesky Ordering: LPREC DLREM DLUND DLAGRI DLFIM
Standard Errors: Monte Carlo (200 repetitions)

Significatif au seuil de 1% (***), 5% (**) et 10% (*). Source : Extrait du logiciel Eviews version 7.

Annexe 3 : Décomposition de la variance

Décomposition de la variance cumulée du groupe A

Variables	Période *h*	LPREC	DLREM	DLUND	DLAGRI	DLFIM
LPREC	10	88.98790	0.019155	9.424992	0.825539	0.742411
DLREM	10	22.08456	76.26030	0.830291	0.338032	0.486815
DLUND	10	1.036480	0.292755	98.19760	0.329018	0.144146
DLAGRI	10	0.318970	4.288906	18.43789	75.66502	1.289213
DLFIM	10	1.013012	0.744795	5.977178	18.95245	73.31257

Décomposition de la variance cumulée du groupe B

Variables	Période *h*	LPREC	DLREM	DLUND	DLAGRI	DLFIM
LPREC	10	80.34267	7.493520	10.27384	0.663162	1.226809
DLREM	10	15.65288	75.44121	2.012868	2.315710	4.577331
DLUND	10	5.078869	12.66012	77.62184	1.286724	3.352443
DLAGRI	10	37.49475	3.620012	7.290757	50.54734	1.047136
DLFIM	10	15.74228	5.770876	5.021674	2.127581	71.33759

Décomposition de la variance cumulée du groupe C

Variables	Période *h*	LPREC	DLREM	DLUND	DLAGRI	DLFIM
LPREC	10	99.41288	0.394984	0.003760	0.061881	0.126491
DLREM	10	1.769559	90.05575	0.568449	7.564609	0.041636
DLUND	10	0.519071	0.772426	92.33075	6.159667	0.218086
DLAGRI	10	4.803251	2.832407	3.798483	88.35507	0.210790
DLFIM	10	3.288040	18.00854	0.832980	11.28074	66.58970

Source : Extrait du logiciel Eviews version 7.

Remittances and food security in the West Africa countries

Abstract - This study aims to better understand the conditions of the impact of migrant remittances on food security and poverty reduction after a climatic shock. To do this, we used a specified VAR (vector autoregressive) model on panel data from seven countries of West African Economic and Monetary Union (WAEMU) classified into three groups according to their rainfall amounts and collected on the period 1990-2010. The results show a positive impact of remittances on the prevalence of undernourishment and poverty reduction in low-rainfall countries, with an agricultural sector dominated by food crops and international migrants mostly from rural areas.

Key-words
Climate
Remittances
Food Security
Poverty
West Africa

Région et Développement

n° 49-2019

www.regionetdeveloppement.org

Un modèle de gravité de la mobilité internationale des demandeurs d'asile

Dimitri KARKANIS*

Résumé – Selon le Haut-Commissariat des Nations Unies pour les réfugiés, une population importante a été forcée de quitter son lieu de résidence ces dernières années. Le présent article applique un modèle de gravité pour évaluer le poids relatif des différents facteurs qui déterminent les flux de personnes ayant demandé l'asile pendant l'année 2014 à l'échelle internationale. L'analyse des données montre qu'il existe une forte relation entre les populations de réfugiés et celles de demandeurs d'asile, les premières représentant la « trace » cumulative des approbations des demandes d'asile des années précédentes. Il ressort aussi que les pays d'origine des réfugiés sont généralement caractérisés par un accès limité à l'eau potable, ce qui concerne plutôt les pays africains et du Moyen-Orient.

Classification JEL

F22, C33

Mots-clés

Modèle de gravité
Demandeurs d'asile
Réfugiés

Je tiens à remercier la direction de la Revue et les évaluateurs pour leurs remarques qui ont permis d'améliorer significativement cet article.

* Université de Thessalie, Grèce ; dkarkanis@uth.gr

INTRODUCTION

Le Haut-Commissariat pour les Réfugiés fait référence à l'existence de 68,5 millions de personnes déplacées de force dans le monde entier, parmi eux 40 millions de personnes déplacées internes, 25,4 millions de réfugiés et 3,1 millions de demandeurs d'asile (HCR, juin 2018). La question des réfugiés ne se limite pas à certains pays spécifiques puisqu'elle concerne, d'une part, les pays d'origine qui sont affectés par des conflits, l'instabilité politique ou des difficultés financières et, d'autre part, les pays d'accueil qui sont amenés à accueillir des populations de réfugiés. Cela oblige bien souvent ces derniers pays à formuler des politiques d'intégration appropriées. Les flux de réfugiés les plus intenses sont observés au Moyen-Orient et en Afrique subsaharienne. La guerre en Syrie (2011) et en Irak (2014) contre l'État islamique, la guerre de l'armée nationale afghane contre les talibans et les djihadistes depuis 2015, ainsi que la guerre civile au Yémen la même année, sont les causes d'une crise humanitaire dans la région conduisant à des pertes énormes en vies humaines, mais aussi à des déplacements forcés de personnes essayant d'échapper aux zones de guerre. Les guerres et l'instabilité politique, ainsi que les sécheresses, la faim et l'émergence d'épidémies figurent parmi les principales raisons de l'augmentation des flux de personnes en Afrique subsaharienne (Soudan du Sud, Somalie, Érythrée, Éthiopie, Burundi, Nigeria, République centrafricaine, République Démocratique du Congo, entre autres). Ces dernières années, des flux intenses sont également observés en Asie du Sud (Pakistan, Bangladesh, Myanmar) ou en Amérique latine (Colombie, Honduras). Les pays de destination sont généralement des pays développés (Union européenne, États-Unis) ou des pays proches de ceux d'origine et qui maintiennent des politiques souvent favorables aux droits des réfugiés.

Dans ce contexte, les causes du gonflement des flux de réfugiés varient en fonction des conditions socio-politiques et économiques décrivant les pays d'origine. Cependant, les raisons du choix des pays de destination ne dépendent pas seulement des facteurs géographiques et économiques, mais aussi des facteurs institutionnels tels que les politiques nationales d'asile, sans négliger les liens (par mail, mobile, réseaux sociaux, etc.) entre les compatriotes du pays de destination et ceux du pays d'origine.

L'objectif du présent article est donc d'apporter des éléments de réponse à la question suivante : quels sont les facteurs d'attraction et de répulsion (*pull-push)* qui seraient les plus déterminants quant à la mobilité des personnes demandant l'asile à l'échelle internationale ? Parmi les divers déterminants, la question des événements violents ne peut naturellement être évitée. Cependant au cours des dernières décennies les causes de l'exode tendent à se multiplier, et des études récentes insistent sur le développement des flux de personnes déplacées pour causes environnementales et/ou climatiques (Beine & Parsons, 2012 ; Dritsas, 2015). Il s'agit d'une vaste question qui dépasse l'objet du présent article. Seul un aspect sera ici examiné, à savoir l'accès à l'eau potable, question qui nous semble d'une importance primordiale car elle conditionne aussi bien les possibilités de développement économique et des capacités d'investissement dans la construction des infrastructures que les conditions sanitaires et de survie des populations (OMS, UNICEF, 2017).

L'approche méthodologique repose sur l'application d'un modèle de gravité afin d'évaluer les facteurs qui déterminent la direction et l'intensité des demandes d'asile dans le monde. Le modèle incorpore un ensemble de variables explicatives associées à des facteurs géographiques, démographiques, économiques, socio-politiques et environnementaux, afin d'estimer le volume des demandes d'asile, représentés par le nombre de demandeurs d'asile enregistrés par pays d'origine et de destination pour l'année 2014. L'ensemble des observations découle d'une table origine-destination de demandeurs d'asile concernant 153 pays et territoires (donnés en annexe 1).

L'article est organisé comme suit. La section 1 donne une revue de la littérature sur l'étude des flux migratoires des demandeurs d'asile. La section 2 présente les variables et les données utilisées. La section 3 est consacrée aux estimations du modèle de gravité considéré et à l'analyse des résultats.

1. LES DÉTERMINANTS DES FLUX DE DEMANDEURS D'ASILE : UNE REVUE DE LA LITTÉRATURE

Selon le HCR, un demandeur d'asile est « une personne qui dit être un(e) réfugié(e) mais dont la demande est encore en cours d'examen » (HCR, 2018). Par conséquent, tous les réfugiés sont à l'origine des demandeurs d'asile, sans nécessairement que tous les demandeurs d'asile obtiennent le statut de réfugié (IGC, 2015). Cela implique que la population des demandeurs d'asile comprend les populations dont les demandes ont été acceptées par les autorités des pays concernés, ainsi que les personnes dont les demandes ont été finalement refusées. Il devient alors évident que la population des réfugiés enregistrés dans un pays de destination ne peut pas représenter de manière adéquate l'intensité des flux des personnes qui revendiquent le statut de réfugié dans un pays de destination.

La littérature sur l'analyse du phénomène des flux de réfugiés est relativement limitée (par exemple, Hatton & Williamson, 2004 ; Iqbal, 2007 ; Alix-Garcia & Saah, 2010 ; Ruiz & Vargas-Silva, 2013, Dreher *et al.*, 2018), dont une partie examine les flux de réfugiés dans le contexte de la guerre en Syrie (Alhanaee & Csala, 2016 ; Najem & Faour, 2018). Par exemple, Brekke *et al.* (2017) étudient les effets de la politique d'asile sur les demandes, en constatant un fort impact du niveau de conflit et de terreur sur l'intensité des flux. En ce qui concerne leur question centrale, ils observent qu'un resserrement des politiques d'asile dans les pays d'accueil réduit le nombre de nouveaux demandeurs d'asile. Dans leur analyse, les flux sont représentés par le nombre de demandeurs d'asile, enregistrés par le HCR. Les critiques sur l'utilisation du nombre des demandes d'asile par pays d'origine et de destination pour l'estimation des flux de réfugiés font référence, d'une part, au fait qu'une partie de demandeurs pourrait bien concerner des migrants économiques (Echevarria, 2016) et, d'autre part, les procédures d'asile varient non seulement entre les pays mais également à l'intérieur des pays (Jones, 2009).

Nestorowicz et Anacka (2018) se réfèrent à la séparation qui existe, en matière d'approche conceptuelle, théorique ou méthodologique, entre les articles scientifiques qui traitent des questions de la migration interne et ceux qui étudient la migration internationale. Ils essaient d'explorer les canaux d'interconnexion entre les deux types de migration, visant à proposer une approche holistique de ce domaine d'étude au carrefour de plusieurs disciplines.

L'utilisation d'un modèle de gravité est devenue fréquente pour évaluer les facteurs qui déterminent la direction et l'intensité des flux en sciences sociales (migration, mobilité) ou en économie régionale ou internationale (commerce bilatéral). Même si les origines de l'introduction du modèle de gravité pour l'observation des tendances migratoires remontent aux travaux de Ravenstein (1889), le recours à ce modèle est largement favorisé aujourd'hui par une disponibilité accrue des données de flux dyadiques (Poot *et al.*, 2016).

En appliquant le modèle de gravité lors de l'examen du phénomène de la migration internationale, Dedeoğlu & Genç (2017) montrent que les flux migratoires provenant d'un pays d'origine donné sont plus intenses, *ceteris paribus*, dans les pays où il existe un nombre important d'immigrants du même pays d'origine. Il y aurait donc un effet d'attraction lié à la proximité socioculturelle ou au phénomène de diaspora. Au contraire, en modélisant la relation entre les demandes d'asile et (i) le PIB, (ii) le taux de reconnaissance du statut de réfugié et (iii) le « stock » de réfugiés dans les pays de l'UE-15, Keogh (2013) constate un effet statistiquement significatif de deux premiers facteurs, ce qui n'est pas le cas pour le dernier. Aux niveaux géographique et culturel, l'existence d'une frontière commune est considérée comme un facteur qui favorise les flux migratoires (Ramos et Suriñach, 2013). Kim & Cohen (2010) constatent des effets statistiquement significatifs du partage d'une frontière et d'une langue minoritaire commune, ainsi que des liens coloniaux entre le pays d'origine et celui de destination, sur les migrations internationales. *Ceteris paribus*, les flux migratoires semblent alors être plus prononcés avec les pays voisins (Karemera *et al.*, 2000 ; Letouzé *et al.*, 2009 ; Dedeoğlu et Genç, 2017 ; Cattaneo et Bosetti, 2017 ; Tuccio, 2017), mais cette relation n'est pas forcément respectée dans le cas de la mobilité des demandeurs d'asile. Aburn et Wesselbaum (2017) observent également un impact positif d'une langue commune sur la migration internationale, cependant ils constatent un effet non significatif d'une frontière commune sur les flux.

Les études sur l'existence de mouvements migratoires pour des raisons environnementales (sécheresse, désertification) tendent à se développer sensiblement. On peut par exemple citer Myers (2002), Bates (2002), Backhaus *et al.* (2015), Dritsas (2015), Damette et Gittard (2017), Cattaneo et Bosetti (2017) ou Beine et Parsons (2015). Ces derniers constatent un impact limité du changement et des variations climatiques sur la migration internationale à long terme, cependant ils ajoutent que les changements environnementaux peuvent avoir une incidence indirecte sur la migration par d'autres canaux. Évaluant les liens entre la pénurie d'eau et le conflit actuel en Syrie, Gleick (2014) trouve que les facteurs associés à la disponibilité limitée de l'eau sont susceptibles de produire encore plus d'instabilité politique, à moins que des mécanismes appropriés (meilleure gestion de l'eau pour l'agriculture, systèmes de surveillance des ressources en eaux souterraines, etc.) existent pour atténuer l'insécurité dans le domaine de l'eau.

2. MÉTHODOLOGIE ET DONNÉES

Dans le modèle, la variable indépendante ($ASYL_d$) représente le nombre demandeurs d'asile par pays d'origine et par pays de destination selon la base statistique du HCR, considérant que cette dernière reflète mieux l'ampleur des demandes d'asile par année[1]. Pour des raisons d'accessibilité et de fiabilité des données et compte tenu des problèmes liés à la multiplication des valeurs manquantes, l'étude se limite aux demandeurs d'asile en 2014. La population de réfugiés par pays d'origine et de destination, c'est-à-dire des personnes étant reconnues comme réfugiés sur la base de la Convention de 1951, ne représente que la « trace » cumulative des demandes d'asile déjà acceptées, ce qui donne à cette population les caractéristiques d'une « masse » d'attraction ou de répulsion, selon la terminologie des sciences naturelles, plutôt que d'un « flux » de ressources humaines. Comme c'est toujours le cas avec les modèles de gravité étendus, la variable indépendante est représentée sous la forme du logarithme naturel.

Les quatre variables concernant la distance entre les pays (*Dist*), la contiguïté (*Contig*), une relation coloniale antérieure entre les pays d'accueil et ceux d'origine (*Colon*) et la langue commune (*Comlang_ethno*) proviennent de la base GeoDist du

[1] C'est d'ailleurs la seule source qui permet de considérer l'ensemble des pays dans le monde alors que Frontex fournit des données selon les « routes » suivies par les migrants à destination de l'Europe uniquement.

CEPII (Mayer & Zignago, 2011). Par définition, la distance est inversement proportionnelle aux flux dans les modèles de gravité (Bergh *et al*, 2015) et, pour cette raison, le signe du coefficient devrait être négatif. Les trois autres variables sont des variables muettes qui prennent la valeur 1 s'il y a une frontière commune, une relation coloniale ou une langue commune, sinon elles prennent la valeur 0. Les trois coefficients sont supposés positifs.

En vue d'évaluer le rôle attractif ou répulsif du niveau de développement des pays sur la mobilité des demandeurs d'asile au niveau international, la variable PIB par habitant (*PIB*) qui provient des estimations du secrétariat de la CNUCED et de la base de données de la Division de statistique ONU DAES (*National Accounts Main Aggregates Database*) est utilisée. Les valeurs sont exprimées aux prix constants de 2010. Les mêmes bases statistiques disposent des données sur la population totale par pays (*POP*) que nous utilisons également comme variable exogène.

Le Haut-Commissariat des Nations Unies pour les réfugiés dispose des données sur la population des réfugiés - ceux qui ont obtenu l'asile dans les pays de destination - par pays d'origine et par pays de destination (*REFUG*). Concernant le traitement des valeurs nulles, afin de permettre le passage au logarithme naturel, nous avons opté pour une méthode souvent utilisée : transformer la variable initiale x comprenant des zéros en une variable $x+a$. Comme le choix de la constante a peut dans certains cas interférer sur les estimations de coefficient du modèle, cette méthode a été à plusieurs reprises critiquée, même si la forme de la distribution de la variable n'est pas changée (Burger *et al*, 2009). Cependant, il est possible de vérifier la pertinence relative de la méthode en comparant les résultats du modèle pour différentes valeurs de la constante a. Si les estimations ne sont pas fondamentalement perturbées par le choix de ces valeurs, on peut alors admettre que ce type de traitement des valeurs nulles est satisfaisant. Nous avons en effet testé trois alternatives pour la valeur de la constante (a=0,1, a=0,5 et a=1). Dans le cas présent, les différences sont suffisamment faibles pour nous permettre d'effectuer une telle transformation (voir annexes 3 et 4). Nous avons retenu pour l'analyse a=1.

Le phénomène des flux de réfugiés est directement lié au déclenchement de guerres et d'autres manifestations de violence dans les pays d'origine. Depuis dix ans, le *Global Peace Index* propose un indice composite qui évalue l'existence de conflits intérieurs et internationaux en cours, le degré de sécurité et la militarisation des pays à l'échelle internationale. Pour l'année d'étude, la valeur minimale de l'indice de paix (*GPI*) est observée en Islande, le caractérisant comme le pays le plus pacifique (1,189), contrairement à la Syrie qui représente le pays le moins pacifique (3,65) dans l'échantillon des 153 pays (voir annexe 1). Dans cette analyse, notre variable explicative GPI_o représente le degré de pacifisme des pays d'origine, calculée comme la valeur inverse de l'indice GPI [2]. Le coefficient de la variable devrait avoir un signe négatif, étant donné que, *ceteris paribus*, plus l'indice GPI_o est faible (donc faible degré de pacifisme) plus les sorties de populations des demandeurs d'asile sont élevées.

La question de l'accès à l'eau est souvent évoquée parmi les facteurs de départ des populations dans les pays confrontés à de graves problèmes de sécheresse ou ceux subissant les conséquences de l'élévation graduelle du niveau de la mer (Dritsas, 2009). La première variable utilisée dans le modèle (WAT_o) représente le volume en mètres cubes des ressources internes renouvelables en eau douce par habitant (Figure 1) ; les données provenant de la base statistique de la Banque mondiale. Le signe attendu du coefficient de cette variable est négatif.

[2] Comme GPI>1, la variable $GPI_o = 1/GPI$ est toujours définie.

La deuxième variable qui s'inscrit dans ce cadre, SEP_o, provient également de la base de données de la Banque mondiale. Elle est définie comme la proportion de la population d'un pays ayant accès aux services de base en eau potable. Comme on pouvait s'y attendre, les proportions les plus faibles en 2014 (Figure 2) sont observées en Papouasie-Nouvelle-Guinée, et en général dans les pays les moins développés, notamment en Afrique subsaharienne.

De manière générale, l'annexe 2 retrace la définition des variables du modèle et leur source.

Figure 1. Ressources internes renouvelables en eau douce par habitant par pays ou territoire en 2014 (<1.000 mètres cubes par hab.) (WAT_o)

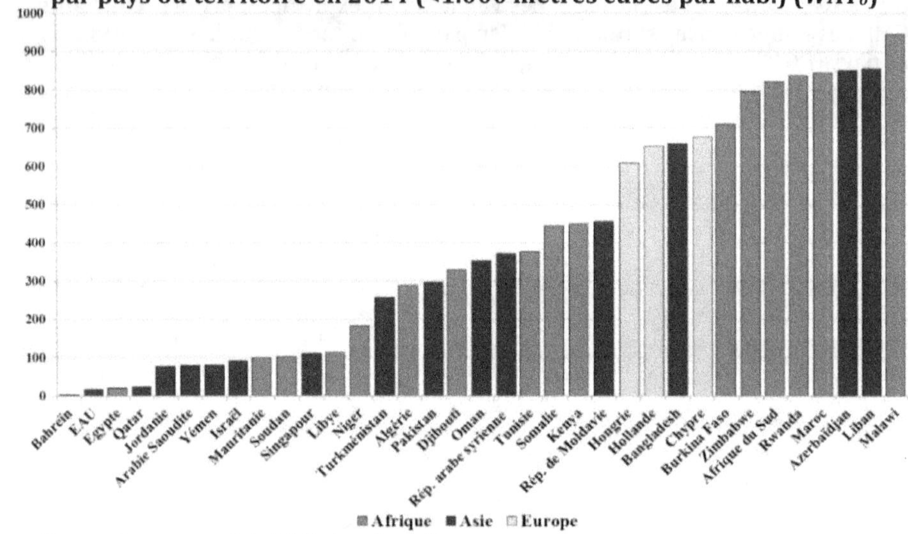

Source : Banque mondiale, 2019, données en ligne.

Figure 2. Proportion de la population (%) par pays ou territoire utilisant au moins les services de base en eau potable en 2014 (<66,67%) (SEP_o)

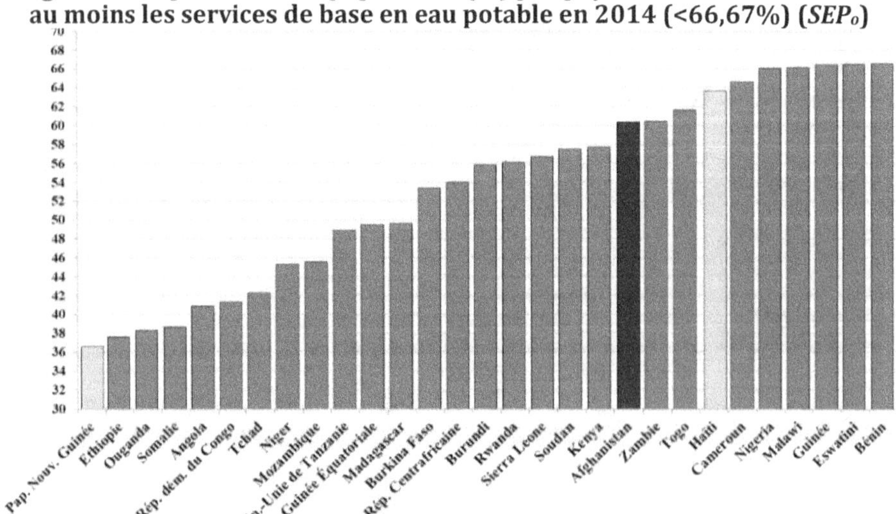

Source : Banque mondiale, 2019, données en ligne.

Plusieurs études ont suggéré l'existence d'un lien entre le changement climatique et le manque de ressources associé et les zones de conflit (Anderson *et al.*, 2000 ; Gleditsch, 2012). Cette hypothèse ne repose pas sur l'idée d'un impact direct des conditions climatiques sur le déclenchement de conflits, mais les conditions climatiques peuvent tendre les relations sociales et par conséquent accroître les probabilités de déclenchement de conflits (Burke *et al.*, 2014). Une telle relation positive et statistiquement significative semble ici se confirmer entre les deux variables d'accès à l'eau potable (WAT_o, SEP_o) et la variable évaluant le niveau de paix dans les pays (GPI_o) (Tableau 1).

Tableau 1. Matrice des corrélations (valeur minimale a=1)

	$ASYL_d$	Dist	Contig	Comlang _ethno	Colon	PIB_d	POP_d	POP_o	$REFUG_d$	WAT_o	SEP_o	GPI_o
$ASYL_d$	1	-.174**	.123**	.116**	.114**	.280**	.190**	.151**	.824**	-.086**	-.156**	-.267**
Dist	-.174**	1	-.396**	-.167**	-.068**	-.029**	.058**	.058**	-.195**	.165**	-,004	-,008
Contig	.123**	-.396**	1	.150**	.105**	-.018**	.047**	.047**	.190**	-,008	-.019**	-.032**
Comlang _ethno	.116**	-.167**	.150**	1	.153**	-.017**	,011	,011	.121**	-.047**	-.039**	-.050**
Colon	.114**	-.068**	.105**	.153**	1	.060**	.052**	.052**	.114**	-,001	.034**	,012
PIB_d	.280**	-.029**	-.018**	-.017**	.060**	1	-.099**	,001	.292**	,000	-,005	-,004
POP_d	.190**	.058**	.047**	,011	.052**	-.099**	1	-,007	.158**	,001	,000	,002
POP_o	.151**	.058**	.047**	,011	.052**	,001	-,007	1	.134**	-.135**	-.070**	-.300**
$REFUG_d$	.824**	-.195**	.190**	.121**	.114**	.292**	.158**	.134**	1	-.067**	-.161**	-.265**
WAT_o	-.086**	.165**	-,008	-.047**	-,001	,000	,001	-.135**	-.067**	1	.029**	.243**
SEP_o	-.156**	-,004	-.019**	-.039**	.034**	-,005	,000	-.070**	-.161**	.029**	1	.421**
GPI_o	-.267**	-,008	-.032**	-.050**	,012	-,004	,002	-.300**	-.265**	.243**	.421**	1

*** Corrélation significative au niveau 0,01. Toutes les variables sauf les variables muettes sont exprimées en logarithmes naturels.*

L'analyse de corrélations indique également une relation inverse des trois variables mentionnées ci-dessus avec l'intensité des flux de réfugiés ($REFUG_d$, $ASYL_d$). Cette constatation suggère que plus les niveaux de paix et d'accès à l'eau potable sont faibles dans certains pays, *ceteris paribus*, plus les flux de réfugiés en provenance de ces pays sont forts.

3. MODÈLE DE GRAVITÉ ET RÉSULTATS

3.1. Description du modèle

Le modèle de gravité estimé représente une forme augmentée de l'équation de gravité de base où la population de demandeurs d'asile est une fonction log-linéaire des facteurs géographiques, culturels, économiques, démographiques, politiques et environnementaux. L'équation de gravité est exprimée comme suit :

$$ASYL_d = \beta_0 + \beta_1\, Dist + \beta_2\, Contig + \beta_3\, Comlang\_ethno + \beta_4\, Colon + \beta_5\, PIB_d + \beta_6\, POP_d + \beta_7\, POP_o + \beta_8\, REFUG_d + \beta_9\, WAT_o + \beta_{10}\, SEP_o + \beta_{11}\, GPI_o + \varepsilon$$

La variable dépendante $ASYL_d$ désigne la taille de la population de demandeurs d'asile dans le pays de destination, exprimée en logarithme naturel. Les variables explicatives *Contig*, *ComLang_ethno* et *Colon* représentent l'existence d'une frontière commune, d'une langue ethnique commune et d'un passé colonial commun entre le pays de destination et celui d'origine. Les variables PIB_d, POP_d, POP_o indiquent respectivement le PIB par habitant du pays de destination, les tailles de la population totale dans le pays de destination et d'origine. La variable $REFUG_d$ représente la taille de la population des réfugiés dans le pays de destination, GPI_o l'indice de paix dans le pays d'origine ; les variables WAT_o et SEP_o représentent le degré de disponibilité de l'eau potable dans le pays d'origine. Les variables explicatives représentant les déterminants économiques et démographiques (PIB_d, POP_d, POP_o, $REFUG_d$), ainsi que celles concernant l'accès à l'eau potable (WAT_o, SEP_o) sont exprimées en logarithmes naturels. Le terme ε représente le terme d'erreur associé à l'estimation OLS.

Pour s'assurer de la robustesse du modèle, nous avons recours à l'une des méthodes d'inférence statistique les plus courantes, à savoir la méthode « bootstrap ». Cette méthode de ré-échantillonnage en un grand nombre d'échantillons (1000) permet de vérifier la fiabilité des résultats puisque, en tant que méthode non paramétrique, les conditions d'application du modèle sont moins restrictives (Palm, 2002, p. 143).

3.2. Les déterminants des mouvements des demandeurs d'asile

L'analyse recouvre les demandes d'asile vers et à partir d'un total de 153 pays et territoires pour l'année 2014 et l'échantillon comprend 23256 observations. Le modèle estimé (Régression 1, Tableau 2) est caractérisé par un R^2 satisfaisant (0,69), il ne présente pas de problèmes de colinéarité (annexe 6) et tous les coefficients des variables explicatives introduites sont statistiquement significatifs aux niveaux de 1% et 5%. L'absence de colinéarité entre les deux variables WAT_o et SEP_o, concernant les effets sur les demandeurs d'asile, pourrait s'expliquer par le fait que les pays caractérisés par des ressources renouvelables en eau douce par habitant limitées se différencient largement des pays où la proportion de la population utilisant les services de base en eau potable est relativement faible.

La distance (*Dist*) exerce un rôle répulsif, comme attendu, sur l'intensité des demandes d'asile. Le signe du coefficient est cohérent avec les résultats obtenus dans d'autres travaux concernant l'analyse des flux de migrants (Kim & Cohen, 2010) ou des demandeurs d'asile (Neumayer, 2005). Néanmoins, et selon le modèle, l'effet de la proximité géographique sur la détermination de la destination des demandes d'asile doit être nuancé. L'effet négatif et statiquement significatif de la variable *Contig* montre que dans certains cas les personnes ne préfèrent pas ou ne peuvent pas – pour des raisons politiques et diplomatiques – demander l'asile dans les pays partageant une frontière commune avec leurs pays d'origine. Ce résultat s'oppose à ceux concernant d'autres travaux qui analysent les déterminants des flux migratoires en général (Karemera *et al.*, 2000 ; Echevarria & Gardeazabal, 2016 ; Tuccio, 2017). Les coefficients de *Dist* et *Contig* sont tous deux statistiquement très significatifs. En résumé, la possibilité de déposer une demande d'asile dans un pays partageant une frontière commune avec le pays d'origine est souvent difficile, et les coûts de déplacement s'imposent alors pour définir le pays de destination.

L'effet de la langue commune (*Comlang_ethno*) sur les flux des demandeurs d'asile est estimé positif et significatif, bien que moins important que les deux facteurs susmentionnés, comme cela a déjà été rapporté dans le cas des modèles de gravité sur les flux migratoires (par exemple, Kim & Cohen, 2010). Ce résultat n'empêche pas le fait qu'une langue commune entre le pays de destination et le pays d'origine encourage, *ceteris paribus*, la demande d'asile dans le pays de destination. L'avantage de la communication par l'intermédiaire d'une langue commune avec les minorités ethniques dans le pays d'accueil contribue à atténuer les problèmes liés aux asymétries de l'information et l'intégration future des personnes sur le marché du travail. Pour des raisons assez similaires, le rôle des liens coloniaux entre les pays de destination et ceux d'origine, représentés par la variable muette *Colon* est réaffirmé ici, comme déjà indiqué dans la littérature (Kim & Cohen, 2010 ; Aburn & Wesselbaum, 2017).

Tableau 2. Résultats (valeur minimale a=1)

Variables indépendantes	**Régr. 1** **$ASYL_d$** *N=23256*	**Coeff. bêta**	**Régr. 2** **$ASYL_d$** *N=23256*	**Coeff. bêta**
Constante	-0,841	0,000	-1,353	0,000
Dist	-0,077 (-9,076)***	-0,044	-0,072 (-8,883)***	-0,041
Contig	-0,474 (-5,964)***	-0,052	-0,471 (-5,932)***	-0,052
Comlang_ethno	0,074 (3,368)***	0,017	0,077 (3,515)***	0,018
Colon	0,205 (3,643)***	0,017	0,190 (3,374)***	0,016
PIB_d	0,052 (11,457)***	0,058	0,051 (11,159)***	0,057
POP_d	0,073 (18,610)***	0,078	0,072 (18,342)***	0,077
POP_o	0,034 (9,578)***	0,036	0,035 (9,913)***	0,038
$REFUG_d$	0,666 (65,308)***	0,772	0,671 (66,686)***	0,778
WAT_o	-0,007 (-3,120)***	-0,011		
SEP_o	-0,056 (-2,271)**	-0,010		
GPI_o	-0,505 (-11,253)***	-0,046		
$WAT'_o x GPI'_o$			-0,362 (-13,892)***	-0,044
R^2 ajusté	0,692		0,692	
F-test	4761,780***		5798,010***	

*Note : Toutes les variables sauf les variables muettes sont exprimées en logarithmes naturels. Les estimations utilisent l'estimateur matriciel de covariance cohérent avec l'hétéroscédasticité de White. Les t-statistiques sont entre parenthèses. L'exposant *** signifie p<0,01 et l'exposant ** signifie p<0,05.*

Le déterminant économique de la mobilité des demandeurs d'asile est principalement exprimé au travers du PIB par habitant des pays de destination, le signe est celui attendu et généralement rapporté dans la littérature (Aburn & Wesselbaum, 2017 ; Tuccio, 2017 ; Dreher *et al.*, 2018). Cela confirme l'impact attractif du niveau de développement économique du pays d'accueil. De manière générale, le besoin urgent d'échapper à la pauvreté et en particulier à la faim qui accompagne souvent le destin des populations touchées par les guerres ou les sécheresses semble laisser peu de place au choix de la direction de ces populations vers des pays, plus riches et/ou des pays assez proches des pays d'origine, qui peuvent leur garantir la sécurité du statut d'asile.

Ceteris paribus, plus la taille de la population d'un pays d'origine est grande, plus le nombre de personnes susceptibles de migrer est élevé, et plus la population du pays de destination est grande, plus le marché du travail est attractif pour les immigrants (Lewer & Van den Berg, 2008). Nos résultats confirment d'une certaine manière l'impact des facteurs économiques dans le cas des flux de réfugiés. La comparaison entre les deux coefficients respectifs montre que la taille des pays de destination joue un rôle relativement plus important que le rôle répulsif de la taille du pays d'origine, reflétant la capacité des pays développés à pouvoir attirer des ressources humaines. Les coefficients et leurs signes sont relativement similaires à ceux observés dans d'autres travaux sur l'étude des flux de réfugiés (Echevarria & Gardeazabal, 2016) ou de la migration (Kim & Cohen, 2010 ; Poot *et al.*, 2016).

Par ailleurs, il ressort du modèle que plus le nombre de réfugiés – personnes ayant déjà obtenu le statut d'asile dans le pays de destination – est grand, plus la population de demandeurs d'asile augmente dans le même pays d'accueil. Le coefficient estimé, très significatif, de *REFUG* tend à illustrer le rôle des politiques d'asile favorables pour les réfugiés des pays d'accueil, mais également l'importance de la présence des « concitoyens » des demandeurs d'asile dans les pays de destination, ce qui rend l'insertion et la familiarisation des personnes avec le nouvel environnement moins difficiles. Il devient alors raisonnable de supposer que cette variable incorpore l'impact positif des réseaux de communication, qui servent souvent à informer les demandeurs d'asile sur les politiques d'accueil favorables – ou non – pour les réfugiés dans les pays de destination.

Au niveau socio-politique, l'effet de l'implication des pays dans des conflits internes ou internationaux (GPI_o) ne peut être que répulsif pour les populations des pays d'origine. Le signe du coefficient est cohérent avec ceux observés dans la littérature concernant les flux de réfugiés (Iqbal, 2007 ; Echevarria & Gardeazabal, 2016) et il est généralement confirmé par l'observation des populations déplacées dans de nombreux pays en guerre dans le monde entier. Cela en aucun cas ne permet de généraliser cette constatation, mais il paraît en tout cas que les conflits et les guerres constituent une cause importante à l'origine de l'augmentation des demandes d'asile à l'échelle mondiale pour l'année 2014.

En ce qui concerne la composante liée à l'accès à l'eau, le coefficient de la variable WAT_o prend un signe négatif et statistiquement significatif au niveau de 1%. Il ressort que plus la disponibilité des ressources internes renouvelables en eau douce par habitant dans les pays d'origine est limitée, plus sont importantes les demandes d'asile provenant de ces pays. Un coefficient équivalent et statistiquement significatif au niveau de 5% est obtenu quant à la proportion de la population pouvant utiliser les services de base en eau potable (SEP_o), même s'il s'agit d'un effet répulsif apparemment plus limité. Ce résultat peut être interprété comme une indication sur l'éventualité du développement des flux de réfugiés pour causes environnementales, spécialement à partir des pays touchés par les sécheresses. Le signe du coefficient de la variable WAT_o est cohérent avec la littérature sur la question (Gleick, 2014 ; Backhaus *et al.*, 2015).

Nous avons ensuite examiné l'effet combiné d'un accès limité à l'eau et des hostilités dans les pays d'origine sur les flux de réfugiés (Régression 2, Tableau 2) et selon les résultats tirés de la matrice des corrélations (Tableau 1), en estimant une variable interactive, définie comme le produit des scores normalisés[3] des variables WAT_o et GPI_o. La variable WAT_o semble mieux représenter la faible disponibilité des ressources en eau (Figure 1), que ce soit en raison des conditions climatiques (Bahreïn, Qatar) ou du manque relatif d'infrastructures de base (Yémen, Soudan). D'ailleurs, le choix de la variable WAT_o dans la variable interactive semble être renforcé par le fait qu'elle s'avère statistiquement significative au niveau de 1% dans toutes les régressions alternatives (Régression 1, Tableau 2 ; Régressions 3 et 4, annexe 5), contrairement à la variable SEP_o. Mais l'inclusion de la variable GPI_o et de la variable interactive dans la même régression ne peut être retenue ici en raison de la colinéarité entre ces deux variables.

Il semble que la deuxième régression (Tableau 2) serve à étendre les conclusions déjà tirées de la première régression, le signe négatif du coefficient de la variable interactive suggérant une intensité accrue des flux de réfugiés lorsque se conjuguent les deux facteurs de répulsion considérés. Au-delà, il convient aussi de remarquer que les poids relatifs des variables $REFUG_d$ et POP_o sont légèrement plus élevés par rapport à ceux estimés précédemment. On peut subodorer qu'il existe un impact plus important des réseaux de communication entre les compatriotes du pays d'origine et ceux de destination sur l'intensité des flux, et en particulier lorsque les risques concernant la survie des réfugiés et de leurs familles se

[3] Normalisation des données mise à l'échelle afin d'éviter des valeurs négatives, sous forme : $x' = (x - x_{min}) / (x_{max} - x_{min})$.

multiplient. *Ceteris paribus*, plus il est urgent d'échapper au pays d'origine, plus le rôle des réseaux sociaux s'avère essentiel. Ceci semble d'autant plus important si nous tenons compte de l'utilisation généralisée des médias sociaux, quel que soit le niveau de vie des personnes.

CONCLUSION

Le présent article a tenté d'évaluer, à l'aide d'un modèle de gravité, l'impact d'un certain nombre de facteurs géographiques, démographiques, économiques ou socio-politiques sur le nombre et la destination des demandes d'asile à l'échelle internationale en 2014.

Comme attendu, le déclenchement des conflits et les guerres dans les pays provoquent des flux migratoires vers des pays plus pacifiques.

Les flux de personnes demandant le droit d'asile sont généralement dirigés vers des pays à niveau de développement élevé et qui respectent les droits fondamentaux des réfugiés et maintiennent des politiques favorables à leur égard. L'impact des réseaux de communication sur les filières de migration semble aussi être confirmé, les demandeurs d'asile cherchant le regroupement avec d'autres membres de la même communauté du pays d'origine.

Comme dans la très grande majorité des modèles de gravité, la distance constitue un facteur répulsif. Dans le cas des réfugiés, la question de la distance est cependant plus complexe, car il apparaît aussi un effet répulsif de la variable « frontière commune ». Il semblerait bien que les migrants forcés ne cherchent pas à s'éloigner très fortement de leur pays d'origine, mais en même temps, pour des raisons souvent politiques, les pays les plus proches ne sont pas toujours les pays d'accueil recherchés. L'utilisation d'une langue commune et une relation coloniale entre le pays de destination et celui d'origine tendent à encourager les flux des demandeurs d'asile.

En revanche, le manque relatif d'accès à l'eau potable n'a pas, pour l'année 2014 considérée, un impact aussi important sur l'augmentation des demandes que les guerres. Cependant, nos résultats suggèrent que l'exode des populations qui demandent l'asile concerne des pays où la disponibilité des ressources renouvelables en eau potable est relativement limitée.

Considérées dans leur ensemble, les constatations ci-dessus confirment que la recherche sur l'identification des facteurs qui déterminent la direction et l'intensité des flux de réfugiés à l'échelle internationale exige d'être abordée par une approche multidisciplinaire. Le modèle de gravité utilisé présente inéluctablement des limites intrinsèques liées au choix des variables retenues. Une des difficultés est aussi l'accès à des données fiables. Enfin, la limite essentielle dans ce type d'approche porte sur l'impossibilité – en l'état actuel des données disponibles – de distinguer le choix volontaire de celui « forcé » des personnes demandant l'asile à un autre pays. Cependant et compte tenu des réserves émises ci-dessus, il n'en demeure pas moins que le modèle fournit certains résultats intéressants quant au comportement de mobilité des demandeurs d'asile et dont l'analyse méritera d'être approfondie dans une approche dynamique.

REFERENCES

Aburn A., Wesselbaum D., 2017, Gone with the Wind: International Migration, *Economics Discussion Papers*, 1708, University of Otago.

Alhanaee A., Csala D., 2016, Motives to Flee: Modelling Syrian Refugee Crisis, Working paper.

Alix-Garcia J., Saah D., 2010, The Effect of Refugee Inflows on Host Communities: Evidence from Tanzania, *The World Bank Economic Review*, 24, 1, 148-170.

Anderson C.A., Anderson K.B., Dorr N., DeNeve K.M., Flanagan M., 2000, Temperature and aggression, *Advances in Experimental Social Psychology*, 32, 63-133.

Backhaus A., Martinez-Zarzoso I., Muris C., 2015, Do climate variations explain bilateral migration? A gravity model analysis, *IZA Journal of Migration*, 4, 3, 1-15.

Bates D.C., 2002, Environmental Refugees? Classifying Human Migrations Caused By Environmental Change, *Population and Environment*, 23, 5, 465-477.

Beine M., Parsons Ch., 2015, Climatic factors as determinants of International Migration, *Scandinavian Journal of Economics*, 117, 2, 723-767.

Bergh A., Mirkina I., Nilsson T., 2015, Pushed by Poverty or by Institutions? Determinants of Global Migration Flows, Research Institute of Industrial Economics, *IFN Working Paper* No. 1077.

Brekke J.P., Røed M., Schøne P., 2017, Reduction or deflection? The effect of asylum policy on interconnected asylum flows, *Migration Studies*, 1-32.

Burger M.J., van Oort F., Linders G.J., 2009, On the specification of the Gravity Model of Trade: Zeros, Excess Zeros and Zero Inflated Estimation, *Spatial Economic Analysis*, 4, 2, 167-190.

Burke M., Hsiang S.M., Miguel E., 2014, Climate and Conflict, *NBER Working Paper No.* 20598.

Caselli G., Vallin J., Wunsch G., 2003, *Démographie : Analyse et synthèse IV, Les Déterminants de la Migration*, INED, Paris.

Cattaneo C., Bosetti V., 2017, Climate-induced international migration and conflicts, Centro Euro-Mediterraneo sui Cambiamenti Climatici, Research Papers RP0284.

Conférence de Plénipotentiaires des Nations Unies sur le Statut des Réfugiés et des Apatrides, 1951, *Acte Final et Convention Relative au Statut des Réfugiés*, Nations Unies, Genève, Suisse.

Conférence des Nations Unies sur le Commerce et le Développement (CNUCED), 2018, base statistique de la CNUCED, données disponibles : http://unctad.org/fr/Pages/Home.aspx.

Damette O., Gittard M., 2017, Changement climatique et migrations : les transferts de fonds des migrants comme amortisseurs ?, *Mondes en développement*, 45, 179, 85-102.

Dedeoğlu D., Genç D.H., 2017, Turkish Migration to Europe: a modified gravity model analysis, *IZA Journal of Development and Migration*, 7, 17, 1-19.

Dreher A., Fuchs A., Langlotz S., 2018, The Effects of Foreign Aid on Refugee Flows, *GLO Discussion Paper*, 195, Global Labor Organization, Maastricht.

Dritsas S.E., 2009, Environmental (climate) refugee or environmental (climatic) migrant? Proceedings of the 2nd Panhellenic Conference of Urban Planning, Regional Planning and Regional Development, Volume III, pp. 1453-1464, University Press of Thessaly, Volos.

Dritsas S.E., 2015, *Organisation et gestion du littoral - évaluation des ressources humaines : réfugiés environnementaux et aménagement du territoire en Europe et en Méditerranée. Etudes de cas : La Gironde (L'estuaire) en France et Thessalonique (Les deltas d'Axios-Loudias-Aliakmonas) en Grèce.* Thèse de doctorat, Bordeaux, Centre de Droit Comparé du Travail et de la Sécurité Sociale / COMPTRASEC, Université de Thessalie.

Echevarria J., Gardeazabal J., 2016, Refugee Gravitation, *Public Choice*, 169, 269-292.

Gleditsch N., 2012, Whither the weather? Climate change and conflict, *Journal of Peace Research*, 49, 1, 3-9.

Gleick P.H., 2014, Water, Drought, Climate Change, and Conflict in Syria, *Weather, Climate, and Society*, 6, 3, 331-340.

Hatton T.J., Williamson J.G., 2004, Refugees, Asylum Seekers and Policy in Europe, *NBER Working Paper*, 10680.

Haut-Commissariat pour les Réfugiés, 2018, site officiel de l'Agence des Nations Unies pour les réfugiés, http://www.unhcr.org/fr/.

IGC, 2015, *Asylum Procedures, Report on Policies and Practices in IGC Participating States*, Intergovernmental consultations on migration, asylum and refugees, Geneva, Switzerland.

Iqbal Z., 2007, The Geo-Politics of Forced Migration in Africa, 1992-2001, *Conflict Management and Peace Science*, 24, 2, 105-119.

Institute for Economics & Peace, 2018, Rapports annuels sur l'indice *Global Peace Index*, http://economicsandpeace.org/reports/.

Jones M., 2009, Refugee status determination: Three challenges. *Forced Migration Review*, 32, 53-54.

Karemera D., Oguledo V.I., Davis B., 2000, A gravity model analysis of international migration to North America, *Applied Economics*, 32, 13, 1745-1755.

Keogh G., 2013, Modelling Asylum Migration Pull-Force Factors in the EU-15, *The Economic and Social Review*, 44, 3, 371-399.

Kim K., Cohen J.E., 2010, Determinants of International Migration Flows to and from Industrialized Countries: A Panel Data Approach Beyond Gravity, *International Migration Review*, 44, 4, 899-932.

Letouzé E., Purser M., Rodríguez F., Cummins M., 2009, Revisiting the Migration-Development Nexus: A Gravity Model Approach, *Human Development Research Paper*, 44.

Lewer J., Van der Berg H., 2008, A Gravity Model of Immigration, *Economics Letters*, 99, 1, 164-167.

Mayer T., Zignago S., 2011, Notes on CEPII's distances measures: the GeoDist Database, *CEPII Working Paper*, 25.

Myers N., 2002, Environmental refugees: a growing phenomenon of the 21st century, *Philosophical Transactions, Royal Society of London, Series B*, 357, 609-613.

Najem S., Faour G., 2018, Debye-Hückel theory for refugees' migration, *EPJ Data Science*, 7, 22, 1-9.

Nestorowicz J., Anacka M., 2018, Mind the Gap? Quantifying Interlinkages between Two Traditions in Migration Literature, *International Migration Review*, 1-25.

Neumayer E., 2005, Bogus refugees? The determinants of asylum migration to Western Europe [online]. London: *LSE Research Online*, http://eprints.lse.ac.uk/archive/00000580.

Organisation mondiale de la Santé, Fonds des Nations Unies pour l'enfance (UNICEF), 2017, *Progrès en matière d'eau, d'assainissement et d'hygiène : mise à jour 2017 et estimations des ODD*. Genève : Organisation mondiale de la Santé et le Fonds des Nations Unies pour l'enfance (UNICEF) ; 2017.

Palm R., 2002, Utilisation du bootstrap pour les problèmes statistiques liés à l'estimation des paramètres, *BASE* [en ligne], 6, 3, 143-153.

Poot J., Alimi O., Cameron M.P., Marée D.C., 2016, The Gravity Model of Migration: The Successful Comeback of an Ageing Superstar in Regional Science, *IZA Discussion Paper* No. 10329.

Ramos R., Suriñach J., 2013, A gravity model of migration between ENC and EU, *Research Institute of Applied Economics (IREA), Working Paper* 17, 26p.

Ravenstein E.G., 1889, The Laws of Migration, *Journal of the Royal Statistical Society*, 52, 2, 241-305.

Ruiz I., Vargas-Silva C., 2013, The Economics of Forced Migration, *The Journal of Development Studies*, 49, 6, 772-784.

Tuccio M., 2017, Determinants of Intra-ASEAN Migration, *Asian Development Review*, 34, 1, 144-166.

ANNEXES

Annexe 1. L'échantillon des 153 pays de destination et d'origine retenus

Afghanistan	Gambie	Nicaragua
Albanie	Géorgie	Niger
Algérie	Ghana	Nigeria
Allemagne	Grèce	Norvège
Angola	Guatemala	Oman
Argentine	Guinée	Ouganda
Arménie	Guinée-Bissau	Pakistan
Australie	Guyane	Panama
Autriche	Haïti	Papouasie-Nouvelle-Guinée
Azerbaïdjan	Hollande	Paraguay
Bahreïn	Honduras	Pérou
Bangladesh	Hongrie	Philippines
Bélarus	Islande	Pologne
Belgique	Inde	Portugal
Bénin	Indonésie	Qatar
Bhoutan	Iran	Roumanie
Bolivie	Irak	Royaume-Uni
Bosnie Herzégovine	Irlande	Russie
Botswana	Israël	Rwanda
Brésil	Italie	Arabie Saoudite
Bulgarie	Jamaïque	Sénégal
Burkina Faso	Japon	Sierra Leone
Burundi	Jordanie	Singapour
Cambodge	Kazakhstan	Slovaquie
Cameroun	Kenya	Slovénie
Canada	Rép. pop. dém. de Corée	Somalie
Rép. centrafricaine	République de Corée	Afrique du Sud
Tchad	Kirghizistan	Espagne
Chili	Laos	Sri Lanka
Chine	Lettonie	Soudan
Colombie	Liban	Swaziland (Eswatini)
Congo	Lesotho	Suède
Rép. dém. du Congo	Libéria	Suisse
Costa Rica	Libye	Syrie
Côte d'Ivoire	Lituanie	Tadjikistan
Croatie	Macédoine du Nord	Tanzanie
Cuba	Madagascar	Thaïlande
Chypre	Malawi	Togo
Tchéquie	Malaisie	Trinidad et Tobago
Danemark	Mali	Tunisie
Djibouti	Mauritanie	Turquie
République Dominicaine	Maurice	Turkménistan
Equateur	Mexique	Ukraine
Egypte	Moldavie	Emirats Arabes Unis
États Unis	Mongolie	Salvador
Guinée Équatoriale	Maroc	Uruguay
Estonie	Mozambique	Venezuela
Ethiopie	Myanmar	Viet Nam
Finlande	Namibie	Yémen
France	Népal	Zambie
Gabon	Nouvelle-Zélande	Zimbabwe

Annexe 2. Définitions des variables et sources de données

Variable	Définition	Source
$ASYL_d$	Population de demandeurs d'asile dans le pays de destination (ln)	HCR (2019)
$REFUG_d$	Population de réfugiés dans le pays de destination (ln)	HCR (2019)
POP_d	Population du pays de destination (ln)	ONU DAES, CNUCED (2018)
POP_o	Population du pays d'origine (ln)	ONU DAES, CNUCED (2018)
PIB_d	PIB par habitant du pays de destination à prix constant (ln)	ONU DAES, CNUCED (2018)
Dist	Distance entre le pays d'origine et le pays de destination (ln)	CEPII, base de données GeoDist (2018)
Contig	Variable muette, valeur 1 = contigüité entre le pays d'origine et celui de destination, sinon 0	CEPII, base de données GeoDist (2018)
Comlang_ethno	Variable muette, valeur 1 = langue ethnique commune entre le pays d'origine et celui de destination, sinon 0	CEPII, base de données GeoDist (2018)
Colon	Variable muette, valeur 1 = relation précoloniale entre le pays d'origine et de destination, sinon 0	CEPII, base de données GeoDist (2018)
WAT_o	Ressources internes renouvelables en eau douce par habitant, en mètres cubes (ln)	Banque mondiale (2019), données en ligne
SEP_o	Proportion (%) de la population utilisant au moins les services d'eau potable de base (ln)	Banque mondiale (2019), données en ligne
GPI_o	$\frac{1}{GPI}$, où GPI est l'indice de paix du pays d'origine	*Global Peace Index*, Institute for Economics & Peace (2018)

Annexe 3. Résultats (valeur minimale a=0,5)

Variables indépendantes	**Régr. 1** **$ASYL_d$** *N=23256*	**Coeff. bêta**	**Régr. 2** **$ASYL_d$** *N=23256*	**Coeff. bêta**
Constante	-1,205	0,000	-1,827	0,000
Dist	-0,092 (-9,498)***	-0,046	-0,086 (-9,187)***	-0,042
Contig	-0,494 (-5,682)***	-0,047	-0,490 (-5,628)***	-0,047
Comlang_ethno	0,090 (3,670)***	0,018	0,094 (3,818)***	0,019
Colon	0,254 (4,155)***	0,018	0,236 (3,851)***	0,017
PIB_d	0,063 (12,433)***	0,062	0,061 (12,058)***	0,060
POP_d	0,087 (19,337)***	0,081	0,085 (19,018)***	0,080
POP_o	0,040 (9,774)***	0,037	0,041 (10,087)***	0,039
$REFUG_d$	0,671 (72,312)***	0,765	0,677 (73,967)***	0,772
WAT_o	-0,008 (-2,796)***	-0,010		
SEP_o	-0,070 (-2,507)**	-0,011		
GPI_o	-0,615 (-11,903)***	-0,048		
$WAT'_o \times GPI'_o$			-0,436 (-14,462)***	-0,046
R^2 ajusté	0,691		0,690	
F-test	4728,246***		5754,871***	

*Note : Toutes les variables sauf les variables muettes sont exprimées en logarithmes naturels. Les estimations utilisent l'estimateur matriciel de covariance cohérent avec l'hétéroscédasticité de White. Les t-statistiques sont entre parenthèses. L'exposant *** signifie p<0,01 et l'exposant ** signifie p<0,05.*

Annexe 4. Résultats (valeur minimale a=0,1)

Variables indépendantes	**Régr. 1** **$ASYL_d$** *N=23256*	**Coeff. bêta**	**Régr. 2** **$ASYL_d$** *N=23256*	**Coeff. bêta**
Constante	-2,095	0,000	-3,045	0,000
Dist	-0,139 (-10,495)***	-0,052	-0,127 (-9,918)***	-0,047
Contig	-0,523 (-4,912)***	-0,038	-0,511 (-4,795)***	-0,037
Comlang_ethno	0,138 (4,237)***	0,021	0,143 (4,388)***	0,022
Colon	0,389 (5,069)***	0,021	0,360 (4,693)***	0,019
PIB_d	0,097 (14,972)***	0,071	0,094 (14,411)***	0,069
POP_d	0,126 (20,559)***	0,088	0,124 (20,131)***	0,087
POP_o	0,056 (9,991)***	0,039	0,058 (10,270)***	0,040
$REFUG_d$	0,667 (85,031)***	0,738	0,674 (87,299)***	0,746
WAT_o	-0,008 (-1,988)**	-0,007		
SEP_o	-0,114 (-2,990)***	-0,014		
GPI_o	-0,945 (-13,325)***	-0,056		
$WAT'_o \times GPI'_o$			-0,653 (-15,587)***	-0,052
R^2 ajusté	0,671		0,669	
F-test	4303,537***		5231,526***	

*Note : Toutes les variables sauf les variables muettes sont exprimées en logarithmes naturels. Les estimations utilisent l'estimateur matriciel de covariance cohérent avec l'hétéroscédasticité de White. Les t-statistiques sont entre parenthèses. L'exposant *** signifie p<0,01 et l'exposant ** signifie p<0,05.*

Annexe 5. Résultats (valeur minimale a=1)

Variables indépendantes	**Régr. 3** **$ASYL_d$** *N=23256*	**Coeff. bêta**	**Régr. 4** **$ASYL_d$** *N=23256*	**Coeff. bêta**
Constante	-1,054	0,000	-0,889	0,000
Dist	-0,077 (-9,059)***	-0,044	-0,081 (-9,882)***	-0,046
Contig	-0,474 (-5,961)***	-0,052	-0,482 (-6,081)***	-0,053
Comlang_ethno	0,074 (3,411)***	0,017	0,074 (3,410)***	0,017
Colon	0,201 (3,567)***	0,017	0,204 (3,615)***	0,017
PIB_d	0,052 (11,413)***	0,058	0,052 (11,466)***	0,059
POP_d	0,073 (18,578)***	0,078	0,073 (18,667)***	0,078
POP_o	0,033 (9,401)***	0,036	0,035 (9,765)***	0,037
$REFUG_d$	0,667 (65,546)***	0,773	0,666 (65,280)***	0,772
WAT_o	-0,007 (-2,899)***	-0,010		
SEP_o			-0,051 (-2,085)**	-0,010
GPI_o	-0,556 (-13,358)***	-0,050	-0,536 (-12,200)***	-0,049
R^2 ajusté	0,692		0,692	
F-test	5236,009***		5235,643***	

*Note : Toutes les variables sauf les variables muettes sont exprimées en logarithmes naturels. Les estimations utilisent l'estimateur matriciel de covariance cohérent avec l'hétéroscédasticité de White. Les t-statistiques sont entre parenthèses. L'exposant *** signifie p<0,01 et l'exposant ** signifie p<0,05.*

Annexe 6. Test de colinéarité – Régression 1 (valeur minimale a=1)

	Statistiques de colinéarité	
	Tolérance	VIF
Constante		
Dist	0,769	1,300
Contig	0,808	1,237
Comlang_ethno	0,937	1,067
Colon	0,954	1,048
PIBd	0,876	1,142
POPd	0,934	1,071
POPo	0,885	1,130
REFUGd	0,742	1,347
WATo	0,895	1,117
SEPo	0,809	1,236
GPIo	0,678	1,476

A gravity model of the international mobility of asylum seekers

Abstract – According to the Office of the United Nations High Commissioner for Refugees, a large population has been forced to leave the place of residence in recent years. The present article applies a gravity model in order to assess the relative weight of the different factors that determine the flows of people who applied for asylum in 2014 at international level. The data analysis reveals a strong and positive relationship between refugee and asylum seeker populations, the former representing the cumulative "trace" of asylum application approvals of previous years. It also appears that the refugees' countries of origin are generally characterized by limited access to drinking water, which is more the case in African and Middle Eastern countries.

Key-words
Gravity model
Asylum seekers
Refugees

Région et Développement

n° 49-2019

www. regionetdeveloppement.org

Interactions fiscales stratégiques entre pays de la CEMAC et flux entrants d'investissements directs étrangers

Bernard MIMBOE NOAH*, Samuel FAMBON**

Résumé - Cet article analyse l'impact des interactions fiscales stratégiques entre les pays de la CEMAC (Communauté Economique et Monétaire de l'Afrique Centrale) sur les flux d'investissements directs étrangers (IDE) que chacun de ces pays accueille. Pour cela, nous estimons d'abord l'effet fiscal stratégique au moyen d'un modèle spatial autorégressif. Puis, à l'aide d'un modèle spatial inspiré du modèle de gravité, nous évaluons la sensibilité des flux entrants d'IDE d'un pays donné à une variation du degré d'interactions fiscales stratégiques entre les pays de la CEMAC. Les résultats des estimations, réalisées par la méthode du maximum de vraisemblance avec effet aléatoire en données de panel, montrent que les pays de la CEMAC développent entre eux des comportements stratégiques sur le plan fiscal, et que ces comportements favorisent l'entrée d'IDE dans chaque pays. De ce fait, loin d'être dommageables, les interactions fiscales stratégiques constituent plutôt un facteur d'attractivité pour les pays évoluant dans une zone d'intégration économique en développement.

Classification JEL

R3, H23, H25, H3

Mots-clés

Interaction fiscale stratégique
Flux entrants d'IDE
CEMAC

Nous remercions le rapporteur anonyme et la direction éditoriale de la Revue qui ont contribué à l'amélioration de cet article.

* FSEG - Université de Yaoundé II ; benmimboe@yahoo.fr
** FSEG - Université de Yaoundé II ; sfambon@yahoo.fr

INTRODUCTION

L'environnement fiscal constitue un des facteurs déterminants à partir desquels les entreprises multinationales fondent leurs décisions de localisation. Conscients des opportunités qu'engendre l'entrée d'investissements directs étrangers (IDE), les Etats tentent d'offrir en ce sens des mesures fiscales incitatives. Mais, dans un contexte marqué par la mobilité accrue des capitaux et par une intégration croissante des économies, l'engagement des Etats à attirer les investissements étrangers se traduit très souvent par des situations d'interactions fiscales stratégiques entre les territoires.

L'interaction fiscale stratégique s'entend comme une situation dans laquelle les gouvernements agissent d'une manière non coopérative, où chacun provoque ou subit, sans avoir l'intention de faire concurrence, les actions des autres (Zodrow et Mieszkowski, 1986 ; Wilson, 1986 ; Wildasin, 1988). A cet égard, l'offre de politique fiscale d'un pays donné sera fonction non seulement de ses caractéristiques socioéconomiques intrinsèques, mais également des niveaux d'offre de politique fiscale des pays voisins (Brueckner, 2002 ; Leprince et al., 2005 ; Birkelöf, 2009 ; Costa et al., 2013 ; Ega, 2007). C'est dans ce sens que ressort le lien de causalité entre les interactions fiscales stratégiques et la localisation des activités économiques étudié au sein des zones d'intégration économique en général.

Sur la base des enseignements issus de la théorie traditionnelle de la concurrence fiscale (Tiebout, 1956 ; Zodrow et Mieszkowski, 1986 ; Wilson, 1986 ; Wildasin, 1988 ; Gordon, 1986 ; Hoyt, 1991 ; Mintz et Tulkens, 1986 ; Jensen et Toma, 1991 ; Bucovetsky et Wilson, 1991 ; Barro, 1974 ; Barros et Cabral, 2000), et de ses extensions à la « théorie du mimétisme»[1] (Salmon, 1987 ; Brueckner, 2002 ; Besley et Case, 1995), cet article aborde le problème du rôle de la concurrence territoriale sur la localisation des activités économiques dans un espace d'intégration économique en développement, la CEMAC (Communauté Economique et Monétaire de l'Afrique Centrale)[2] .

Même s'il est communément admis que les pays sont en permanence en compétition les uns avec les autres pour attirer les investissements étrangers, les études empiriques antérieures (Xing et al., 2018 ; Bénassy-Quéré et al. 2005 ; Guntram, 2006 ; Anastassopoulos, 2007 ; Hansson et Olofsdotter, 2008 ; Hauptmeier et al. 2009 ; Hansson et Olofsdotter, 2010; Ouramdane, 2014) n'ont pu conclure si cette concurrence leur est bénéfique ou pas ; ce d'autant plus qu'au sein d'une zone d'intégration économique, la coordination des politiques économiques est très souvent la règle.

En faisant l'hypothèse que des écarts stratégiques de niveaux d'imposition entre les pays de la CEMAC entraînent une variation des flux entrants d'IDE dans un pays donné, l'objectif de cet article est d'apprécier comment une offre concurrentielle influence les décisions de localisation des firmes multinationales. L'intérêt d'une telle analyse est ainsi de vérifier l'existence et le rôle des interactions fiscales stratégiques. Sur ce plan, il faut noter que, contrairement à différentes zones d'in-

---

[1] Selon Ega (2007), la théorie du mimétisme (*copy-cat theory*) est un comportement par lequel, les juridictions vont toujours essayer d'améliorer leurs performances budgétaires en imitant les politiques économiques adaptables, qui font la réussite des territoires voisins (concurrents). Chaque juridiction ou pays dans ce cas, veut propulser sa structure économique à un niveau qui est convoité par tous les acteurs et une façon d'y parvenir est d'adopter des politiques qui sont considérées comme succès ailleurs.

[2] La CEMAC est née des cendres de l'ancienne Union Douanière et Economique de l'Afrique Centrale (UDEAC) en 1964, précédée par l'Union Douanière Equatoriale (UDE) en 1959. Avec une population estimée à 51,8 millions habitants, elle compte actuellement six pays: Cameroun, Gabon, Congo, Guinée équatoriale, Tchad, République centrafricaine.

tégration économique développées ou émergentes, la CEMAC n'a pas encore fait l'objet d'analyse du phénomène d'interactions fiscales stratégiques et de leur impact sur la localisation des IDE.

Cet article s'articule en quatre sections. Après avoir présenté quelques faits stylisés (1), nous décrivons le modèle retenu (2). Puis, à partir des résultats (3), nous avançons quelques implications de politique économique (4).

1. LES FAITS STYLISÉS

Une vue d'ensemble est donnée ici, d'une part, sur le niveau de pression fiscale observé dans la CEMAC et, d'autre part, sur les flux entrants d'IDE.

1.1. Les incitations fiscales dans la CEMAC

Place des pays de la CEMAC

La crise économique de la seconde moitié des années 1980 a entrainé une panoplie de réformes budgétaires qui ont touché aussi le secteur fiscal (IMF, 2011). Dans les années 1990, les ajustements fiscaux qui vont être entrepris par les pays durement frappés par la crise économique ont été perçus comme une démarche de modernisation du système fiscal en vue de le rendre plus performant. Dans la même période, la décentralisation est apparue comme un moyen de redistribution efficace, avec la particularité de construire un développement socioéconomique à partir des territoires. La décentralisation fiscale qui verra alors le jour permettra de définir un champ fiscal propre aux collectivités locales. Dans les pays francophones d'Afrique, cette fiscalité propre s'appuie sur les quatre impôts locaux de base à savoir : le foncier bâti, le foncier non bâti, la taxe d'habitation et la patente (Yatta, 2009). Certes la décentralisation fiscale n'est pas sans influence sur la fiscalité globale d'un pays, mais dans cet article nous considérons uniquement les impôts gérés par les gouvernements centraux des pays de la CEMAC.

A défaut d'avoir des données assez récentes sur les principales variables fiscales mobilisées dans cette étude, Pwc et World Bank (2018) proposent, dans une analyse détaillée des systèmes fiscaux de 190 économies, une variable permettant d'avoir une lecture assez précise de l'environnement fiscal de chaque pays : il s'agit du taux global d'imposition et de cotisations sociales (*Total Tax & Contribution Rate, TTCR*). Il comprend l'impôt sur le résultat commercial des entreprises, l'impôt sur le travail et les autres taxes. Sa composition permet donc d'avoir une information plus ou moins réelle de la dynamique fiscale de chaque pays et donc sur la fiscalité des pays de l'espace CEMAC. Le classement qui en résulte donné au tableau 1 permet d'apprécier dans une certaine mesure l'attractivité fiscale de chaque pays.

D'après le tableau 1, les pays de l'espace CEMAC occupent des positions très peu enviables. Avec un TTCR de 45,2%, le Gabon occupe le 30e rang continental et est premier en zone CEMAC, suivi du Congo (54,3%) qui est au 41e rang au niveau africain. Le Cameroun arrive en troisième position. Dans ce classement, la Guinée Equatoriale apparait comme étant le territoire le moins attractif de la zone sur le plan fiscal, avec un TTCR de 79,4%.

De manière générale, on peut dire que la situation fiscale des pays d'Afrique n'est pas très reluisante. L'Afrique est la deuxième région du monde où le taux global d'imposition et cotisations obligatoires est le plus élevé (47,1%), après l'Amérique du sud avec 52,6%, alors que la moyenne à l'échelle mondiale est de 40,5%. La CEMAC se caractérise avec un TTCR moyen de 62,23%, largement au-dessus de la moyenne africaine.

Tableau 1. Taux global d'imposition et cotisations obligatoires (TTCR) : classement 2017 des pays de la CEMAC

Pays	TTCR (%)	Rang au niveau africain	Rang au niveau de la CEMAC
Gabon	45,2	30e	1e
Congo	54,3	41e	2e
Cameroun	57,7	44e	3e
Tchad	63,5	46e	4e
République centrafricaine	73,3	50e	5e
Guinée équatoriale	79,4	51e	6e
Taux global moyen CEMAC	62,2		
Taux global moyen Afrique	47,1		
Moyenne mondiale	40,5		

Source : Pwc et World Bank (2018) et traitement des auteurs.

Appréciation des écarts d'imposition entre pays de la CEMAC

Le tableau 2 fait apparaître une tendance tantôt à la hausse, tantôt à la baisse des taux d'imposition entre 2005 et 2016. Cette variation du TTCR en zone CEMAC montre que les taux d'imposition ne sont pas statiques mais varient en fonction de la conjoncture économique de chaque territoire. Aussi, l'on relève des écarts fiscaux non négligeables entre les pays sur la période 2005-2016.

Tableau 2. Taux global d'imposition et cotisations obligatoires des pays de la CEMAC entre 2005 et 2016

	CMR	GAB	CON	GUE	TCH	RCA	Moy. CEMAC
2005	50,6	44,6	64,5	47,1	74,0	65,7	57,7
2006	50,8	44,2	64,5	47,1	74,0	68,7	58,2
2007	58,8	44,2	64,5	47,1	74,0	68,7	59,5
2008	50,4	44,2	64,5	47,1	71,3	68,7	57,7
2009	48,8	44,2	64,5	47,1	71,3	68,7	57,4
2010	48,8	43,0	64,5	47,1	75,8	68,7	58,0
2011	48,8	43,0	63,1	47,1	75,8	54,6	55,4
2012	48,8	43,0	64,5	47,1	75,7	67,4	57,7
2013	48,8	43,2	55,8	47,1	72,4	73,3	56,8
2014	48,8	40,1	55,0	47,1	63,5	73,3	54,6
2015	48,8	45,2	56,0	47,1	63,5	73,3	55,6
2016	57,7	45,2	54,3	79,4	63,5	73,3	62,2
Ecart 2005-2016	8,9	4,5	10,2	32,3	12,3	18,7	7,6
Moy. pays	50,8	43,7	61,3	49,8	71,2	68,7	57,6

Note : CMR = Cameroun ; GAB = Gabon ; CON = Congo; GUE = Guinée équatoriale; TCH = Tchad; RCA = République centrafricaine.

Source : World Development Indicators (WDI, 2017) et traitement des auteurs.

Le graphique 1 montre une variation modérée du TTCR moyen entre 2005 et 2015, alors que l'on enregistre une hausse importante en 2016. Ceci peut raisonnablement être lié à une conjoncture particulièrement difficile que la majorité des pays de la CEMAC traversent depuis 2014/2015. En effet, suite à la baisse des cours de leurs principaux produits d'exportation, certains pays ont été contraints de procéder à des ajustements fiscaux pour préserver les revenus de l'Etat et l'équilibre des finances publiques. Dans une perspective d'élargissement de l'assiette fiscale, le Cameroun par exemple a pris différentes mesures, concernant notamment le couplage du paiement de la vignette automobile à la souscription de l'assurance automobile, la taxe foncière, la taxe d'hébergement dans les hôtels, la taxe sur les communications électroniques, etc.

Graphique 1. CEMAC : évolution moyenne du taux global d'imposition et cotisations obligatoires (TTCR) entre 2005 et 2016

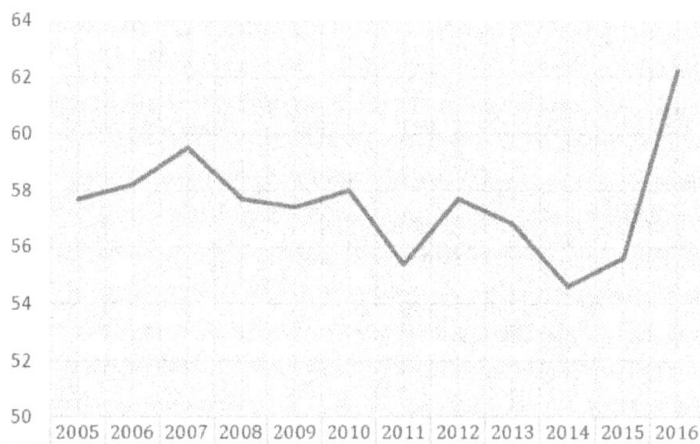

Source : auteurs, à partir des données WDI (2017).

1.2. Les flux entrants d'IDE dans la CEMAC

Evolution dans les années 2000 des flux d'IDE dans la CEMAC

D'après le graphique 2, l'on observe que le flux d'IDE en direction de la CEMAC croît de manière lente et progressive entre 2000 et 2005. Par la suite, il va s'accélérer pour atteindre un pic de 4535,41 millions de dollars US en 2010, avant de commencer à décroitre lentement pour s'établir à 3482,41 millions de dollars US en 2016. La faiblesse des cours du pétrole et les effets néfastes de la crise des produits de base se sont soldés par une contraction des flux d'IDE en Afrique, particulièrement dans les grands pays exportateurs de produits de base. Selon la CNUCED (2018), les flux d'IDE vers l'Afrique centrale ont chuté de 22 % à 5,7 milliards de dollars US entre 2016 et 2017. Cette tendance baissière des flux entrants d'IDE est également visible au niveau de la CEMAC.

De manière générale, la CEMAC est très loin d'être la première destination des IDE dans le monde. Sa particularité est liée au fait qu'elle accueille majoritairement les IDE du secteur primaire. Ce qui la rend quelque peu vulnérable aux chocs liés à la détérioration des termes de l'échange des produits de base.

La phase de relance observée entre 2000 et 2010 est consécutive à un vaste programme de réformes économiques mis en place dans les années 1990, pour essayer de juguler la crise économique à laquelle ont été confrontées les économies d'Afrique centrale. Au rang de ces réformes figurent la privatisation des entreprises publiques ; la dévaluation, pour avoir un taux de change compétitif et relancer les exportations ; la libéralisation des échanges commerciaux ; la déréglementation, pour supprimer les barrières à l'entrée et à la sortie des marchés ; les réformes fiscales allant dans le sens de l'élargissement de l'assiette fiscale et la réduction des taux d'imposition marginaux ; la promotion des droits de propriété pour faciliter la création des richesses ; etc.

Graphique 2. CEMAC : évolution des flux entrants d'IDE entre 2000 et 2016 (en millions de dollars US)

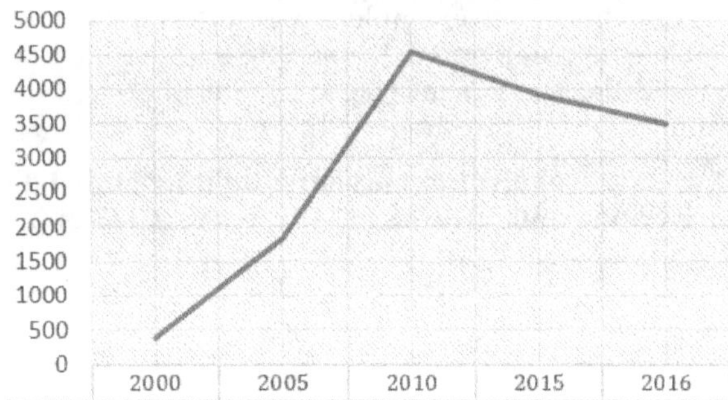

Source : auteurs, à partir des données UNCTADstat (2017).

Bien que ces réformes aient produit des résultats très mitigés du point de vue de l'amélioration des conditions de vie, il faut néanmoins relever que leur mise en place a contribué à stabiliser l'équilibre des finances publiques et à favoriser dans une certaine mesure la construction d'un environnement économique propice aux investissements privés. A cet égard, la privatisation des entreprises publiques et la réduction des taux d'imposition marginaux, par exemple, ont facilité une entrée importante de capitaux étrangers. De même, la dévaluation du FCFA en 1994 va encourager l'accroissement des investissements des multinationales dans l'exploitation des ressources naturelles, notamment le bois, le pétrole et les métaux précieux.

Au-delà, il convient de relever que la situation reste contrastée d'un pays à l'autre.

Graphique 3. CEMAC : évolution des flux entrants d'IDE par pays entre 2005 et 2016

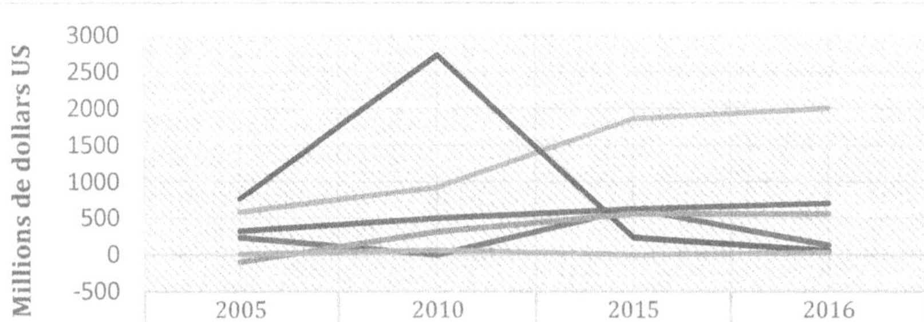

	2005	2010	2015	2016
CMR	234,01	-0,55	627,44	128,2
GAB	326,16	499	623,89	703,19
CON	585,16	928,44	1866	2006
GUE	769,15	2734	233,32	53,96
TCH	-99,34	313	559,64	559,86
RCA	10,1	61,52	3	31,2

Source : auteurs, à partir des données CNUCED, 2017.

Des disparités dans la répartition

Le graphique 3 fait apparaître un certain nombre d'écarts d'un pays à l'autre. Ceci tient à la spécificité de chaque territoire en termes d'actions publiques et à la survenance d'un certain nombre d'événements économiques propres au pays. La Guinée Equatoriale par exemple va commencer l'exploitation de son pétrole dans les années 2000, le Tchad commencera la sienne vers 2002 avec la construction du pipe-line Tchad-Cameroun, etc. ; c'est ainsi que ces pays vont drainer en un temps record un nombre important de capitaux. L'atteinte du point d'achèvement de l'initiative PPTE[3], en avril 2006, va permettre au Cameroun d'avoir plus de marge de manœuvre en termes de stabilisation de l'équilibre des finances publiques pour « un nouveau départ » (Touna Mama, 2008). Ce sera de ce point de vue un indicateur pour attirer davantage les investisseurs étrangers, après avoir privatisé un certain nombre d'entreprises publiques.

2. MODÈLE EMPIRIQUE

2.1. Interactions fiscales stratégiques : mesure de l'intensité

Les interactions fiscales stratégiques dont il est question ici sont celles qui s'observent entre les gouvernements centraux des pays de la CEMAC. Nous ne faisons donc pas cas des interactions fiscales entre les collectivités locales décentralisées de ces pays, qui constitueraient une autre étude.

L'analyse des phénomènes d'interdépendance spatiale se fait généralement de plusieurs manières : soit à l'aide d'un modèle autorégressif spatial avec variable endogène décalée, soit à l'aide d'un modèle régressif croisé avec variable exogène décalée, la combinaison des deux permettant d'obtenir le modèle Durbin spatial. Une autre façon d'analyser l'interaction spatiale se fait à travers la spécification d'un processus spatial pour les erreurs. Cependant, Gibbons et Overman (2012) montrent que l'interaction spatiale s'appréhende mieux à travers les décalages spatiaux des variables explicatives provenant des juridictions voisines plutôt que par les décalages spatiaux de la variable endogène. Mais dans cette étude, ne pouvant pas avoir les données sur les variables exogènes susceptibles de faire l'objet de décalages spatiaux pour mieux saisir le phénomène d'interactions fiscales stratégiques entre les pays de la CEMAC, nous nous limiterons au modèle spatial autorégressif avec variable endogène décalée.

En effet, parler d'interaction fiscale stratégique revient à dire que le niveau d'imposition d'un pays i dépend non seulement de ses caractéristiques socioéconomiques intrinsèques, mais aussi des niveaux d'imposition des pays concurrents voisins j. Dans cette situation, les gouvernements agissent d'une manière non coopérative, où chacun provoque ou subit, sans avoir l'intention de faire concurrence, les actions de ses rivaux. A cet égard, la fonction de réaction fiscale d'un pays i est donnée par la relation (2.1) ci-dessous :

$$T_{it} = R_i(T_{jt}, X_{kit}) \quad (2.1)$$

où T_{it} représente le vecteur d'imposition du pays i à la période t ; X_{kit} le vecteur des autres caractéristiques économiques et sociodémographique (variables de contrôle) du pays i à la date t. T_{jt} représente le vecteur des niveaux moyen d'imposition des pays voisins j ($j \neq i$) à la date t. Pondéré par une matrice d'interactions spatiales W, nous obtenons le poids moyen des taux d'imposition des pays voisins, soit $WT_{jt} = \sum_{j \neq i} w_{ij} T_{jt}$ et l'équation (2.1) devient :

[3] Pays pauvres très endettés.

$T_{it} = \beta_0 + \lambda \sum_{j \neq i} w_{ij} T_{jt} + \beta_k X_{kit} + \varepsilon_{it}$ (2.2)

où λ représente le paramètre autorégressif spatial, c'est-à-dire la pente de la fonction de réponse fiscale. La valeur et le signe de λ indiqueront respectivement l'existence ou pas d'interactions fiscales stratégiques entre les pays de la zone CEMAC, et le sens de ces dernières ; ε_{it} est le terme d'erreur.

2.1.1. Technique d'estimation

Partant du fait que le niveau d'imposition d'un pays *i* au cours d'une période dépend du niveau d'imposition du pays *j* au cours de la même période et vice versa, il vient que les pays ont des fonctions de réaction réciproques. De ce fait, le terme WT_{jt} est endogène au modèle et corrélé avec le terme d'erreur :

$E(\varepsilon_{it} WT_{jt}) \neq 0$ (2.3)

Dans ce cas, les conséquences économétriques de la présence d'interactions spatiales ne se limitent pas seulement à la variable expliquée (autorégression spatiale), mais concernent aussi la partie aléatoire du modèle (autocorrélation spatiale des résidus).

Pour éviter des conclusions incorrectes et tester séparément la présence des deux phénomènes spatiaux (l'autorégression et l'autocorrélation), il convient donc de modéliser explicitement le fait que les résidus peuvent être liés selon la relation suivante :

$\varepsilon_{it} = \delta W \varepsilon_{it} + \mu_{it}$ soit sous forme matricielle $\varepsilon = \delta W \varepsilon + \mu$ (2.4)

avec δ le coefficient d'autocorrélation spatiale entre les résidus, et μ le terme d'erreur supposé i.i.d[4].

La corrélation entre les erreurs et les niveaux d'imposition des territoires voisins implique que l'estimation des fonctions de meilleure réponse fiscale ne peut être effectuée par la méthode des moindres carrés ordinaires et requiert l'utilisation de méthodes capables d'estimer des modèles avec autorégression spatiale, c'est-à-dire dans lesquels la variable expliquée dépend en chaque point de ses valeurs en d'autres points de l'espace.

Pour obtenir des estimateurs efficaces et sans biais, des techniques d'estimation telles que la méthode du maximum de vraisemblance, la technique des variables instrumentales (Cliff et Ord, 1973 ; Anselin, 1988 ; Kelejian et Robinson, 1993), la méthode des doubles moindres carrés généralisés (Kelejian et Prucha, 1998) et la méthode des moments généralisés (Kelejian et Prucha 1999, 2006), sont plus indiquées. Il faut néanmoins rappeler que certaines de ces méthodes (les variables instrumentales, les moments généralisés, les doubles moindres carrés) ont été remises en cause par Gibbons et Overman (2012). Lyytikäinen (2012) pense même que les méthodes d'économétrie spatiale standard peuvent avoir tendance à surestimer le degré d'interdépendance spatiale. Dans le cadre de cette étude, nous employons la méthode du maximum de vraisemblance qui a été moins critiquée et du fait de sa simplicité ; elle a d'ailleurs inspiré bon nombre d'auteurs, en l'occurrence Besley et Case (1995), Bordignon et al., (2003), Brueckner (2003), Ega (2007), Foucault et al. (2008), entre autres.

2.1.2. Spécifications spatiales

La modélisation de l'interaction fiscale stratégique passe par la construction d'une matrice d'interaction spatiale *W*. C'est une matrice carrée ayant autant de lignes et de colonnes qu'il y a de zones géographiques. Cette construction se fait généralement selon plusieurs critères (Hamadou et al., 2012) : le critère géogra-

[4] Indépendant et identiquement distribué.

phique (comme la contiguïté ou la distance), le critère économique (basé sur le PIB), le critère social (comme l'Indice de développement humain), entre autres. Toutefois, il n'est pas possible de déterminer a priori la mesure la plus efficace. Dans le cadre de cette étude, quatre types de matrices de poids ont été retenus à savoir : une matrice de distance à vol d'oiseau, une matrice de contiguïté, une matrice de poids élaborée à partir du PIB et une matrice d'interactions spatiales construite à partir du PIB par tête.

La matrice de distance à vol d'oiseau (W^D)

Selon le critère de distance, on suppose que l'intensité de l'interdépendance entre deux pays *i* et *j* dépend de la distance entre les centroïdes de ces pays (ici les différentes capitales). Ainsi la matrice W^D est une matrice telle que :

$$w_{ij}^{d} = \begin{cases} \frac{1}{d_{ij}} si\ i \neq j \\ 0\ sinon \end{cases} \quad (2.5)$$

D'après les estimations de l'Institut National de Cartographie-Cameroun, d_{ij} représente la distance à vol d'oiseau.

La matrice de contiguïté (W^C)

La matrice de contiguïté W^C est une matrice telle que :

$$w_{ij}^{c} = \begin{cases} 1\ si\ i\ et\ j\ sont\ voisins \\ 0\ sinon \end{cases} \quad (2.6)$$

Le critère économique basé sur le PIB (W^{PIB})

La construction de cette matrice a comme éléments de base le PIB moyen de chaque pays entre 1981 et 2010. Ainsi, W^{PIB} est une matrice telle que :

$$w_{ij}^{pib} = \frac{1}{|PIB_i - PIB_j|} \Big/ \sum \frac{1}{|PIB_i - PIB_j|} \quad (2.7)$$

Le critère économique basé sur le PIB par tête (W^{PIBPT})

La matrice W^{PIBPT} est construite sur la base du PIB par tête moyen de chaque pays de la CEMAC entre 1981 et 2010 telle que :

$$w_{ij}^{pibpt} = \frac{1}{|PIBpt_i - PIBpt_j|} \Big/ \sum \frac{1}{|PIBpt_i - PIBpt_j|} \quad (2.8)$$

Pour des raisons de simplification, ces différentes matrices seront représentées de la manière suivante :

$W^{PIB} = W1$ $\quad$ $W^{D} = W3$

$W^{PIBPT} = W2$ $\quad$ $W^{C} = W4$

2.2. Description des variables

La variable dépendante (T_{it})

La variable d'intérêt est essentiellement constituée des données fiscales regroupées en différentes catégories d'impôts telles que spécifiées dans la base de données de Mansour (2014) :

Impôt sur les sociétés (IS) : il est appliqué sur les bénéfices des sociétés et autres entités économiques à l'exception des activités extractives dans les secteurs pétrolier, gazier et minier. Les recettes issues de ces impôts sont exprimées en pourcentage du PIB.

Impôt sur le commerce international (ICI) : il s'agit des tarifs douaniers externes, des frais de service ad valorem encore appelés frais statistiques dans certains pays et des prélèvements spéciaux sur les exportations et les importations destinés à certains usages. Les recettes issues de cet impôt sont exprimées en pourcentage du PIB.

Impôt sur le revenu des personnes physiques (IRPP) : cet impôt s'applique sur le revenu des particuliers dans les pays où les individus sont soumis à un impôt sur le revenu commercial ou non commercial, y compris l'impôt sur les bénéfices (en pourcentage du PIB).

Impôts indirects (II) : ils sont essentiellement constitués de toutes les taxes intérieures sur la consommation telle que la taxe sur la valeur ajoutée (TVA) et les droits d'accises (en pourcentage du PIB).

Impôts directs (ID) : ils regroupent les impôts sur toute source de revenu (les salaires, les revenus de portefeuille, les bénéfices des entreprises, les revenus immobiliers, les plus-values, etc.). Les recettes provenant de ces impôts sont exprimées en pourcentage du PIB.

Les variables indépendantes (WT_{jt} et X_{kit})

La variable endogène décalée (WT_{jt})

C'est la moyenne des niveaux d'imposition des pays (*j*) voisins de *i* (*j≠i*), pour les quatre types d'impôts.

Les variables économiques et démographiques ($\sum_{k=1}^{n} X_{kit}$)

- La taille du marché captée par le PIB de chaque pays de la CEMAC, et exprimé en dollars US courants (PIB) (en logarithme et en différence d'ordre 3).
- La population totale (POP), qui mesure le poids démographique de chaque pays (et permet de capter d'une autre manière la taille potentielle du marché) (en logarithme et en différence seconde).
- Le PIB par tête exprimé en dollar US courant (PIBPT), qui est égal à PIB/POP (en logarithme et en différence première).
- L'investissement public global de chaque pays exprimé en pourcentage du PIB (INVPUB) (en différence première).
- La densité de la population (DENSPOP) : le nombre d'habitants au kilomètre carré (en logarithme et en différence seconde).

Les données

Les données utilisées dans cette étude sont des données de panel. Elles ont pour avantage de fournir une large échelle d'informations. Ce qui accroit les degrés de liberté tout en réduisant l'effet de colinéarité entre les variables explicatives. Ces données couvrent les six pays de l'espace CEMAC sur une période allant de 1981 à 2010.

Les données fiscales proviennent de la base de données de Mansour (2014). La base de données WDI (2017) fournit les données sur les variables de contrôle, notamment le PIB, le PIB par tête, la densité de population, la population totale entre 1981 et 2010.

2.3. Interactions fiscales stratégiques et flux entrants d'IDE : mesure de l'impact

Présentation du modèle

La plupart des travaux empiriques (mentionnés en introduction) ont eu recours au modèle de gravité pour analyser l'impact des écarts d'imposition sur les IDE entre pays d'origine et pays d'accueil. Mais comme ici nous ne prenons pas en compte le lieu de provenance des IDE, le modèle mobilisé est simplement un modèle spatial s'inspirant du modèle de gravité.

Le modèle de gravité, qui est une adaptation de la loi d'attraction universelle, est un modèle qui permet de déterminer le volume d'échanges de deux pays par leur poids économiques (PIB ou PIB par habitant) et par la distance qui les sépare[5] (Luo, 2001). De manière formelle, on a :

$$EXP_{ij} = A\frac{Y_i^{\beta_1}Y_j^{\beta_2}}{D_{ij}^{\beta_3}} \qquad (2.9)$$

où EXP_{ij} est le niveau des exportations du pays *i* vers le pays *j* ; *A* est une constante ; Y_i est le PIB du pays *i* ; Y_j est le PIB du pays *j* ; D_{ij} représente la distance du pays *i* vers le pays *j*.

Partant de là, nous déduisons qu'il est également possible de simuler les flux de capitaux qu'un pays *i* accueille sur son territoire par son propre poids économique et par les interactions stratégiques qui existent entre ce dernier et ses voisins (*j*). Ce qui nous permet d'établir la relation suivante :

$$FK_{ei} = A\frac{Y_i^{\beta_1}}{WT_j^{\beta_2}} \qquad (2.10)$$

où FK_{ei} est le flux de capitaux entrants du pays *i* ; $WT_j = \sum_{j\neq i} w_{ij}\, T_j$ est la variable d'interactions spatiales stratégiques. Dans cette variable, w_{ij} représente la matrice de connectivité spatiale entre le pays *i* et ses voisins *j*, tandis que T_j est le poids moyen de la variable économique d'intérêt, c'est-à-dire l'instrument de politique économique sur lequel se fonde le comportement stratégique des territoires. Il peut s'agir de la fiscalité ou de l'investissement public en infrastructures. Dans le cas présent, *T* va représenter le poids moyen des niveaux d'imposition entre pays concurrents.

Pour que nous puissions interpréter les coefficients de chaque variable explicative en termes d'élasticité, nous mettons l'équation (2.10) en forme logarithmique :

$$LnFK_{ei} = LnA + \beta_1 Ln\, Y_i + \beta_2 Ln\, WT_j \qquad (2.11)$$

L'entrée des capitaux dans le pays i n'étant pas influencée uniquement par ces deux facteurs, nous ajoutons d'autres déterminants potentiels (X_{ki}) afin d'élargir le modèle. Il s'agit précisément du PIB, de la population totale, de l'investissement public, du PIB par habitant et de la densité de population. Ceci permet de réduire le risque de biais dans les estimations des coefficients, pouvant provenir de l'omission de variables pertinentes. Ainsi on aura :

$$LnFK_{ei} = LnA + \beta_1 Ln\, Y_i + \beta_2 Ln\, WT_j + \sum_{k=3}^{K} \beta_{3k}\, LnX_{ki} + \varepsilon_i \qquad (2.12)$$

Etant en panel dynamique et en remplaçant FK_{ei} par le flux d'IDE entrant ($FIDE_e$) du pays i, *LnA* par β_0, on obtient finalement l'équation :

[5] Ce modèle fut introduit pour la première fois en économie par Walter Isard en 1954.

$$LnFIDE_{eit} = \beta_0 + \beta_1 Ln\, Y_{it} + \beta_2 Ln\, WT_{jt} + \sum_{k=3}^{K} \beta_{3k}\, LnX_{kit} + \varepsilon_{it} \quad (2.13)$$

avec ε_{it} le terme d'erreur.

La technique d'estimation mobilisée est le maximum de vraisemblance avec effet aléatoire.

3. ANALYSE DES RÉSULTATS

3.1. L'ampleur de la concurrence fiscale

Dans l'ensemble, la présence d'interactions fiscales stratégiques est avérée pour les cinq catégories d'impôts retenues. Les résultats obtenus n'étant pas significatifs pour toutes les matrices de poids considérées ici, nous nous limiterons à analyser uniquement les cas significatifs. L'essentiel de ces résultats est résumé dans le tableau 3.1. Les résultats exhaustifs figurent en annexe.

L'impôt sur les sociétés (IS)

Le paramètre spatial autorégressif pour la matrice de poids W2 (PIB par habitant) est statistiquement significatif à 1%. Ce résultat montre que chaque pays de la CEMAC tend à augmenter (baisser) l'impôt sur les sociétés de 0.48 % en réponse à une augmentation (baisse) de 1 % dans les pays de niveau de vie comparable. Avec la matrice de poids W4 (contiguïté), le paramètre λ_1 est de 0.20 % pour un taux de significativité statistique de 5 %. Les taux supérieurs moyens de l'IS en Afrique subsaharienne ont connu une réduction de plus de 5 points depuis 2000 (FMI, 2018) et la dynamique d'imposition en zone CEMAC semble marquée par des comportements stratégiques entre les pays. Ainsi chaque pays, tout en cherchant à améliorer les revenus issus de l'impôt sur les sociétés, se préoccupe également d'améliorer son positionnement fiscal par la prise en compte des caractéristiques socioéconomiques extrinsèques.

L'impôt sur le revenu des personnes physiques (IRPP)

S'agissant de l'IRPP, la pente de la fonction de réaction fiscale est positive avec la matrice de poids W1 (PIB) pour un taux de significativité statistique de 1 %. D'après ce résultat, chaque pays CEMAC augmentera (baissera) l'IRPP de 0.23 % suite à une hausse (diminution) de 1 % dans les pays similaires en termes de taille économique. On observe ainsi un effet de complémentarité des niveaux d'imposition. En Afrique subsaharienne, le taux supérieur moyen de l'IRPP est passé de 44 % environ à 32 % depuis 2000 (FMI, 2018).

L'impôt sur le commerce international (ICI)

En matière d'impôt sur le commerce international, la pente de la fonction de réponse fiscale est positive pour les quatre matrices de poids W1, W2, W3 et W4, représentant respectivement les matrices de poids économique (W1 et W2), la matrice de distance à vol d'oiseau (W3) et la matrice de contiguïté (W4). Avec un taux de significativité statistique de 1 % pour les deux premiers cas, les résultats montrent que chaque pays de la CEMAC apporte une variation de l'ICI de 0.45 % et de 0.34 % respectivement, en réponse à une variation de 1 % dans les pays à poids économique proche.

Les impôts directs (ID)

D'après les résultats, les pentes des fonctions de réaction fiscale sont positives avec les matrices de poids W3 et W4. Avec un taux de significativité statistique de 1 % pour la matrice de poids W3, la valeur du paramètre spatial autorégressif montre que chaque pays de la CEMAC augmente (baisse) ses impôts directs de 0.39 % en réponse à une hausse (baisse) de 1 % dans les pays voisins.

Tableau 3.1. Résultats des estimations de l'équation (2.2) par la technique du maximum de vraisemblance avec effet aléatoire

Variable dépendante	Valeur du paramètre spatial autorégressif (λ) en fonction des différentes matrices de poids			
	W1	W2	W3	W4
IS	-0.004 (0.03)	0.477 (4.58)***	0.182 (1.37)	0.201 (2.12)**
IRPP	0.228 (2.66)***	-0.037 (0.41)	0.062 (0.41)	0.023 (0.19)
ICI	0.448 (7.23)***	0.339 (3.34)***	0.267 (2.42)**	0.228 (1.95)*
ID	-0.045 (0.36)	0.105 (1.01)	0.386 (2.89)***	0.179 (1.80)*
II	-0.337 (5.74)***	-0.037 (0.30)	-0.581 (3.88)***	-0.308 (2.71)***

**p<0.1 ; ** p<0.05; *** p<0.01.*

IS = impôt sur les sociétés ; IRPP = impôt sur le revenu des personnes physiques ; ICI = impôt sur le commerce international ; ID = impôts directs ; II = impôts indirects ; W1 et W2 = matrices de poids construites sur la base des critères économiques (PIB et PIBPT) ; W3 et W4 = matrices de poids construites sur la base des critères de distance à vol d'oiseau et de contiguïté.
Source : auteurs.

Les impôts indirects (II)

Les résultats des estimations réalisées avec les matrices de poids W1, W3 et W4 affichent des pentes de réactions fiscales négatives sur les impôts indirects. La significativité statistique des résultats est de 1 %. Pour le premier cas, la valeur du paramètre spatial autorégressif indique que chaque pays abaisse les impôts indirects de 0.34 % en réponse à un accroissement de 1 % dans les autres pays. La réduction atteint 0.58 % avec la matrice de poids W2 et se situe à 0.30 % avec la matrice de poids W4. Il est vrai que les impôts indirects ne touchent pas directement l'activité économique mais ils peuvent avoir un impact sur la compétitivité des biens et services marchands. La TVA et les droits d'accise par exemple influencent directement les prix des marchandises.

Ega (2007), après avoir analysé le phénomène d'interactions spatiales stratégiques en Afrique subsaharienne et en zone SADC[6], avait suggéré le cas de la CEMAC comme une piste de recherche future. Finalement, au vu des résultats présentés ci-dessus, il ressort que dans l'ensemble le phénomène d'interactions fiscales stratégiques se trouve largement avéré dans la CEMAC. Sur les différentes catégories d'impôts ciblées, le paramètre spatial autorégressif est significatif. La question qui se pose alors est de savoir de quelle manière le phénomène en question influence les flux entrants d'IDE dans la CEMAC.

3.2. L'impact des interactions fiscales stratégiques sur les flux d'IDE entrants

La sensibilité des IDE entrants par rapport à une variation du degré d'interdépendance stratégique entre pays de la CEMAC est analysée pour chaque catégorie d'impôt. L'essentiel des résultats est résumé dans le tableau 3.2. Les résultats exhaustifs figurent en annexe (tableau A2).

[6] Southern African Development Community.

Tableau 3.2. Résultats des estimations de l'équation (2.13) par la technique du maximum de vraisemblance avec effet aléatoire (variable dépendante FIDEe)

Valeur du coefficient β_2 en fonction des différentes matrices de poids				
Matrice de poids W1				
IS	IRPP	ICI	ID	II
6.129 (3.35)***	5.553 (4.46)***	-0.659 (1.16)	2.848 (3.15)***	2.984 (4.02)***
Matrice de poids W2				
-0.950 (0.70)	4.084 (1.65)*	-0.900 (1.38)	-0.150 (0.11)	2.508 (1.79)*
Matrice de poids W3				
-3.598 (1.15)	9.531 (2.34)**	-0.793 (1.32)	-4.239 (1.98)**	3.417 (1.65)*
Matrice de poids W4				
-3.092 (1.31)	9.571 (3.45)***	-0.936 (1.18)	-2.633 (1.49)	6.007 (4.42)***

*Note : IS = impôt sur les sociétés ; IRPP = impôt sur le revenu des personnes physiques ; ICI = impôt sur le commerce international ; ID = impôts directs ; II = impôts indirects ; FIDEe = flux d'investissements directs étrangers entrants. * p<0.1 ; ** p<0.05; *** p<0.01. Source : auteurs.*

L'impôt sur les sociétés (IS)

Des résultats obtenus, il ressort que l'impact de l'interaction fiscale stratégique sur les IDE entrants est net avec la matrice W1 (PIB). Une variation de l'intensité interactionnelle de 1 % entraîne dans un pays donné une variation de flux d'IDE de 6.13 %. Or on a vu plus haut que la pente de réponse fiscale est positive. On en déduit alors que l'interdépendance fiscale stratégique vue sous cet angle est plutôt bénéfique sur l'attraction des IDE pour les pays de la CEMAC.

L'impôt sur le revenu des personnes physiques (IRPP)

D'après le tableau 3.2, il apparaît que l'interdépendance fiscale stratégique influence la localisation des IDE. Les résultats obtenus avec la matrice de poids W1 montrent que chaque pays de la CEMAC connaît une augmentation de flux d'IDE entrants de 5.55 % suite à une hausse du degré d'interactions fiscales stratégiques de 1 % entre pays de la CEMAC. La hausse est de 9.57 % avec la matrice de poids W4, 9.53 et 4.10 % avec les matrices de poids W3 et W2 respectivement. Comme il a été observé plus haut que chaque pays de la CEMAC varie l'IRPP de 0.23 % en réponse à une variation de 1 % dans les pays voisins, on en déduit alors que l'interdépendance fiscale stratégique observée sur l'IRPP peut favoriser l'entrée des IDE dans chaque pays.

L'impôt sur le commerce international (ICI)

L'impact de l'interaction fiscale stratégique sur l'entrée des IDE n'apparaît pas significatif. Or les résultats observés plus haut font état d'une situation d'interdépendance stratégique sur l'ICI. L'influence sur les flux entrants d'IDE n'étant pas significative, il serait avantageux pour les pays de rechercher un cadre fiscal plus harmonisé, en évoluant vers un tarif extérieur commun par exemple.

Les impôts directs (ID)

Au regard des résultats, il ressort que les flux d'IDE entrants ne sont pas insensibles aux interactions stratégiques observées dans cette catégorie d'impôts. Pour un degré de significativité statistique de 1 % avec la matrice de poids W1, les résultats montrent que chaque pays bénéficiera d'une augmentation de flux d'IDE de 2.85 % suite à un accroissement du degré d'interdépendance stratégique de 1 %, entre pays voisins de ce point de vue.

Les impôts indirects (II)

Dans cette catégorie d'impôts, l'impact des interdépendances fiscales stratégiques sur l'entrée des IDE est sensible notamment avec les matrices de poids W1 et W4 dont les résultats sont statistiquement significatifs à 1 %. Pour le premier cas, il apparaît que chaque pays bénéficiera d'une hausse de flux d'IDE entrants de 2.98 % suite à un accroissement de l'intensité interactionnelle de 1 %.

4. RECOMMANDATIONS DE POLITIQUE ÉCONOMIQUE

4.1. Promouvoir l'interdépendance fiscale stratégique entre pays

En remettant en cause le phénomène de concurrence fiscale, de nombreuses études théoriques ont vivement recommandé l'harmonisation des politiques fiscales. Or d'après les résultats de la présente étude, il ressort que l'amélioration du positionnement fiscal d'un pays appartenant à la CEMAC passe moins par la coordination fiscale que par l'interdépendance fiscale stratégique. A cet égard, chaque pays de la CEMAC pourrait davantage évoluer dans une situation d'interaction fiscale stratégique avec ses voisins pour non seulement améliorer son environnement fiscal, mais aussi et surtout influencer positivement l'entrée des IDE sur son territoire. Ainsi, plus un pays prendra conscience des effets de voisinage liés à la fiscalité, mieux il construira son environnement fiscal et plus il sera susceptible d'attirer les investissements directs étrangers, toutes choses restant égales par ailleurs. Mais, de manière opérationnelle, cette démarche suppose que soit préalablement élaboré un audit fiscal stratégique.

L'audit fiscal stratégique est une condition sine qua non de toute opération d'interaction fiscale stratégique réussie. Son but est d'évaluer avec précision la capacité fiscale théorique d'un pays en vue d'une amélioration conséquente de son effort fiscal (recettes fiscales effectives), et par voie de conséquence le perfectionnement de ses capacités attractives et compétitives. C'est un exercice qui consiste à identifier en termes de forces et de faiblesses, de menaces et d'opportunités, toutes les variables susceptibles d'influencer la construction d'un environnement fiscal attractif et compétitif.

4.2. Asseoir l'élaboration de la politique fiscale sur une démarche participative et mettre sur pied un dispositif de veille fiscale stratégique

La construction d'un environnement fiscal attractif passe par une offre de politique fiscale appropriée, selon une démarche participative. L'approche participative ici suppose que soit créée au sein de chaque territoire une plateforme de concertation fiscale permanente entre les principaux acteurs économiques parmi lesquels les pouvoirs publics, les producteurs/investisseurs, les institutions bancaires et les consommateurs. Ces échanges qui devront par ailleurs précéder l'élaboration du projet de loi des finances publiques, auront pour finalité d'aboutir à une situation de consensus fiscal, avec la particularité de refléter l'environnement économique réel du territoire. Mais, l'impact économique des propositions issues du consensus fiscal sera d'autant plus pertinent que l'effectivité de leur mise en œuvre sera réelle. L'enjeu majeur étant d'améliorer la compétitivité fiscale des territoires, socle de la compétitivité-prix des entreprises, aussi bien étrangères que nationales, la durabilité d'une telle démarche passe inéluctablement par la mise sur pied d'un dispositif de veille fiscale stratégique au niveau de chaque pays.

Les centres de veille fiscale stratégique devront œuvrer dans la collecte, le traitement et la publication de l'information fiscale à temps réel. Ils devront être composés de plusieurs divisions en fonction des types d'impôts devant faire l'objet d'études stratégiques. Dans un contexte d'interactions fiscales stratégiques, le rôle capital joué par un centre national de veille fiscale stratégique ne se limitera pas uniquement au plan interne, mais aura également pour mission de suivre l'évolution des réformes fiscales provenant des pays voisins. Finalement, l'enjeu des centres nationaux de veille fiscale stratégique est d'amener les pays à évoluer dans une stratégie de différenciation territoriale active et compétitive, au bénéfice des investisseurs étrangers et nationaux.

CONCLUSION

Cet article avait pour objectif de montrer de quelle manière les interdépendances fiscales stratégiques influencent la localisation des IDE au sein de la Communauté Economique et Monétaire de l'Afrique Centrale. Des résultats issus des estimations réalisées, il ressort d'abord que le phénomène d'interactions fiscales stratégiques est avéré, avec toutefois la particularité d'être de faible intensité. Ces résultats se situent ainsi en droite ligne avec la plupart des travaux empiriques effectués en la matière dans d'autres zones. Ensuite il s'est avéré sur la base des résultats obtenus que ces interactions favorisent l'entrée d'IDE dans les pays de la CEMAC.

Ainsi, loin d'être dommageable, la concurrence territoriale vue sous cet angle, est plutôt « souhaitable » (Friedman, 1998)[7]. Elle apparaît comme une opportunité que les pays de la CEMAC pourraient saisir pour orienter leurs politiques d'attracti-compétitivité. A cet effet, l'élaboration préalable d'un diagnostic fiscal stratégique est nécessaire. La construction d'une plateforme de concertation fiscale entre les principaux acteurs économiques de chaque territoire devra favoriser l'élaboration et la mise en œuvre d'une politique fiscale plus consensuelle. Enfin, des centres nationaux de veille fiscale stratégique dans le but d'affiner le positionnement interactionnel doivent être mis en place. De cette manière, l'interdépendance fiscale stratégique pourra donner à chaque pays la possibilité d'accueillir sur son territoire les IDE que ses capacités lui permettent d'attirer.

[7] Milton Friedman dans *Wall Street Journal Europe*, 29 July 1998.

REFERENCES

Anastassopoulos G., 2007, Countries' international competitiveness and FDI: An Empirical analysis of selected EU member-countries and regions, *Journal of Economics and Business*, 10(1).

Anselin L., 1988, *Spatial econometrics: Methods and models*, Springer.

Barro J.R., 1974, Are government bonds net wealth?, *Journal of Political Economy*, 82.

Barros P.P., Cabral L., 2000, Competing for Foreign Direct Investment, *Review of International Economics*, 8(2), 360-371.

Benassy-Quere A.L., Fontagne A., Lahreche-Revil, 2005, How Does FDI React to Corporate Taxation?, *International Tax and Public Finance*, 12.

Besley T., Case A., 1995, Incumbent behavior: Vote seeking, tax setting and yardstick competition, *American Economic Review*, 85.

Birkelöf L.C., 2009, Spatial interaction and Local Government Expenditures for Functionally Impaired in Sweden, *Economic Studies*, 798.

Bordignon M., Cerniglia F., Revelli F., 2003, In search of yardstick competition: a spatial analysis of Italian municipality property tax, *Journal of Urban Economics* 54 (2), 199-217.

Brueckner J.K., 2003, Strategic interaction among governments: An overview of empirical studies, *International Regional Science Review*, 26(2), 175-188.

Bucovetsky S., Wilson J.D., 1991, Tax competition with Two Tax Instruments, *Regional Science and Urban Economics*, 21.

Case A. C., Rosen H.S., Hines J.R., 1993, Budget spillovers and fiscal policy interdependence: Evidence from the states, *Journal of Public Economies*, 52, 285-307.

Cliff A., Ord J., 1973, *Spatial auto correlation*, London, Pion.

Costa H., Veiga L.G., Portela M., 2013, Interactions in local governments' spending decisions: Evidence from Portugal, *Regional Studies Association*.

Ega Mbakile-Moloi, C., 2007, Copycat Theory: Testing for Fiscal Policies Harmonization in the Southern African Development Community (SADC) and Sub-Saharan Africa (SSA), A Dissertation Submitted for the Degree of Doctor of Philosophy in the Andrew Young School of Policy Studies of Georgia State University.

Fonds Monétaire International, 2018, *Perspectives économiques régionales pour l'Afrique subsaharienne : mobilisation des recettes fiscales et investissement privé*, Washington, DC.

Fonds Monétaire International, 2011, Réformes des administrations fiscales dans les pays francophones d'Afrique sub-saharienne, *IMF Working Paper*.

Foucault M., Madies T., Paty S., 2008, Public spending interactions and local politics: Empirical evidence from French municipalities, *Public Choice*, 137.

Gibbon S., Overman H., 2012, Mostly pointless spatial econometrics?, *Journal of Regional Science*, 52(2), 172-191.

Gordon R., 1986, Taxation of investment and savings in a world economy, *American Economic Review*, in Wilson J.D.,1999, Theories of Tax Competition, *National Tax Journal*, 52.

Guntram B. W., 2006, Foreign direct investment in the enlarged EU: Do taxes matter and to what extent?, Discussion Paper, series 1: Economics Studies, N° 13, Deutsche Bundesbank.

Hamadou H., Paty S., Savona M., 2012, Strategic interactions in public R&D across EU-15 countries: A spatial econometric analysis, WP 1223, Groupe d'Analyse et de Théorie Economique Lyon-St Etienne.

Hansson A., Olofsdotter K., 2008, Foreign Direct Investment in Europe: Tax Competition and Agglomeration Economies, Working Paper, Lund University, Sweden.

Hansson A., Olofsdotter K., 2010, Tax differences and foreign direct investment in the EU 27, Department of Economics, Lund University, Sweden.

Hauptmeier S., Mittermaier F., Rincke J., 2009, Fiscal Competition over Tax and Public Inputs: Theory and Evidence, Working Paper Series, N° 1033/march 2009, European Central Bank.

Hoyt W. H., 1991, Competitive Jurisdiction, congestion, and the Henry George Theorem: When should Property Be taxed Instead of land?, *Regional Science and Urban Economics*, 21.

Jensen R., Toma E.F., 1991, Debt in a model of tax competition, *Regional Science and Urban Economics*, 21.

Kelejian H. H., Robinson D.P., 1993, A suggested method of estimation for spatial interdependent models with auto correlated errors and an application to a county expenditure model, *Papers in Regional Science*, 72, 297-312.

Kelejian H. H., Prucha I.R., 1998, A generalized spatial two-stage least squares procedure for estimating a spatial autoregressive model with autoregressive disturbances, *Journal of Real Estate Finance and Economies*, 17, 99-121.

Kelejian H. H., Prucha I.R., 1999, A generalized moments estimator for the autoregressive parameters in a spatial model, *International Economic Review*, 40, 2.

Kelejian H. H., Prucha I.R., 2006, Specification and estimation of spatial autoregressive models with autoregressive and heteroskedastic disturbances, In: Ega Mbakile-Moloi, C., 2007, *Copycat Theory: Testing for Fiscal Policies Harmonization in the Southern African Development Community (SADC) and Sub-Saharan Africa (SSA)*, A Dissertation Submitted for the Degree of Doctor of Philosophy in the Andrew Young School of Policy Studies of Georgia State University.

Leprince M., Paty S., Reulier E. 2005, Choix d'imposition et interactions spatiales entre collectivités locales : Un test sur les départements français, *Recherches Economiques de Louvain*, 71(1).

Lyytikäinen T., 2012, Tax competition among local governments: Evidence from a property tax reform in Finland, *Journal of Public Economics*, 96, 584-595.

Luo X., 2001, La mesure de la distance dans la modèle de gravité : une application au commerce des provinces chinoises avec le Japon, *Région et Développement*, 13, 163-180.

Mansour M., 2014, Une base de données sur les recettes fiscales en Afrique sub-saharienne, 1980-2010, *Revue d'Economie du Développement*, 22, 99-128.

Mintz J., Tulkens H., 1986, Commodity Tax Competition between Member State of a Federation: Equilibrium and Efficiency, *Journal of Public Economics*, 29.

Ouramdane S., 2014, La concurrence fiscale et les investissements directs étrangers, Mémoire, en vue de l'obtention du diplôme de Magister en Sciences économiques, Université Mouloud Mammeri de Tizi-Ouzou.

PWC, World Bank, 2018, Paying taxes 2018.

Salmon P., 1987, Decentralisation as an incentive scheme, *Oxford Review of Economic Policy*, 3(2), 24-43.

Tiebout C.M., 1956, A Pure Theory of Local Expenditures, *The Journal of Political Economy*, 64, 5.

Touna Mama, 2008, *L'économie camerounaise: pour un nouveau départ*, Afrédit, 472 p.

Wildasin D.E, 1988, Nash equilibrium in models of fiscal competition, *Journal of Public Economics*, 35, 229-240.

Wilson J.D., 1986, A theory of inter-regional tax competition, *Journal of Urban Economics*, 19.

World Development Indicators (WDI), 2017, World Bank.
http://datatopics.worldbank.org/world-development-indicators/

Xing J., W. Cui, X. Qu, 2018, Local tax incentives and behavior of foreign enterprises: evidence from a large developing country, Singapore Management University, Research Paper series, 16(1).

Yatta F. P., 2009, *La décentralisation fiscale en Afrique*, Karthala.

Zodrow, G.R., P.M. Mieszkowski, 1986, Pigou, Tiebout property taxation and the under provision of local public goods, *Journal of Urban Economics*, 19.

ANNEXES

Tableau A1. Statistiques descriptives

Variable	Obs	Mean	Std. Dev.	Min	Max
Impôt sur les sociétés (IS) (en pourcentage du PIB)	180	1.0822	.8480	0	5.0
Impôt sur le revenu des personnes physiques (IRPP) (en pourcentage du PIB)	180	1.4861	.6878	0	3.1
Impôt sur le commerce international (ICI) (en pourcentage du PIB)	180	3.5317	3.0555	0	22.2
Impôts directs (ID) (en pourcentage du PIB)	180	2.4033	1.2348	0	6.8
Impôts indirects (II) (en pourcentage du PIB)	180	2.7789	1.5548	0	7.0
Investissement public (INVPUB) (en pourcentage du PIB)	180	3.0705	2.2721	0.1105	11.4295
PIB (en dollars US)	180	5.15e+09	5.57e+09	3.67e+07	2.64e+10
PIB par tête (PIBPT) (en dollars US)	180	2011.093	3307.282	136.0106	22742.38
Population (POP)	180	4906965	4899743	270063	2.00e+07
Densité de la population (DENSPOP)	180	12.2548	10.1254	2.9013	42.2468
Flux entrants d'IDE (FIDE) (en pourcentage du PIB)	180	5.7706	16.6334	-8.5894	161.8238

Source : auteurs, à partir des données du Fonds Monétaire International (FMI), de la Banque Africaine de Développement (BAD), de la Banque Mondiale (WDI, 2017) et de la base de données sur les recettes fiscales en Afrique sub-saharienne (Mansour, 2014).

Tableau A2. Résultats des estimations des équations (2.2) et (2.13) par le maximum de vraisemblance (avec effet aléatoire)

Résultats des estimations de l'équation 2. 2				
Variables	Matrices			
	W1	W2	W3	W4
	Impôt sur les sociétés (IS)			
λ	-0.004 (0.03)	0.477 (4.58)***	0.182 (1.37)	0.201 (2.12)**
DINVPUB	0.061 (2.28)**	0.064 (2.57)*	0.059 (2.23)**	0.055 (2.07)**
D3lnPIB	-0.000 (0.18)	-0.000 (0.80)	-0.000 (0.30)	-0.000 (0.33)
DlnPIBPT	0.000 (1.42)	0.000 (1.76)*	0.000 (1.45)	0.000 (1.42)
D2lnPOP	0.000 (1.69)*	0.000 (2.40)**	0.000 (1.82)*	0.000 (1.42)
D2lnDENSPOP	-0.049 (2.44)*	-0.052 (2.51)**	-0.050 (2.50)**	0.048 (2.40)**
Const.	0.994 (3.18)**	0.347 (0.90)	0.800 (2.55)**	0.741 (2.43)**
Sigma _u const	0.553 (3.10)**	0.542 (18.60)***	0.560 (3.23)***	0.562 (3.22)***
Sigma _e const	0.579 (18.60)**	0.542 (18.60)***	0.576 (18.63)***	0.572 (18.63)***
Obs.	180	180	180	180
	Impôt sur le revenu des personnes physiques (IRPP)			
λ	0.228 (2.66)***	-0.037 (0.41)	0.062 (0.41)	0.023 (0.19)
DINVPUB	-0.055 (2.53)**	-0.052 (2.29)**	-0.053 (2.36)**	-0.054 (2.41)**
DlnPIB	0.000 (2.89)***	0.000 (2.51)**	0.000 (2.73)***	0.000 (2.66)***
DlnPIBPT	-0.000 (3.22)***	-0.000 (2.12)**	-0.000 (2.53)**	-0.000 (2.38)**
D2lnPOP	-0.000 (0.37)	0.000 (0.35)	0.000 (0.14)	0.000 (0.08)
D2lnDENSPOP	0.023 (1.55)	0.022 (1.26)	0.021 (1.22)	0.024 (1.46)
_cons	0.947 (4.09)***	1.153 (4.79)***	1.083 (4.30)***	1.121 (4.88)***
sigma _u _cons	0.254 (1.58)	0.403 (2.07)**	0.309 (1.98)**	0.369 (1.73)
sigma _e _cons	0.489 (17.82)***	0.491 (18.18)***	0.493 (18.13)***	0.493 (17.89)***
Obs.	180	180	180	180
	Impôt sur le commerce international (ICI)			
λ	0.448 (7.23)***	0.339 (3.34)***	0.267 (2.42)**	0.228 (1.95)*
DINVPUB	0.067 (0.95)	-0.022 (0.27)	-0.023 (0.26)	-0.012 (4.12)
D3lnPIB	-0.000 (1.11)	0.000 (0.62)	0.000 (0.81)	0.000 (0.93)
DlnPIBPT	0.000 (4.57)***	0.000 (2.25)**	0.000 (1.54)	0.000 (1.57)***

D2lnPOP	0.000 (10.47)***	0.000 (7.74)***	0.000 (7.13)***	0.000 (6.91)***
D2lnDENSPOP	-1.018 (14.96)***	-0.885 (12.20)***	-0.809 (10.43)***	-0.839 (11.10)***
_cons	3.899 (1.04)	4.898 (1.46)	5.277 (1.78)	6.000 (2.02)**
sigma _u _cons	9.088 (3.39)***	7.963 (3.35)***	6.916 (3.33)***	7.013 (3.33)***
sigma _e _cons	1.519 (18.64)***	1.684 (18.63)***	1.716 (18.63)***	1.725 (18.63)***
Obs.	180	180	180	180
	Impôts directs (ID)			
λ	-0.045 (0.36)	0.105 (1.01)	0.386 (2.89)***	0.179 (1.80)*
DINVPUB	0.031 (0.85)	0.028 (0.77)	0.017 (0.48)	0.019 (0.50)
D3lnPIB	-0.000 (0.74)	-0.000 (0.94)	-0.000 (0.99)	-0.000 (0.81)
DlnPIBPT	0.000 (2.34)**	0.000 (2.67)***	0.000 (2.67)***	0.000 (2.15)**
D2lnPOP	0.000 (3.26)***	0.000 (4.00)***	0.000 (4.27)***	0.000 (3.88)***
D2lnDENSPOP	-0.150 (4.10)***	-0.157 (4.69)***	-0.153 (4.91)***	-0.149 (4.50)***
_cons	2.568 (4.30)***	2.139 (3.31)***	1.476 (2.47)**	1.976 (3.46)***
sigma _u _cons	1.083 (2.75)***	1.265 (2.86)***	1.065 (3.02)***	1.103 (2.95)***
sigma _e _cons	0.798 (18.49)***	0.792 (18.52)***	0.781 (18.57)**	0.791 (18.55)***
Obs.	180	180	180	180
	Impôts indirects (II)			
λ	-0.337 (5.74)***	-0.037 (0.30)	-0.581 (3.88)***	-0.308 (2.71)***
DINVPUB	-0.022 (0.47)	0.003 (0.07)	-0.025 (0.55)	-0.006 (0.13)
D3lnPIB	0.000 (2.63)***	-0.000 (0.050)	-0.000 (0.69)	-0.000 (1.09)
DlnPIBPT	-0.000 (6.08)***	-0.000 (2.72)***	-0.000 (2.66)***	-0.000 (1.93)*
D2lnPOP	-0.000 (4.19)***	-0.000 (2.93)***	0.000 (2.25)**	0.000 (3.74)***
D2lnDENSPOP	0.071 (5.31)***	0.009 (0.22)	0.054 (1.30)	0.008 (0.19)
_cons	3.691 (11.42)***	1.585 (1.96)**	3.082 (3.69)***	2.087 (2.36)**
sigma _u _cons	0.000 (0.00)	1.675 (2.92)***	1.625 (3.01)	1.959 (3.05)***
sigma _e _cons	1.135 (18.97)***	1.023 (18.54)***	0.983 (18.56)***	0.997 (18.57)***
Obs.	180	180	180	180

Note : DINVPUB = investissement public en différence première ; D3lnPIB = logarithme du produit intérieur brut en différence d'ordre 3 ; DlnPIBPT = logarithme du produit intérieur brut par tête en différence première ; D2lnPOP = logarithme de la population en différence seconde ; D2lnDENSPOP = logarithme de la densité de la population en différence seconde.

Résultats des estimations de l'équation 2.13				
	Impôt sur les sociétés (IS)			
β_2	6.129 (3.35)***	-0.950 (0.40)	-3.598 (1.15)	-3.092 (1.31)
DINVPUB	0.267 (0.46)	0.606 (0.95)	0.613 (0.96)	0.692 (1.08)
D3lnPIB	-0.000 (0.11)	-0.000 (0.35)	-0.000 (0.21)	-0.000 (0.25)
DlnPIBPT	-0.001 (2.20)**	-0.002 (2.22)**	-0.002 (2.37)**	-0.002 (2.32)**
D2lnPOP	-0.000 (2.55)**	-0.000 (2.35)**	-0.000 (2.66)***	-0.000 (2.64)***
D2lnDENSPOP	0.771 (4.27)***	1.183 (3.58)***	1.293 (3.90)***	1.220 (3.81)***
_cons	-1.340 (0.36)	4.443 (0.93)	6.882 (1.36)	7.060 (1.43)
sigma _u _cons	0.000 (0.00)	4.426 (1.88)	4.531 (2.01)**	4.419 (1.95)
sigma _e _cons	14.530 (18.97)***	14.487 (18.48)***	14.430 (18.45)***	14.424 (18.43)***
Obs.	180	180	180	180
	Impôt sur le revenu des personnes physiques (IRPP)			
β_2	5.553 (4.46)***	4.084 (1.65)*	9.531 (2.34)**	9.571 (3.45)***
DINVPUB	0.401 (0.70)	0.371 (0.57)	0.728 (1.16)	0.152 (0.23)
D3lnPIB	0.000 (0.37)	0.000 (0.15)	-0.000 (0.44)	-0.000 (0.46)
DlnPIBPT	-0.002 (3.00)***	-0.002 (2.70)***	-0.002 (2.79)***	-0.002 (2.78)***
D2lnPOP	-0.000 (3.56)***	-0.000 (2.69)***	-0.000 (2.01)**	-0.000 (2.65)***
D2lnDENSPOP	0.907 (5.40)***	1.405 (3.46)***	0.886 (2.33)**	1.043 (3.76)***
_cons	-2.785 (0.78)	-1.025 (0.20)	-6.917 (1.13)	-6.816 (1.44)
sigma _u _cons	0.000 (0.00)	5.655 (2.16)**	5.773 (2.36)**	3.557 (1.85)
sigma _e _cons	14.212 (18.97)***	14.282 (14.42)***	14.162 (18.50)***	14.103 (18.50)***
Obs.	180	180	180	180
	Impôt sur le commerce international (ICI)			
β_2	-0.659 (1.16)	-0.900 (1.38)	-0.793 (1.32)	-0.936 (1.18)
DINVPUB	0.609 (0.96)	0.726 (1.12)	0.609 (0.93)	0.747 (1.14)
D3lnPIB	-0.000 (0.17)	-0.000 (0.66)	-0.000 (0.57)	-0.000 (0.57)
DlnPIBPT	-0.002 (2.46)**	-0.002 (2.11)**	-0.002 (2.17)**	-0.002 (2.25)**
D2lnPOP	-0.001 (2.17)**	-0.000 (2.19)**	-0.000 (2.61)***	-0.000 (2.57)**

D2lnDENSPOP	1.385 (2.96)***	1.160 (3.55)***	1.176 (4.15)***	1.208 (3.94)***
_cons	6.121 (1.15)	7.077 (1.49)	6.978 (1.55)	6.837 (1.42)
sigma _u _cons	6.563 (1.94)	4.75 (2.03)**	3.729 (1.85)	4.182 (2.00)**
sigma _e _cons	14.282 (18.23)***	14.411 (18.46)***	14.484 (18.49)***	14.457 (18.49)***
Obs.	180	180	180	180
	Impôts directs (ID)			
β_2	2.848 (3.15)***	-0.150 (0.11)	-4.239 (1.98)**	-2.633 (1.49)
DINVPUB	0.378 (0.64)	0.617 (0.97)	0.610 (0.96)	0.751 (1.17)
D3lnPIB	-0.000 (0.07)	-0.000 (0.31)	-0.000 (0.17)	-0.000 (0.35)
DlnPIBPT	-0.001 (2.18)**	-0.002 (2.25)**	-0.002 (2.56)**	-0.002 (2.34)**
D2lnPOP	-0.000 (2.53)**	-0.000 (2.28)**	-0.000 (2.94)***	-0.000 (2.56)**
D2lnDENSPOP	0.779 (4.29)***	1.190 (3.48)***	1.461 (4.28)***	1.223 (3.79)***
_cons	-2.153 (0.54)	3.742 (0.73)	12.813 (2.08)**	9.933 (1.65)*
sigma _u _cons	0.000 (0.00)	4.583 (1.92)	4.675 (2.19)**	4.633 (2.04)**
sigma _e _cons	14.579 (18.97)***	14.480 (18.40)***	14.311 (18.51)***	14.385 (18.45)***
Obs.	180	180	180	180
	Impôts indirects (II)			
β_2	2.984 (4.02)***	2.508 (1.79)*	3.417 (1.65)*	6.007 (4.42)***
DINVPUB	0.734 (1.24)	0.363 (0.54)	0.830 (1.30)	0.105 (0.19)
D3lnPIB	0.000 (0.11)	0.000 (0.33)	-0.000 (0.13)**	-0.000 (0.24)
DlnPIBPT	-0.002 (2.70)***	-0.002 (2.51)**	-0.002 (2.62)***	-0.002 (3.01)***
D2lnPOP	-0.000 (3.28)***	-0.000 (3.23)***	-0.000 (1.97)**	-0.000 (3.80)***
D2lnDENSPOP	0.974 (5.76)***	1.290 (4.25)***	1.033 (2.70)***	1.027 (6.10)***
_cons	-5.077 (1.24)	-1.379 (0.29)	-5.918 (0.80)	-11.486 (2.32)**
sigma _u _cons	0.000 (0.00)	3.339 (1.49)	5.450 (1.93)	0.000 (0.00)
sigma _e _cons	14.346 (18.97)***	14.467 (18.34)***	14.298 (18.31)***	14.224 (18.97)***
Obs.	180	180	180	180

*$p<0.1$ ** $p<0.05$; *** $p<0.01$.*

Strategic tax interactions among EMCCA countries and foreign direct investments inflows

Abstract - This paper analyses the impact of strategic tax interactions between Economic and Monetary Community of Central Africa (EMCCA) countries on the Foreign Direct Investments (FDI) that each of these countries welcomes in its territory. To do this, we first estimate the degree of strategic tax interaction by using spatial autoregressive model. Then, using a particular spatial model inspired by the gravity model, we assess the sensitivity of FDI inflows of a given country to a change in the degree of strategic tax interactions between EMCCA countries. The results of the estimates carried out by the random-effect maximum likelihood method in panel data show that the EMCCA countries are developing strategic tax behaviors among themselves, and that these behaviors promote the entry of FDI in each country. Thus, far from being damaging, strategic tax interactions are rather an attractiveness factor for countries evolving in a developing economic integration zone.

Key-words

Strategic tax interaction
FDI inflows
EMCCA

REVUE RÉGION ET DÉVELOPPEMENT

Site Web : www.regionetdeveloppement.org

Recommandations aux auteurs

La Revue Région et Développement publie en français ou en anglais des articles originaux, des notes et documents et des comptes rendus de lecture. Pour soumission à publication, l'auteur doit adresser à la rédaction de la revue le texte par courrier électronique (ou le manuscrit dactylographié en deux exemplaires). La présentation des chapitres, des références bibliographiques et des notes de bas de page doit être conforme à celle de la revue. Les articles doivent être accompagnés d'un résumé en français et en anglais d'une dizaine de lignes, des mots-clés correspondants et de la classification du JEL. Le nom de l'auteur, l'institution à laquelle il appartient et l'adresse complète doivent figurer en page de garde.
Les articles proposés à la revue Région et Développement sont évalués par le Comité de rédaction puis soumis de manière anonyme à un ou deux referees. L'auteur reçoit un rapport d'évaluation, lui aussi anonyme, concluant à publication, révision ou refus.
Après avis favorable à la publication dans la revue, il sera demandé à l'auteur un envoi par mail du texte en Word (y compris figures, tableaux et formules mathématiques compatibles avec Word 2010).

Les propositions d'articles doivent être adressées à la rédaction de la revue :

Professeur Maurice Catin

Revue Région et Développement
Université de Toulon
Laboratoire d'Economie Appliquée au Développement (LEAD)
Faculté de Sciences Économiques et de Gestion
70 Avenue Roger Decouvoux - 83000 Toulon

Mail : maurice.catin@univ-tln.fr

BULLETIN D'ABONNEMENT

Revue Région et Développement

• **Je désire souscrire un abonnement pour l'année 2019 (deux numéros) :**

☐ France, DOM-TOM : 44 € ☐ Étranger : 47 €

• **Règlement :**

Pour la France

- Chèque bancaire
- Virement sur le compte *CCP 23 625 44 N Paris*
- Paypal sur le lien *paiement.harmattan.fr*
- Carte Bancaire sur le lien *paiement.harmattan.fr*

Pour l'étranger

- Virement (en euros uniquement) sur le compte *CCP 23 625 44 N Paris*
- Paypal sur le lien *paiement.harmattan.fr*
- Carte Internationale Visa/Mastercard sur le lien *paiement.harmattan.fr*

Nom et Prénom : ....
Adresse : ....
....
Code Postal : .... Ville : ....
Pays : ....

Date : Signature :

Ce bulletin d'abonnement à la revue Région et Développement et votre règlement sont à retourner à :

Éditions L'HARMATTAN - 7, rue de l'École-Polytechnique, 75005 PARIS
Tél. : 01 40 46 79 14 - fax : 01 43 29 86 20 - site web : www.editions-harmattan.fr

Abonnement annuel : 2 numéros
France, DOM-TOM : 44 € ; Étranger : 47 €

Structures éditoriales du groupe L'Harmattan

L'Harmattan Italie
Via degli Artisti, 15
10124 Torino
harmattan.italia@gmail.com

L'Harmattan Hongrie
Kossuth l. u. 14-16.
1053 Budapest
harmattan@harmattan.hu

L'Harmattan Sénégal
10 VDN en face Mermoz
BP 45034 Dakar-Fann
senharmattan@gmail.com

L'Harmattan Cameroun
TSINGA/FECAFOOT
BP 11486 Yaoundé
inkoukam@gmail.com

L'Harmattan Burkina Faso
Achille Somé – tengnule@hotmail.fr

L'Harmattan Guinée
Almamya, rue KA 028 OKB Agency
BP 3470 Conakry
harmattanguinee@yahoo.fr

L'Harmattan RDC
185, avenue Nyangwe
Commune de Lingwala – Kinshasa
matangilamusadila@yahoo.fr

L'Harmattan Congo
67, boulevard Denis-Sassou-N'Guesso
BP 2874 Brazzaville
harmattan.congo@yahoo.fr

L'Harmattan Mali
Sirakoro-Meguetana V31
Bamako
syllaka@yahoo.fr

L'Harmattan Togo
Djidjole – Lomé
Maison Amela
face EPP BATOME
ddamela@aol.com

L'Harmattan Côte d'Ivoire
Résidence Karl – Cité des Arts
Abidjan-Cocody
03 BP 1588 Abidjan
espace_harmattan.ci@hotmail.fr

L'Harmattan Algérie
22, rue Moulay-Mohamed
31000 Oran
info2@harmattan-algerie.com

L'Harmattan Maroc
5, rue Ferrane-Kouicha, Talaâ-Elkbira
Chrableyine, Fès-Médine
30000 Fès
harmattan.maroc@gmail.com

Nos librairies en France

Librairie internationale
16, rue des Écoles – 75005 Paris
librairie.internationale@harmattan.fr
01 40 46 79 11
www.librairieharmattan.com

Librairie l'Espace Harmattan
21 bis, rue des Écoles – 75005 Paris
librairie.espace@harmattan.fr
01 43 29 49 42

Lib. sciences humaines & histoire
21, rue des Écoles – 75005 Paris
librairie.sh@harmattan.fr
01 46 34 13 71
www.librairieharmattansh.com

Lib. Méditerranée & Moyen-Orient
7, rue des Carmes – 75005 Paris
librairie.mediterranee@harmattan.fr
01 43 29 71 15

Librairie Le Lucernaire
53, rue Notre-Dame-des-Champs – 75006 Paris
librairie@lucernaire.fr
01 42 22 67 13

www.ingramcontent.com/pod-product-compliance
Lightning Source LLC
LaVergne TN
LVHW021229061026
849535LV00008B/2990